LOST AND FOUND II
REDISCOVERING IRELAND'S PAST

LOST AND FOUND II
Rediscovering Ireland's past

Edited by
JOE FENWICK

Wordwell

First published in 2009
Wordwell Ltd
PO Box 69, Bray, Co. Wicklow
Copyright © the authors

ISBN 978 1 905569 26 7

British Library Cataloguing-in-Publication Data.
A catalogue record for this book is available from the British Library.

Cover design: Rachel Dunne and Nick Maxwell

Typeset in Ireland by Wordwell Ltd

Copy-editor: Emer Condit

Printed by Graficas Castuera, Pamplona

Contents

Acknowledgements

I would first of all like to express my gratitude to the authors who so generously contributed their time, enthusiasm and talents to this book, and particularly for their forbearance in permitting me the liberty to tinker, chop and change where necessary. My thanks, too, as always, to my friends and colleagues in the Department of Archaeology, NUI Galway, especially Professor John Waddell, for help, advice and encouragement when it was most required. My wife Lisa also deserves special mention for her patience and understanding, and for the many unprompted cups of tea (with occasional chocolate biscuit) provided throughout the protracted editorial process, much of which took place at home during our valued 'free time' at evenings and weekends.

I am particularly indebted to the staff of Wordwell Ltd, most especially to Nick Maxwell for resolutely holding to his high standards of layout, presentation and production despite the current economic climate, and to Emer Condit for her diligent copy-editing skills. This publication, like the first volume, has received welcome financial support from the Heritage Council under the 2009 Publications Grant Scheme, for which I am most grateful.

Finally, while the editor takes full responsibility for any errors and omissions, I would like to remind readers that he bears no responsibility whatsoever for the thoughts and personal opinions expressed by individual authors (even those with which he wholeheartedly agrees). Furthermore, any similarities that may exist between jokes contained in these pages and current or long-expired jokes that you may have heard elsewhere (however bad or politically incorrect) is entirely coincidental.

Joe Fenwick
(February 2009)

Foreword

When Joe Fenwick got the brilliant idea of producing a collection of essays written by archaeologists and historians, all experts in their profession, that would share with the reader the thrill, novelty and interest of a 'discovery', each written with the minimum use of footnotes and suchlike, which tend to smother such excitement 'in the dry format required of academic publication', he ended up with a fascinating book which he called *Lost and found: discovering Ireland's past.* He might well have added to his request to prospective authors: 'Now's your chance to say what you've wanted to say for years!'

The idea appealed to the authors, and the resultant book, copiously illustrated with colour and black-and-white photographs, clearly appealed to the general public too. Launched in November 1993, in good time for the Christmas presents to all one's friends, it proved such a success that it soon ran 'out of print'. Its success demanded a 'folly-yer-upper' (a term used in the 1930s and 40s, when I was very young, to describe short cowboy films that cinemas showed as a series to entice juveniles to squander their pocket-money on a weekly return to 'the fillums')!

But is this new book, *Lost and found II: rediscovering Ireland's past,* a folly-yer-upper? Well, 'yes' and 'no'. Its aims and its terms of reference are broadly the same (though the range of authors has expanded to embrace anthropologists, geographers, Celticists and noted writers), but only two of the authors are the same as those in *Lost and found* (one being, of course, the editor himself), and the themes indicated by the various titles do not suggest much of any sequel to any of those in the first collection . . . only the last essay in this second collection could perhaps provide a link between the 31 essays in the first book and the 28 in this one, and that we won't know if we have not read them *all* first! You may learn as much, perhaps more, about the authors as about their subject-matter, but take that as a bonus. I look forward to doing so, and am confidently waiting for a folly-yer-upper in the next few years, when I hope to produce a folly-yer-upper to my last effort, published as the concluding contribution in the first volume—maybe the editor will make it No. 1 next time?

I feel confident that this collection of essays will be every bit as successful as those in the first book, so rush out and get extra copies for presents before it, too, goes 'out of print'. A third collection will certainly materialise . . . it must!

Meanwhile, *go n-éirí an leabhar seo libh uile, go mór-mhór leo-san atá gan suim at bith san seandálaíocht—agus ná déan dearmad: an rud is annamh is iontach!*

Etienne Rynne

ix

Introduction

Lost and found II: rediscovering Ireland's past is the second of what I hope will be three edited volumes on the theme of discovering Ireland's past. This is unashamedly a 'popular' publication, intended to appeal to everyone who shares a curiosity in those dimly illuminated corners of Ireland's distant past and whose thirst for adventure and discovery is sated only by the deep and satisfying draught of scientific fact without the froth of fiction or fantasy. This anthology, therefore, in common with the first volume, *Lost and found: discovering Ireland's past*, contains an eclectic mix of copiously illustrated essays, written by recognised experts in their field, each of whom has embraced a novel aspect of the world of Irish archaeology, history, anthropology, geography, Celtic studies or other related disciplines.

It is apparent that the authors, unconstrained by formal academic convention and free to write in a relaxed style on a subject of their choosing, have relished the opportunity to share with you, the reader, a personal experience, insight or 'discovery', and with it their unselfconscious enthusiasm for their chosen professions. The term 'popular' in this instance is not, then, to be confused in any way with 'lightweight entertainment', as the subject-matter, while topical and absorbing in its own right, is well informed, factual and entirely new to publication. One concession to academia is the inclusion of a short bibliography of further reading at the end of most essays, should you wish to explore the subject in more detail. Indeed, I hope the contents of this volume will prompt you to explore for yourself the extraordinary wealth of cultural and natural heritage that we are privileged to share on this little island—and perhaps your insight, experience or discovery may contribute to the subject-matter of the next volume!

This book has been a privilege to edit. I have little doubt that you will find it a pleasure to read.

Joe Fenwick
(February 2009)

1

Archaeology in Ireland: recollections of an external examiner

Dennis Harding

I first met Ruaidhrí de Valéra in 1975 in the foyer at Newcastle airport. He was a tall man, more heavily built than his father, and I had no difficulty recognising the figure I had been instructed to meet, in a long black overcoat and with strikingly dark brown eyes. It was his first visit to the north-east of England, and as I drove him to visit sites along Hadrian's Wall I gathered that his archaeological interests did not extend much outside Ireland, and notably did not include the Roman military occupation of northern England. At a personal level he was warm and friendly, and it was this initial acquaintance that subsequently led to my appointment as Extern Examiner to the National University of Ireland.

Among personal reminiscences, he recalled a number of incidents from his childhood, and took evident pride in the fact that his birth certificate, dated 1916, recorded his father's place of residence as Maidstone Gaol. I liked his account of his father's advice when he joined the Irish Civil Service, describing the tactics to be adopted when recommending proposals to his superiors. I have heard the story since attributed to others, but in 1975 I have every reason to believe his version was authentic. First, he counselled, you propose the scheme that you yourself least wish to see adopted, for this first proposal you can be sure will be rejected on principle. The second scheme you offer should be the one you calculate *they* would find least acceptable, which will therefore likewise be rejected. The third proposition should be the one you had favoured from the outset; despairing of ever reaching a satisfactory outcome, the establishment will embrace this with relief, and your cause will be won.

Politics was endemic to Irish archaeology, and it was impossible to be in the company of Ruaidhrí Dev without being conscious of the shadow of politics. But he also played to the gallery, as he did one night in a taxi in Dublin when we were discussing the contrasting distributions of La Tène Iron Age metalwork, concentrated in the northern half of Ireland, and the stone fort distribution in the south and west. Irish archaeologists were at that time beginning to discuss the significance of this division between the La Tène and non-La Tène culture zones of Iron Age Ireland. The idea that Ireland had been culturally divided 2,000 years ago seemed ironic enough, but for Ruaidhrí the point of the discussion was that the dividing line in prehistory seemed to be only just north of Dublin. With a confidential stage whisper, he leaned across and added, 'and don't you go telling *that* to Ian Paisley!'

It was a cause of great sadness to me that Dev died suddenly in Enniskillen the year I was appointed Extern, since I had looked forward to visiting the chambered tombs of Ireland in his company. Nevertheless, I met him in Dublin several times prior to taking up that appointment, notably on the occasion of my lecture to the Historical Society in 1978. I had been booked into a hotel near UCD, and at the appointed time left my room to meet him in the lobby downstairs. As I entered the lift on the fourth floor with two others, I spotted a small notice indicating a maximum capacity of six persons. At the third floor three more individuals stepped in, to be joined at the second floor by two more. I thought briefly of pointing out that the lift was now overloaded, but a combination of British reserve, together with an instinctive trust that such equipment was designed to cope with loads well beyond the specified threshold, persuaded me that there was no cause for concern. Even while I was reflecting on the matter, the lift jolted to a halt at the ground floor, and the doors refused to open. Someone pressed the emergency button, and a crowd gathered in the lobby outside. One fellow was on his knees trying to prise the door apart with his fingers, and a nun at the back was repeating 'Hail Marys' and having the vapours. Eventually, the problem was identified. Being overweight, the lift had stopped six inches below the level of the floor outside, hence the doors were jammed closed. In the middle of the hubbub of recriminations and arguments over what should now be done came one of those sudden natural pauses, just as a broad Irish voice from the back of the lift suggested: 'Do you suppose if we all jumped up together . . . ?' I was unable to complete the tale as Dev and the Historical Society audience collapsed in uncontrolled laughter. The lecture seemed like a harmless interlude, and in his vote of thanks Dev responded with tales of Gordon Childe's visit to Ireland in his last year as Abercromby Professor at Edinburgh in 1946. We shook hands on the stage, and the audience thumped its approval.

*   *   *   *

Examining in Ireland demanded a strong constitution, physical as well as mental. The workload was substantial, involving the three constituent colleges of Dublin, Galway and Cork. Apart from a selection of papers, there were numerous dissertations to be marked on a wide range of topics that would have tested the knowledge of an academic polymath. The weight of Irish scholarship, in pounds avoirdupois at any rate, was prodigious, each MA thesis commonly running to two or three volumes. Packed into several suitcases, they were back-breaking to lift, while the cumbersome empty cases invariably baffled customs officers on the return trip. On one occasion the largest case broke the luggage scales at Edinburgh airport—the needle swung to maximum so violently that it sprung off onto the floor, leaving me to fumble my apologies as the queue behind became more and more impatient. On arrival it was vital to grab a pair of trolleys, which were invariably in short supply when needed. Arriving late one night in Dublin, we could find none, and the absence of any staff on duty added to the frustration of the passengers. One elderly nun plainly could not handle her luggage single-handed. A lone clerk behind a desk insisted that it was not his business, and there was nothing he could do about it. With mounting indignation, I marched off along a corridor towards the baggage manoeuvring area, opened a door marked 'No Entry; Staff Only' and found myself in a service bay where there was just one very large trolley of the kind normally attached to a tractor. Dragging it back to the passenger area, we loaded our luggage collectively on the trolley and, with the nun perched on the top, hauled it away through customs. The clerk protested that we could not do this, only to be told bluntly that it was not his business and there was nothing he could do about it— his words, as we recalled. Even the customs officer seemed too stunned at the spectacle to intervene. In the outer hall we parted company, leaving the duty staff next morning to work out how such a piece of equipment came to be in the main concourse.

The host colleges of the National University were generous in their hospitality, but the programme of examining, including the hotly contested competition for the Travelling Postgraduate Studentship, was extremely demanding, and the combination of the two was a recipe for nervous and physical exhaustion. Even for an experienced drinker and air traveller the return journey across the Irish Sea could prove to be something of an ordeal. I was certainly not unique in my recollection of the experience. One of my predecessors as Extern, Professor Charles Thomas, told me that his departure from home for Ireland was like a scene from a Victorian melodrama, in which the children, clutching their mother's apron, begged their father not to succumb again to the evils of intemperance. Yet the Colleges and the NUI itself were very self-conscious in the matter of academic standards, and the new professors in

Dublin and Galway were evidently anxious to maintain their Departments' reputations. In Dublin George Eogan, whom I had first met when I was a postgraduate in Oxford, was an exacting interviewer, and was not averse to telling a candidate in no uncertain terms that his or her answer was 'just not good enough'. So it was a great pleasure for me in my second term to be Extern in Dublin's *annus mirabilis*, the year that no less than six MA students were awarded Firsts. The examinations, and the vivas in particular, could be very exacting for the students, who were remarkably resilient in the face of protracted questioning. On one occasion at Galway, as one candidate withdrew after an extended cross-examination, the next slipped into the room without waiting for an official summons, bearing a tray with a bottle of Paddy and half a dozen glasses and, beaming at us, declared: 'After all this talking, I expect you'll be fancying something to drink?' In my entire university career I cannot recall a more brazen attempt to soften up a Board of Examiners! I would not wish to leave the impression that examining in Ireland was a continuous indulgence in alcohol—there were certainly intervals of sobriety, however brief. But I have to confess that after a taxing day of interviews, as the chill autumn drizzle drifted across the Dublin campus, a round of hot Paddys in the staff bar seemed entirely medicinal rather than recreational. Here we would exchange notes on the latest progress in field research, or on the relative iniquities of our respective governments in their policies towards higher education. Seamus Caulfield, who I suspected had modelled for the Duns Scotus image on the Irish five punt note, had recently extended his pioneering work on Irish beehive querns to an equally important contribution to Scottish broch studies (1978). His ground-breaking research on the Céide Fields of County Mayo was of particular interest to us working in the Western Isles of Scotland, where similar traces were being exposed beneath the peat. Seamus's forthright views frequently invoked the spirit of St Fechan, whose patronage, I recall thinking, was never quite as potent in St Vigean, his Scottish counterpart.

*   *   *   *

Archaeologists in Ireland were as colourful a bunch as you could meet anywhere. Senior among them after Dev's death was Brian O'Kelly from Cork, whom I had come to know well when he was External Examiner in Durham. To the British, he was an archetypal Irishman of pronounced features and twinkling eye, and his beguiling manner in interview left many candidates uncertain whether it had gone well or badly. On one occasion in Durham he had referred to an Irish custom in which six brass screws on the lid of a coffin were removed immediately before its lowering into the grave, inviting the candidate to consider a reason for this practice. The student was plainly thrown by this ethnographic analogy to the archaeological case under review, but gamely mumbled something about releasing the spirit from the grave. 'You think so?', mused O'Kelly, and instead of revealing the answer, with head tilted back and gazing over the high arch of his nose, added solemnly, 'All I can tell you is that I would not wish to be buried without those six brass screws being loosened on my coffin'.

I was never required in my first term as Extern to viva candidates from Cork, since O'Kelly preferred to bring his scripts and dissertations to Dublin. After Peter Woodman's appointment I did indeed visit Cork, and greatly enjoyed the company of the Cork archaeologists and visiting that delightful city. Indeed, I subsequently revisited Cork with my wife to experience the pleasure of dining at the Ballymaloe House at Shanagarry. In odd moments of fantasy I speculated whether O'Kelly's candidates actually existed, or whether he had written the dissertations himself as part of some arcane joke. In fact, I think he was simply over-protective of his students, as he showed on occasions in the Dublin interviews for the Travelling Studentship, where even his candidates could not avoid being represented in person. His style of questioning nevertheless hardly left much opportunity for the candidate to display independent initiative: 'Wouldn't you say, Rose, that an important factor in . . . ?', he would lead, to elicit the response, 'Well, yes, professor, I would'. 'Splendid!' In September, when the MA examinations took place, he was excavating at Newgrange, which he had reconstructed as a shining white mausoleum—some suspected, uncharitably, for his own future use. The last time I saw him was in Cork, when we were appointing his successor to the Chair from which he had just retired. He himself played no part in the appointment, of course, but we spoke briefly as he hovered in the college quadrangle in dark glasses like some local mafioso. The other External Assessor was Michael Duignan, whom I had met at a Celtic Art symposium in Oxford in 1972, when he launched his perceptive interpretation of the Turoe stone, revealing what everyone else had looked at and not seen—the four-sided basis of its ornament (Duignan 1976). O'Kelly died shortly afterwards, before he could attend a celebration dinner that was being planned in his honour. But he would have appreciated the notice that appeared in the *Cork Examiner,* which reportedly announced that, because of his untimely death, the dinner in his honour had been *postponed*.

The most exuberant and colourful personality among the Irish professoriate was undoubtedly Etienne Rynne, who had succeeded Michael Duignan as incumbent of the Galway Chair (Pl. 1). My first sight of Rynne was late one night in the Great Southern Hotel in Galway, when he appeared long after closing time, peering through the rain-smeared glass and rattling the bar door. As a host he was generous and hospitable, as a guide to field monuments of

Pl. 1—Professor Etienne Rynne pointing out detail of decoration on the Turoe Stone.

Galway and County Clare inexhaustible in his enthusiasm, and as an academic colleague stimulating and provocative. He was, however, never tempted to join the latest fashionable bandwagon, and could never be accused of being 'politically correct'. But as Christopher Hawkes once said at a conference with characteristic *double entendre,* 'I am always delighted when Professor Rynne gets up to speak, because it gives me a chance to think'.

No recollection of Rynne would be complete without reference to his driving, so indelibly is the experience imprinted upon the consciousness of those who have witnessed it and survived to tell the tale. It was five past four when we left Galway for Athenry, and the Dublin train that we had intended to take, and for which we had both been ready for several hours before we contrived to miss it, had a five-minute start on us. Needless to say, there was a 'quick route' by country lanes, with hidden farm entrances and unexpectedly sharp bends, down which he now propelled us, oblivious to dogs, hens, tractors or suchlike countryside flotsam. To make matters worse, we parted company with the exhaust system somewhere along the way, which I suppose afforded some advance warning to others of our progress but at the time served only to heighten the prospect of disaster. Approaching Athenry, it was clear that the train had already arrived, and Aideen and children were struggling to the station with our luggage in anticipation of our last-minute arrival. Abandoning the car, we fled to the station. Scarcely pausing for goodbyes, I grabbed my suitcase and doubled over the footbridge to the eastbound platform, where a tearful child was pleading with the train-driver not to go without daddy and his friend. Reflecting upon this moving scene, I collapsed into a seat, only to realise that Rynne was not with me. Conscious of the increasing impatience of the rest of the passengers, I went to the carriage door and looked back. There on the bridge recriminations were in full spate—professor, wife, train-driver, tearful child, passengers—and above all the confusion I caught the words, 'My mother always said . . .'.

*   *   *   *

One of the undoubted perks of examining in Ireland was the pleasure and privilege of visiting innumerable sites in the company of the foremost archaeological authorities on them. I visited Tara and the Boyne Valley on several occasions with George Eogan, and the Burren and the Aran Islands with Etienne Rynne. I was shown Rath Gall and Dún Ailinne by Barry Raftery, at a time when the late Bronze Age origins of insular hillforts were just beginning to be appreciated, among many other instructive and memorable trips of discovery. Among the most memorable was a visit to the Aran Islands in the company of Rynne and Tom Fanning, an immensely knowledgeable man in a schoolmasterly way. The short flight from Oranmore to the Aran Islands was in a small Fokker aircraft, the pilot of which was also German, though evidently long resident in Ireland. The twin-engined, high-wing plane was well suited to the short grass strips that served as the islands' runways. On this occasion the aircraft was full, and I was accommodated in the co-pilot's seat. Being briefed not to touch anything untoward with hands or feet, I must have indicated that I was aware of the controls, as I held a current pilot's licence. This information seemed to be well received by the pilot, who explained that he needed to make an urgent call at Inishmaan before proceeding to Inishmore according to schedule. He would simply land, taxi to the terminal—a wooden hut in the corner of the field—to allow a passenger to disembark, and would take off again without further delay. Unfortunately (and by this stage I felt there had to be a point to the narrative) the brake shoes on the starboard wheel were sticking once the brakes were applied, as on landing, and needed a sharp kick to release them again for take-off. Since it was on my side, could I perhaps oblige?—watching out, of course, for the propeller, which would be idling at 800rpm a couple of feet in front of

Pl. 2—Professor Etienne Rynne at the ceremonial enclosure of Dún Aengus.

Pl. 3—Professor George Eogan at Newgrange.

Pl. 4—Professor George Eogan taking a photograph from the summit of a satellite tomb at Knowth.

the wheel. I duly put the boot in, and quickly climbed back into my seat before the unbraked aircraft started to roll. For me the highlight of the trip was of course the stone forts, and Rynne's interpretation of Dún Aengus as a ceremonial centre (Pl. 2). Regarded with some scepticism when eventually published (1992), the ritual viewpoint is now very much in fashion with the younger generation of ethno-archaeologists, a development that would probably cause Etienne to recoil in horror.

$$* \qquad * \qquad * \qquad *$$

I was back in Ireland for a second term as Extern in 1989. By this time I had assumed the responsibilities of vice-principal in Edinburgh as well as maintaining departmental duties. On this occasion I had the pleasure, in the company of George Eogan, of revisiting Knowth (Pl. 4) and Newgrange (Pl. 3), where I saw at first hand the problems of conserving ancient monuments for public display. Decorated stones of the peristalith at Newgrange that I had photographed ten years earlier had visibly deteriorated through exposure to the elements, and efforts to screen the stones had evidently introduced further problems rather than resolving them (Pl. 5a–b). The Boyne Valley project must

Pl. 5—Newgrange: decorated kerbstone K52,
    (a) (above) photographed in 1979, and
    (b) (below) photographed in 1989.

Pl. 6—Professor George Eogan at Knowth, discussing a feature under excavation with Liam O'Connor, site foreman.

be among the foremost archaeological initiatives in Europe, and the Knowth excavation is surely the most important single excavation conducted in Ireland or Britain in the past century (Pl. 6). Only perhaps Danebury is in the same league, but without the spectacular finds or the important public dimension.

The following year I visited Ireland on three occasions, the first in connection with the appointment of a new lecturer at UCG, now translated back to Cork as professor. After a strenuous day's interviewing, I might have hoped for a lie-in on the following morning, but inactivity was never on the agenda in the Rynne household. It began with voices outside my bedroom door at what seemed like the crack of dawn, and Father O'Malley asking whether we would like to go for a walk in County Mayo. I had not appreciated that the walk in question was around eleven miles, from the Doolough to Louisburgh, in commemoration of a disastrous hunger march in the 1840s at the time of the potato famines. Several hundred walkers took part, and the whole jamboree was hyped up by the media and local political figures. Father Michael took much pleasure at the idea of my participation as a symbol of British national penance, and by the end it was penance indeed, since both soles of my feet were blistered and bloodied for lack of appropriate walking shoes. Relief was at hand, however, not from the first-aid post that had been set up for receiving casualties but, at Rynne's insistence, in the local convent. Here, sat in a chair with my feet on a stool, I was administered to by Sister Mary Magdalene, who very capably bathed and bandaged my feet. The scriptural analogy prompted Father Michael into a salutary warning 'not to go getting ideas above your station . . .'. The whole episode at the time seemed absurd, but I nevertheless harboured just a small sense of satisfaction in that I finished the course just a few minutes ahead of Etienne Rynne. The following day, I recall, we visited Knock without the slightest discomfort in walking, as my feet seemed to have healed remarkably quickly . . .

Less than a month later I was back for the summer diet of examinations, and during the visit we had planned to go by boat to Inishkea. Unfortunately the boatman cried off, on the pretext of winds blowing up from the south-east—a reference, we concluded, to Ireland's forthcoming match in the World Cup in Italy. Our alternative was Inisheer, the only one of the Aran Islands that I had not previously visited. The archaeology was certainly worth the effort, seeing hitherto unrecorded stone ringforts that had only recently been detected among the myriad of walls that dominated the island landscape. But I shall never again depend upon the time-keeping of the Doolin ferry, which was about as erratic as my host's. In fact, it was hard to tell whether the service was an hour behind schedule or an hour ahead. The experience tested even Rynne's patience, prompting him at the end of a tiring day to urge the boatman to 'buy himself a bloody watch', which must rank as the all-time example of a pot calling the kettle black.

In September I was back again to lecture to the Royal Society of Antiquaries on recent field research in the Western Isles of Scotland. We drove from Dublin via Clonmacnois, arriving there as the sun was setting over the Shannon. The atmosphere of serenity was stunning. That evening I joined an unforgettable Rynne family celebration over oysters and Guiness at Clarinbridge.

My first visit to Ireland was more than 40 years ago, when I toured the Early Christian sites of Glendalough, Kells and elsewhere in the company of Ian Blake, then a student at TCD and shortly afterwards a highly controversial archaeological correspondent for the *Irish Times*. I have returned on many occasions since, prompted by a desire to explore further the wealth of field monuments and to keep abreast of the most important landmarks in archaeological achievement. I have always regarded Irish concern for the archaeological heritage as exemplary, and in many ways much more enlightened than Britain's. It has therefore been a source of dismay to me personally to follow the recent desecration of the environment of Tara, which I can only liken to the wilful destruction of the canons and prefatory pages of the Book of Kells. Not actually part of the Gospels themselves, they are nevertheless integral to the Book as a whole, just as the landscape around a major field monument is integral to its archaeology. It is easy for politicians to succumb to the pressures of contemporary interests; the verdict of posterity will doubtless be more severe.

References

Caulfield, S. 1978 Quern replacement and the origin of brochs. *Proceedings of the Society of Antiquaries of Scotland* **109**, 129–39.

Duignan, M. 1976 The Turoe stone: its place in insular La Tène art. In P. M. Duval and C. Hawkes (eds), *Celtic art in ancient Europe: five protohistoric centuries,* 201–12. London.

Rynne, E. 1992 Dún Aengus and some similar Celtic ceremonial sites. In A. Bernelle (ed.), *Decantations: a tribute to Maurice Craig,* 196–207. Dublin.

2

Finding the Clonmore shrine

Cormac Bourke

My subject, the Clonmore shrine (Pl. 7), is the oldest known example of Irish Christian metalwork and one of the treasures of the Ulster Museum. The shrine, which held relics of the saints, consisted originally of nine copper-alloy plates and is just 8cm long, 8cm high and 3cm deep. The outer surfaces are tinned and decorated with spirals, crescents and trumpet curves reserved against a background of hatching. The decoration is hand-cut, though in part compass-drawn, and the golden colour of the recessed surfaces contrasts with the silvery patterns in relief. Such ornament has Iron Age roots but compares with that of the seventh-century Book of Durrow; the shrine must be approximately contemporary and is a major, if miniature, work of art. Clonmore is only 15km from Armagh, and the shrine might have housed some of the imported apostolic relics that Armagh promoted in the seventh century in support of its primatial claims.

I first encountered the Clonmore shrine in the kitchen of Brendan Bradshaw's house at Aghagallon, Co. Antrim, in September 1990. Four of its component plates had come to light the previous month and were shown to me by Eamon McCurry, one of the two finders; the other (whom I was later to meet) was James Walshe. They saw, correctly, the affinity between the decoration on the plates and that on the Iron Age sword-scabbards from Lisnacrogher, Co. Antrim, but were not at all sure of their function. Fresh as I was from playing a (minor) part in the installation of the *Work of Angels* exhibition in London and Dublin, tomb-shaped shrines were never far from my thoughts. Thus I recognised the plates as parts of a shrine or reliquary of the tomb-shaped class, but with decoration that was unparalleled (in my experience) on any such container. All of this I conveyed to Eamon, who took it calmly, never having doubted the significance of his find.

What had been found were the upper and lower front plates (identified as

Pl. 7—The Clonmore shrine: (a) front; (b) back (M. McKeown).

such by their 'windows' of blue glass), the upper back plate and one lower end plate. The base, the lower back plate, the second lower end plate and both of the upper end plates (i.e. the hips of the roof) were unaccounted for.

Several conversations later, I was introduced to the find-spot of the four plates, the corner of a large field in the aptly named townland of Clonmore (*an chluain mhór*, 'the big meadow') beside the River Blackwater in north County Armagh. The plates had been recovered from the old river dredgings that constituted the field surface. With the help of the original finders (and several other people), and with the cooperation of the landowners, the Donaghy and McKee families, I organised a systematic metal-detector search for the missing pieces. This was in February 1991. Nothing being found, I initiated the mechanical stripping of part of the relevant area. But it was a mistake to do so with a light bulldozer and in what turned out, not surprisingly, to be wet weather. Again we found nothing, and the lesson learned is that two things essential to a successful metal-detector search are dry weather and a heavy bulldozer (at least D5 or equivalent) with plenty of pushing power and a wide blade. Nevertheless, two further pieces, both decorated *en suite* with the shrine itself, were found that summer below the regraded surface by Eamon McCurry and Dominic Quinn. One of these is an oblong mount with flanged edges that was designed to receive a leather strap and must be one of an original pair that allowed the shrine to be carried (Pl. 8). The other is a flat strip with a hole at each end (Pl. 9a); it can only have been attached to a flat and rigid background and suggests the existence of a box in which the shrine itself was housed. This whetted appetites, so back we went in August with a heavy 'dozer and in dry weather.

In the business of mechanical stripping and

Pl. 8—The Clonmore shrine: strap-attachment and right-hand end plate with suspension fitting superimposed (M. McKeown).

a

b

Pl. 9—The Clonmore shrine: associated mounts (M. McKeown).

metal-detecting, the machine is used to strip perhaps 15cm at a time and is then reversed over its own tracks with dropped blade to create a smooth surface. You lay out lines on each fresh surface to create parallel lanes and then walk (slowly) up and down with a metal-detector, hoping for a signal as a fisherman hopes for a bite. Wednesday 21 August 1991 was the fateful day when I heard the wished-for signal in my headphones and dug a spade's depth in the sandy soil. I soon had in my hand the lower back plate of the shrine, instantly recognisable as such from its shape, and was thrilled to discover that it was complete and undistorted. I guessed it to be decorated but had to wait a few days while it was professionally cleaned. On seeing it cleaned I wasn't disappointed. Here was a balanced pattern of roundels and curves, an obvious counterpart to the upper back plate with its related but asymmetrical scheme (Pl. 7b). The discovery put pep in our step and we were able to recover in the following weeks another of the flat, strip-like mounts, which, I speculate, may have been attached to a box (Pl. 9b). We also recovered two small castings—flat bars with projecting hinge loops that were originally soldered to the tops of the end plates (Pls 8 and 10). It was with these that the flanged strap-attachment(s) must have engaged, although the requisite linking elements have never turned up. Passing through a hole in one of the bars is part of the pin with which the shrine was locked; a separate find was the other end of the same pin still joining the interlocking tabs that had originally been mounted on the adjacent internal edges of the front plates (Pl. 10). This evidence that the shrine could be opened and closed was confirmed by our discovery of half, or one side, of the hinge—a piano-hinge in today's terminology (Pl. 11). It's worth noting that some of these pieces were found during the process of

Pl. 10—The Clonmore shrine: suspension fitting and lock (M. McKeown).

0   5cm

Pl. 11—The Clonmore shrine: hinge (M. McKeown).

reinstatement. The turning over and spreading of the spoil-heaps offered a second chance to create, and systematically search, fresh surfaces. We had excavated to a maximum depth of 70cm (to the old ground level) over an area of some 1500m² and had moved, I suppose, hundreds of tons of stuff.

It had been established, meanwhile, that parts of a comparable shrine had come to light in the 1980s in Bobbio in the north of Italy, the famous foundation of the Irish monk Columbanus, who died there in 615. These had been studied (in 1988) and were soon to be published by Michael Ryan. The 1991 campaign having produced enough pieces to allow the Clonmore shrine to be understood, I made arrangements to travel to Bobbio in March the following year. This turned out to be a most rewarding visit, but an obvious difficulty was posed by the separation of the parts of the shrine in two institutions (the Archivi Storici Bobiensi and the Museo dell'Abbazia), so that they could not be studied *ensemble*. Having made the necessary contacts in 1992, it proved possible to bring all the pieces together on the occasion of a second visit in 1994 and to reassemble them temporarily. I took the notes and Moira Concannon took the photographs (Pl. 12). The similarity between the two shrines was brought home to me as never before, and not just in terms of their form and decoration. They

19

Pl. 12—The Bobbio shrine: front (M. Concannon).

were similarly hinged and locked, and so similar are their plates in weight and feel as to convince me that the Bobbio shrine was made in Ireland rather than in Italy under Irish influence. Because its decoration is confined to the upper and lower front plates and is less complex than that of the Clonmore shrine, the Bobbio shrine may be the later of the two. But both are products of the same tradition and confirm that metalworking in Ireland flourished under Church patronage in the seventh century.

The original dredgings had been spread far and wide at Clonmore and large areas had still been no more than superficially searched. Circumstances beyond my control delayed a return to the site until 2000, in which year we stripped an area twice the size of that already excavated, and succeeded in finding the base and the second lower end plate (Pl. 13). This is the left-hand end plate and, as expected, it has a (torn) hole in the top right-hand corner through which the locking pin originally passed. Surprisingly, the base and end plate were made in one piece but had broken on the line of the original right-angled bend. The frustrated hope of finding one of the upper end plates (the hips of the roof) brought us back to Clonmore in 2001. Our frustration continued, but was alleviated by the discovery of the second half of the hinge (Pl. 11).

And there things stand. We have *most* of the Clonmore shrine, and haven't abandoned hope of finding at least one of the missing hips. The fame of the

Pl. 13—The Clonmore shrine: the base and left-hand end plate as found in 2000, (a) before and (b) after cleaning. The base was subsequently straightened and the end plate restored to its original curvature by Ian McIntyre of the British Museum (M. McKeown).

shrine is both local and international. It has been the subject of a string of short publications, as well as of numerous passing references, and has illustrated three book-covers. It will, I hope, be published definitively soon, with reference not just to the Bobbio shrine but also to others of Continental manufacture, specifically those from Beromünster (Switzerland), from the district of Overbetuwe (Netherlands) and from Ennabeuren (Germany). The signs are that, contrary to what I first thought, both the Clonmore and Bobbio shrines belong to the late, rather than the early, seventh century.

The Ulster Museum is preparing as I write (June 2006) for a period of closure and redevelopment, and a grand reopening is scheduled for 2009. The Clonmore shrine figures substantially in our plans.

Acknowledgements

Thanks are due to the many people who joined in the search for the Clonmore shrine, and especially to the finders of its various parts: Dean Hughes, Eamon McCurry, Dominic Quinn, the late Albert Trenier, James Walshe and Martina Wisdom. Thanks are also due to the Donaghy and McKee families for permission to excavate on their lands; to the Hayes family for generously granting a right of way; to the Environment and Heritage Service (DoE), the licensing authority, for financial and other support; to Ian McIntyre (British Museum) for his expert intervention; and to Michael McKeown and Moira Concannon (Ulster Museum) for their photography. Thanks are due, finally, to the authorities in Bobbio for facilities afforded in 1992 and 1994, and to the British Academy for a travel grant in the latter year. Plates 7–13 are reproduced by permission of the Trustees of National Museums Northern Ireland.

Further reading

Bourke, C. 1991 The Blackwater shrine. *Dúiche Néill* 6, 103–6.

Bourke, C. 1994–5 The early Irish reliquary in Bobbio. *Archivum Bobiense* 16–17, 287–99.

Bourke, C. 1995 Further notes on the Clonmore shrine. *Seanchas Ardmhacha* 16 (2), 27–32.

Bourke, C. 2001 Ireland's earliest Christian metalwork: the Clonmore shrine. *Minerva* 12 (6), 6–7.

Bourke, C. 2001–2 Clonmore and Bobbio, two seventh-century shrines. *Dúiche Néill* 14, 24–34.

Bourke, C. and Warner, R. 1991 A seventh-century reliquary from County Armagh. *Archaeology Ireland* 5 (2), 16.

Ryan, M. 1991a Decorated Irish metalwork in Bobbio, Italy. *Archaeology Ireland* 5 (2), 17.

Ryan, M. 1991b Decorated metalwork in the Museo dell'Abbazia, Bobbio, Italy. *Journal of the Royal Society of Antiquaries of Ireland* 120 (1990), 102–11.

Youngs, S. (ed.) 1989 *'The work of angels': masterpieces of Celtic metalwork, 6th–9th centuries AD*. London.

3

Murder mystery at Dundrum Castle, Co. Dublin

Elizabeth O'Brien

During my many years of researching and working with human skeletal remains I have come across many odd situations, and while one is always prepared to expect the unexpected, the event described below is the most unusual and bizarre I have encountered to date.

Background

Dundrum Castle in south County Dublin, on the crest of an east-facing ridge overlooking a valley with a small river known locally as the Slang, has had a long and varied history. It starts *c.* 1170 when, after the Norman occupation of Dublin, the lands around Dundrum were granted to John de Clahella. The building of the castle at Dundrum commenced sometime around 1200 (pieces of oak planking nailed together, recovered from the base of a probable garderobe outlet, were examined by David Brown at Queen's University, Belfast, and have produced an estimated felling date of AD 1187 ± 9). In 1239 Dundrum passed from John de Clahull to his brother Hugh de Clahull, but from 1246 until 1268, after the death of Hugh de Clahull, Dundrum became part of the possessions of the then bishop of Meath. By 1268 Dundrum had become the possession of Sir Robert Bagod of Baggotrath, and by 1326 it had been acquired by a member of the Fitzwilliam family. The Fitzwilliams lived at Dundrum until 1490, when they moved their residence to Baggotrath Castle, and the castle at Dundrum was allowed to fall into disrepair. It was rebuilt by Sir Thomas Fitzwilliam in 1590 and was occupied by his family until the wars of 1641–59, when it again fell into disrepair. The castle was restored by Lt. Col. Isaac Dobson, an officer of the Parliamentary army to whom it was leased in 1653, and continued to be inhabited up until the close of the eighteenth century. In 1887/8 it is described as a roofless ivy-covered ruin with flower-beds in the interior. From 1923 to 1926 a Captain Goff, whose father, Dr Goff, occupied the nearby Dundrum House, operated a butcher's shop from inside the castle. This business was continued for a further period of time by a Captain de Caen, and finally during the 1940s part of the castle was converted into a cow byre by a local dairyman. An article in the Property Section of the *Irish Times* for 16 March 1984 reported that Dundrum Castle was to be refurbished for use as office accommodation. Instead, however, the castle was purchased by David Newman Johnson, whose intention was to restore part of the castle and make it habitable.

Excavation and discovery

As Dundrum Castle and its environs formed a zone of archaeological potential (SMRDu022–23), it became necessary that the area immediately in and around the buildings should be archaeologically excavated before any restoration work could commence.

In 1987 Rathmichael Historical Society agreed to undertake this excavation work as part of their ongoing annual Archaeology Summer School Project, and excavation (E419) continued over five seasons (1987–91) under the direction of the present writer.

Before excavation could properly begin, overgrown bushes and shrubs, together with layers of accumulated rubble, had to be removed from around the ruined buildings (Pl. 14). On 13 August 1987 a group of Summer School volunteers, under the supervision of Tricia Ryan, were allotted the apparently safe and straightforward task of clearing by hand the remains of an old rose-bed located in the angle between the smaller and larger towers of the sixteenth-century part of the castle ('x' on Pl. 14). I was supervising the removal of a dangerous modern wall elsewhere on site when an excited volunteer appeared, informing me that one of the volunteers (David Cubitt) had 'found a skull'. My heart sank; something was very wrong. I immediately inspected the 'find' and trowelled the area. What emerged was the face portion of a human skull (Pl. 15) with, surprisingly, the soft cartilage of the nose still present. The skull fragment had been deposited, face up, in a shallow pit dug into gravelly subsoil beneath the loam of the flower-bed. Other material in the surrounding area consisted of some pieces of clay pipe-stems, clay flowerpot sherds etc. Because this 'find' was obviously not in an archaeological context, the local gardaí had to be informed. With the arrival of three garda cars, and many gardaí, our site became a 'crime scene' for the following few hours. The gardaí, who were as puzzled by the 'find'

Pl. 14—*Dundrum Castle prior to excavation (1978).*

Pl. 15—*The face in the flower-bed.*

25

as we were, insisted that the evidence had to be removed for forensic examination. But, ever the 'complete' archaeologists, we requested that before its removal we should be allowed to fully record the 'find' (E419:53) with coordinates, depths etc., and to our surprise and gratification they agreed to this.

We were very pleased when we learned that our friend the late Dr Máire Delaney had been given permission by the then state pathologist Dr J. Harbison to undertake the forensic examination of the skull. The following are extracts from her subsequent report (Appendix 2 in final excavation report, 2002):

'. . . Sex: Male. Age: 25–30 years (could be older but unlikely). Condition: Incomplete, the mandible is absent. The parietals, occipital, basal bones and right temporal bones are absent. The frontal bone is missing superiorly in a line slanting down from the right side to the left. The left zygomatic [malar, or cheek] bone is roughly broken or hacked just medial to the zygomatic temporal junction. There is a large hole in the left maxilla, behind the zygomatic arch. There are depressed fragments at the apex of this hole. There is a large curved area of damage at the root of the nose extending upwards . . . the front teeth from the right first premolar to the left canine are missing (due to trauma). Most of the above damage was sustained at or around the time of death . . . the anterior portion of the left temporal bone which adjoins the right sphenoid is present. It shows three distinct cut marks . . .'

'Trauma: This fragment of skull shows marks of extreme violence at or around the time of death.'

Dr Delaney then goes on to give detailed descriptions of the various wounds on the skull fragment, to which there were no signs of healing. In her conclusion she states:

'There are at least four wounds inflicted. Two involved cutting the skull into probably four pieces, at a time very close to death. Two involved the use of blunt instruments on the forehead and left zygomatic/maxillary area. These were also inflicted at or near the time of death, and may be associated with the cause of death. These findings suggest that the individual was violently killed with the use of excessive violence. The skull may then have been cut vertically and horizontally, while fresh . . . the presence of the left temporal with the rest indicates that the skull was fresh when buried as it would have separated if much decay had set in.'

It would seem, therefore, that the face of this victim had been removed and buried in order to prevent identification.

Based on the fact that the victim's oral hygiene was poor, with evidence of periodontal disease associated with tooth loss, and on his moderately coarse diet, which included some sugars but less than in a modern diet and did not include a large amount of grit, fibre or very coarse meat, Dr Delaney suggested that the individual had lived more than 60 years ago (prior to 1987). This would place this unsolved murder at some time in the early twentieth century. One cannot but wonder whether the availability of butchering equipment in the vicinity of the castle at that time contributed in some measure to this mysterious crime.

During our subsequent four seasons of excavation at the castle, no further human bone was recovered.

While our rather gruesome find became a two- or three-day wonder for the local papers and the general public, I must confess that the most exciting discoveries at Dundrum Castle, as far as those directly involved in the excavation were concerned, included the evidence we uncovered for the original date of the castle's construction, the discovery of the moat, the base of the gate-tower, and the three beam-slots for the counterbalanced drawbridge entrance to the thirteenth-century castle.

Postscript

The ruined Dundrum Castle is now enveloped on its north, west and south sides within a gated development complex of houses and apartments. To the east, the valley with its river and mills which the Castle once overlooked has now been replaced by the busy 'Wyckham bypass' (beneath which the culverted river flows) and the vast new shopping mall known as the Dundrum Town Centre.

Acknowledgements

The final report on the excavations at Dundrum Castle, containing many specialist reports, was completed in 2000 with the aid of a generous grant from the Heritage Council.

I also gratefully acknowledge the input to the excavations of the Rathmichael Historical Society and its members, especially the late Joan Delany. Thanks are due to the many volunteers, who included several now professional archaeologists who 'cut their archaeological teeth' at Dundrum; to Tricia Ryan, the late Paddy Healy, the late Leo Swan and the late Dr Máire Delaney for their valuable input; and to David Newman Johnson for providing the Castle site for excavation.

Further reading

Ball, F.E. 1903 *A history of the county Dublin*, Vol. II, pp 64–73. Dublin.

Cunningham, G. 1987 *The Anglo-Norman advance into the south-west midlands of Ireland 1185–1221*. Roscrea.

Gilbert, J.T. (ed.) 1889 *Calendar of ancient records of Dublin*, Vol. I. Dublin.

McNeill, C. (ed.) 1950 *Calendar of Archbishop Alen's register c. 1171–1534*. [Extra volume of the *Journal of the Royal Society of Antiquaries of Ireland* for 1949.] Dublin.

Nolan, J. 1982 *Changing faces (a local history of Dundrum)*. Dublin.

O'Brien, E. 1988 Dundrum Castle, Dundrum, Co. Dublin. In I. Bennett (ed.), *Excavations 1987*, 13–14. Dublin.

O'Brien, E. 1989 Dundrum Castle, Dundrum, Co. Dublin. In I. Bennett (ed.), *Excavations 1988*, 14–15. Bray.

O'Brien, E. 1990 Dundrum Castle, Dundrum, Co. Dublin. In I. Bennett (ed.), *Excavations 1989*, 19. Bray.

O'Brien, E. 1991 Dundrum Castle, Dundrum, Co. Dublin. In I. Bennett (ed.), *Excavations 1990*, 25–6. Bray.

O'Brien, E. 1992 Dundrum Castle, Dundrum, Co. Dublin. In I. Bennett (ed.), *Excavations 1991*, 15–16. Bray.

O'Brien, E. 2000 Excavations at Dundrum Castle, Co. Dublin, E419 (1987–1991); final report, including specialists' reports. Unpublished report, lodged with the Heritage Council, Dúchas and the National Museum of Ireland.

Pembroke Estate Papers. Gilbert Library, Dublin, and National Archive, Dublin.

Simington, R.C. (ed.) 1945 *The Civil Survey 1645/56 Co. of Dublin*, Vol. VII. Dublin.

4

Where have all the wolves gone?

Kieran Hickey

One of the fascinating aspects of doing research on any topic is the curious material you come across, often not directly related to what you are looking for but terrifically interesting in its own right. From both my early days as a student and from my climate history research I became vaguely aware that there had been real wild wolves in Ireland right up until late medieval times. Wolves, apparently, had survived longer in Ireland than in England, Wales or Scotland. This fact absolutely fascinated me and, being aware that very little had been done on native Irish wolves before, the germ of a little side-research project began to take shape at the back of my mind. It was my intention from the outset simply to gather as much information as I could on the subject to see where it would lead me. For the first four years I just gathered information as I came across it and stuck it in a folder, telling no one, almost embarrassed to admit to my newfound interest in wolves. This extra research also kept me amused while trawling through vast numbers of history volumes looking for climate references to Ireland. Nearly ten years later I am still at it—so much for a little side-project to keep me amused. In the beginning I expected to get no more than a hundred references to wolves in Ireland, possibly a few more if I was lucky. The current total is over 500 and still rising. The initial avenues of investigation have broadened out in a variety of ways that I could never have even imagined when I first started out.

A number of questions dominated my thinking from the very start of the project. These were very simple but, given the nature of the evidence available to me, not very easy to answer. The first issue was how many wolves were likely to have existed in Ireland at any one time, and where they were located. Was I going to be dealing with a small number of wolves isolated in a few remote corners of Ireland, or were they much more widespread than that? Secondly, I wanted to establish why they had died out in Ireland. In particular, I wanted to know the factors that contributed to their demise and whether I could clearly identify the very last date at which a native Irish wild wolf was recorded.

Two publications were of immense use to me when I first started out on this quest. The first was a book (probably long forgotten) by J. E. Harting called *British animals extinct within historic times*, written in 1880. In this great work there is a large section devoted to wolves, including Irish wolves. This provided me with a range of material on which to start my work.

The second publication, by James Fairley, a former Professor of Zoology at NUI Galway and still going strong, was entitled *An Irish beast book: a natural history of Ireland's furred wildlife*. Indeed, Professor Fairley has published a number of very important books of bibliography on the subject of Irish wild mammals, including wolves, in addition to other books on Irish wild mammals and a whole range of other publications.

But, as the wolves might say—yes, there is an Irish tradition for talking wolves too—enough of the preamble; where is the meat in the story? Just to indicate the range of evidence available on the subject of wolves in Ireland I will give you a few brief examples under the headings of archaeology, folklore, place-names and history.

Archaeological evidence

There is no doubt that wolves have been present in Ireland for at least 20,000 years; we know this because of the dating of wolf bones found in a number of caves throughout the country, where they were preserved in the cave-floor sediments. Unfortunately, few of these caves have been scientifically excavated and only a small number of the bones have been radiocarbon-dated to determine their age. These caves, however, have given us a great insight into the animals that were present during the last Ice Age at a time when the ice sheets only covered the northern two-thirds of the country; this period, known as the Midlandian, ended around 13,000 years ago. These animals included the giant Irish elk (now extinct), reindeer, bears and other mammals no longer found in Ireland.

There is no doubt that during the great era of ringfort-building, between about AD 500 and 1000, many were constructed primarily for the protection of domestic animals during the night, to prevent them from being taken by raiders but also to protect them from wolves. In County Tyrone, according to Allen, where wolves were such a plague in Cromwell's time (during the mid-seventeenth century), they even raided the stone enclosures made to protect sheep. This practice of bringing animals in at night is still carried on in many

Pl. 16—A wolf approaches a sheep pen as the shepherd sleeps in this illustration from a thirteenth-century bestiary (reproduced by kind permission of the Fitzwilliam Museum, Cambridge, England).

countries in Eastern Europe, for example, where there remains a significant wolf population and therefore a continuing threat to the domestic animals (Pl. 16).

Folklore

Wolves play a very important role in Irish folklore, myth and legend. Stories about encounters with wolves are relatively common; many early Irish saints seemed to attract wolves with ease. Other accounts tell of the use of wolf parts as medicine and charms against evil and ill health. Wolves were generally considered to be evil creatures associated with the devil, hence the depiction of a wolf in the Book of Kells (Pl. 17).

In the realm of medicine there are a number of bizarre concoctions, involving different wolf body parts and even wolf dung, for treating a variety of illnesses. For example, the wearing of a band of wolfskin like a girdle was considered a preventative for the falling sickness (epilepsy). Pickering records that hanging a wolf's tail over a barn door would keep other wolves away, whereas, more bizarrely, eating a dish of wolf meat will prevent a person from seeing ghosts, and sleeping with a wolf's head under the pillow will ward off nightmares.

Pl. 17—The wolf from f. 76v of the eighth-century Book of Kells in the Library of Trinity College, Dublin (reproduced by kind permission of the Board of Trinity College, Dublin).

Discomfort aside, I should think that anyone who sleeps with a wolf's head under their pillow is more likely to have nightmares.

There is even a strong werewolf tradition in Irish folklore. One of the most surprising folklore aspects was the belief that a man and woman from the barony of Ossory, lying predominantly in County Kilkenny, became wolves for a period of seven years, and this helps to explain beliefs in such supernatural creatures as werewolves. I mentioned talking wolves earlier and there are a surprisingly large number of references to this phenomenon. O'Flaherty notes that the Annals of Clonmacnoise for the year AD 688 record a reference to a wolf speaking with a human voice. Similarly, in his *Life of Molaise*, also known as St Laisren, Kenny notes that, some 50 years after the saint's death, amongst other strange occurrences was a wolf heard to speak with a human voice, to the horror of all.

Even today some curious customs survive from a time when wolves were ever present. One such custom relates to funerals at the Gate Cemetery, Ogonnelloe, Co. Clare. This cemetery, medieval in date, is walled and located in the centre of a field. The mourners carry the coffin around the cemetery and place it at intervals on the ground outside the walls, so that the wolves would not know where the corpse was finally buried. This tradition suggests the rather gruesome possibility and perhaps real fear (in the past) that wolves might disturb freshly dug graves in their search for food. In western Scotland many graveyards were on offshore islands for the same reason.

Place-names

A considerable number of place-names in Ireland are associated with wolves. A few of these are in English, e.g. Wolf Island in Lough Gill, Co. Sligo (Fig. 1). The vast majority, however, are 'hidden' in Irish place-names. This is because there are

Fig. 1— Location map of the English-language wolf place-names in Ireland (drawing by Dr Siubhán Comer).

33

a number of Irish words for wolves, including *Mac-tire* ('son of the country'—
e.g. the townland of Isknamacteera in County Kerry) and *faolchu* ('evil hound'—
e.g. Feltrim Hill, Co. Dublin), and numerous place-names contain *breagh* (wolf)
and its variations, e.g. Breaghy (wolf plain/field) in Drumcree, Co. Armagh, and
Breaghva (wolf plain/field) in Kilrush, Co. Clare. So far I have discovered that
over twenty of the 32 counties of Ireland have place-names linked to wolves.
There are even a few surnames associated with wolves in Ireland, including
O'Connell, originally a County Kerry name that translates as 'strong as a wolf'.

Historical

There is a vast array of historical documentary information relating to wolves in
Ireland. The first, inscribed in ogham (an early form of writing using a simple
alphabet composed of lines and notches, dating from between the fourth and
seventh centuries) on standing stones, overlap with references in the earliest
monastic annals, dating from the sixth and seventh centuries, and other accounts
that record the presence of native wolves right up to the end of the eighteenth
century. These sources include lists of animals found in Ireland in the monastic
annals; Brehon laws (ancient Gaelic legal system); legislation and bounties; early
natural histories and descriptions of the country; descriptions of wolf
encounters, the hunting of wolves, wolf attacks on farm animals and, more
rarely, on humans; and letters and diaries. This historical evidence suggests that
wolves occurred throughout the island of Ireland, and no part of it is without
some reference to them. Below are a selection of the several hundred historical
references to wolves in Ireland to give you an idea of the sorts of encounters that
occurred between humans and wolves.

In the eighth century the monk Nennius, describing the wonders of Ireland,
states that, with the exception of the mouse, the wolf and the fox, Ireland was
not inhabited by any noxious animals.

The wolf was considered the principal predator of livestock, particularly
lambs and calves. As a result, wolf-hunting was considered a public duty:
according to a ninth-century Brehon law-text, a client must hunt wolves once a
week.

The Annals of Connacht for 1420 state that many persons were killed by
wolves in that year (Kelly 1997).

In a written description of Ireland compiled for Sir John Perrot, the lord deputy
of Ireland, in January 1584 it was suggested that leases for tenants should include
provision for the trapping and killing of what were described as ravening and
devouring wolves, and this was to be done with traps, snares or other devices.

Lord William Russell, lord deputy of Ireland, records in his diary that on 26 May 1596 he and Lady Russell went wolf-hunting at Kilmainham, which at that time was quite close to Dublin city, although it would now be considered very much part of the central city area.

In a letter dated to 1611, Roger Braben of Kinalmeaky, Co. Cork, writes of matters largely concerning his horse stud, but also states, as a matter of fact, that one of his colts had been killed by a wolf.

It is stated in the description attached to the Down Survey map of Ballybay, Co. Offaly (1655–6), that few sheep were kept in that barony on account of the prevalence of wolves.

In 1698 the stock book of William Conyngham in County Down notes that a two-year-old from his herd of black cattle was killed by a wolf, without any indication that the incident was particularly remarkable.

In 1710 or 1714 (depending upon author) a last presentment was made by Brian Townsend to the grand jury in County Cork for killing wolves (i.e. to claim the bounty).

One of the last wolves in Ireland was killed near Louisburg, Co. Mayo, in 1745.

It is asserted by many persons of weight and veracity that a wolf was killed in the Wicklow Mountains as recently as 1770.

How did wolves survive in Ireland in the historical period?

Wolves survived in Ireland up to the end of the eighteenth century owing to a number of factors. The first of these was the extensive wilderness areas that existed around the island at least until 1700. These included extensive mountain ranges and large forests with few human inhabitants. Ireland's human population in the 1600s was probably around 1.5 million. So there were extensive areas for wolves to hunt and breed, unaffected or only lightly affected by human interference.

The Irish evidence suggests that pack sizes were small, probably consisting of no more than the dominant breeding pair and one or two other adult wolves, a few juveniles and that year's cubs. This small pack size was an adaptation to the relative scarcity of large mammals such as deer and the absence of farm animals in many of the forest and mountain areas. Wolves are opportunistic feeders and will eat just about anything, including insects, worms, rodents, fish and crabs, in addition to carrion of any type. Interestingly, like urban foxes today, there is evidence to show that wolves were skulking around the outskirts of Dublin city and Cork city scavenging for food. In a letter dated 1698, for example, Herbert

Fig. 2—Illustration of an ancient carved stone in bas-relief from Ardnaglass Castle, Co. Sligo, supposedly depicting a dog attacking a wolf (from Webber 1841).

notes that one J. Howel, an alderman of Cork city, states that wolves were still present in his locality but that they were now considered as game and as a diversion as opposed to noxious and hateful. This also indicates that their numbers were in significant decline in this area at the time.

Remarkably, and somewhat sadly, no wolf skeletons, heads or skins seem to have survived from the time when they were part of Ireland's landscape. In addition, there are almost no illustrations of wolves from Ireland, and all that we know about what they looked like comes from a few scattered references and a number of ecclesiastical and other carvings allegedly showing wolves. One possible exception to this is an ancient carved stone in rude bas-relief from Ardnaglass Castle, Co. Sligo (Fig. 2). According to Fairley, this supposedly depicts a dog attacking a wolf. The carved stone was presented to the Royal Irish Academy in 1841 by Mr Charles Webber and is said to commemorate the destruction of the last wolf in Ireland. The stone, however, appears to be medieval in date and therefore pre-dates the destruction of the last wolves in Ireland by a number of centuries.

Population estimates

Based on a number of indirect sources of evidence and information that we have at our disposal, it is possible to make a rough estimate of wolf population numbers in Ireland over several periods. The first approach is to examine the records of trade and export of wolfskins from Ireland. The murage charter of 1361 for Galway city, for instance, lists the taxable commodities in full. Included in it, among many other things, arc wolfskins. This indicates that wolfskins were seen as a common enough commodity to be worth listing in a tax charter. The evidence of the export trade comes primarily from the port books of key Irish trading ports like Bristol. The Bristol accounts alone show an average of between 100 and 300 wolfskins exported from Ireland per year throughout the 1500s. Most astonishingly, in the tax year 1558–9 a high figure of 961 wolfskins were exported from Ireland into the port of Bristol alone. This indicates a very substantial wolf population in Ireland throughout the 1500s.

The second approach uses a habitat availability assessment based on the landscape and a human population assessment of Ireland for the period in and around 1600, equating this with the requirements of a wolf pack in terms of territory and food resources. At this time there were still large tracts of wilderness areas, including forest and mountains, ideally suited for wolves. It is estimated, based on an average pack size of between five and ten individuals, that these areas could have supported a wolf population of between 400 and 800 individuals.

The third approach was to look at the figures paid out for bounties. It is interesting to note that in 1653 the Cromwellian government set bounties of £6 for a female, £5 for a male, £3 for a hunting juvenile and 10s. for a cub. These were very substantial amounts of money at the time. The records for payment of only two bounties have survived, however, and these date from 1649–56 and from 1655 or 1665 (date not legible).

In the first, the sum of £3,847 5s. is enumerated for bounties for all of Ireland, and this was paid out between July 1649 and November 1656, a period of seven and a half years. This represents an average annual payment of £513, indicating a wolf kill of between 200 and 400 individual animals. Clearly, to sustain this loss the actual population of wolves must have been considerably larger than this, possibly between 600 and 800 or more individuals.

In the second bounty figure, a total payment of £243 5s. 4d. was made for wolves killed in the counties of Galway, Mayo, Sligo and parts of Leitrim alone. Unfortunately no breakdown of the numbers of animals is given, but it can be assumed that the figure represents a mixture of females, males, juveniles and cubs, as it is likely that wolves would have been hunted pack by pack. This figure can be taken to represent a wolf kill of between 75 and 150 wolves and indicates a significant wolf population in this part of the country—bearing in mind that this area represents less than 25% of the land mass of Ireland.

Putting all these sources of information together, it is clear that Ireland had a very significant wolf population during the 1500s and early 1600s, possibly well in excess of a thousand individuals. By the mid-1600s it was probably less than a thousand, and a rapid decline followed throughout the late 1600s and 1700s until the last one was dispatched, most likely in the year 1786. You can imagine my amazement to discover that wolves were once so widespread in Ireland and my delight at being able to estimate their numbers with relative confidence.

Causes of extermination

The extermination of the wolf from the Irish landscape resulted from a number of factors. These include significant landscape change, in particular the loss of most of the remaining tracts of native oak forest, and the encroachment of farming activity into areas not previously involved in agriculture during the late 1600s and 1700s, with the resulting growth in population. The areas in which wolves could breed undisturbed would have been significantly reduced, intensifying the pressure on the existing wolf population.

A major role was also played by legislation and bounties, in particular those of the Cromwellian government in Ireland in the 1650s. The new settlers from England and Scotland were horrified to discover that there was a significant wolf population in the country and perceived this as a serious threat to themselves and their livestock. In some of the literature at this time Ireland is even referred to as 'Wolf-land'. Very substantial bounties were introduced for wolf kills, and this led to the systematic hunting of wolves and their clearance from areas around the country, until at last large areas were devoid of wolves throughout the latter half of the 1600s. A number of professional wolf-hunters even came to Ireland to help carry out the extermination. In 1653 Captain Edward Piers was granted land in County Meath on condition that he destroy fourteen wolves over five years or forfeit £100 annually—a very considerable sum.

By the early 1700s the wolf population in Ireland was in terminal decline and probably confined only to a few small isolated areas, well away from human interference. The very last reference to the killing of a wolf in Ireland for which I have clear evidence occurred in 1786. There are a few references to wolves stretching up to 1810, but these have proved very difficult to authenticate and it is most likely that the dates are erroneous.

The last authenticated date for the killing of a wolf in Ireland, therefore, is 1786. This occurred on Mount Leinster, Co. Carlow, after a farmer had a number of sheep killed by a lone wolf, which was subsequently hunted down and killed by the wolfhounds of John Watson of Ballydarton, Co. Carlow.

As a result of the long history of wolves in Ireland there is an enormous wealth of evidence of their existence. Much of this has been overlooked in the past, partly because some of the material is hidden in early Irish sources and is therefore not readily accessible to some researchers but also on account of the scattered and incidental nature of the information. This includes evidence from a wide variety of sources, including archaeology, folklore, place-names, monastic annals and a great number of other later historical documentary data. Of course, the existence of a specially bred Irish wolf dog or wolfhound is itself evidence of a significant wolf population stretching back thousands of years.

This brief article perhaps gives a small flavour of the information accumulated on wolves and is part of my ongoing research into the natural and cultural history of wolves in Ireland, which will be published shortly as a book. A few short publications have come out on the topic so far, however (Hickey 2000; 2003; 2005). I would hope that, like Harting in 1880 and Fairley in 1984, someone will come along in a hundred years' time and say that Hickey's stuff on wolves is very interesting, though, no doubt, they will also comment that it's a shame he missed out on so much material—such is the nature of research. Obviously, any references to wolves in Ireland that you can bring to my attention will be greatly appreciated.

Bibliography

Allen, F.A. 1909 The wolf in Scotland and Ireland. *Transactions of the Caradoc and Severn Valley Field Club* **5**, 68–74.

Fairley, J. 1972 *Irish wild mammals: a guide to the literature*. Galway.

Fairley, J. 1983 Exports of wild mammal skins from Ireland in the eighteenth century. *Irish Naturalists' Journal* **21** (2), 75–9.

Fairley, J. 1984 *An Irish beast book: a natural history of Ireland's furred wildlife* (2nd edn). Belfast.

Fairley, J. 1992 *Irish wild mammals: a guide to the literature* (2nd edn). Galway.

Harting, J.E. 1880 *British animals extinct within historic times*. London.

Herbert, T. 1885 Wolves in Ireland. *Zoologist* **3** (9), 268.

Hickey, K.R. 2000 A geographical perspective on the decline and extermination of the Irish wolf *Canis lupus*—an initial assessment. *Irish Geography* **33** (2), 185–98. [Available online at www.ucd.ie/gsi/journal.html and then look up Vol. 33, No. 2, where there is a downloadable PDF file of the complete article.]

Hickey, K.R. 2003 Wolf: forgotten Irish hunter. *Wild Ireland* **3**, 10–13. [Available online at www.nuigalway.ie/geography/wolf.pdf.]

Hickey, K.R. 2005 The history of wolves in Ireland. *Wolfprint* **24**, 10–13.

Kelly, F. 1997 *Early Irish farming: a study based mainly on the law-texts of the 7th and 8th centuries AD*. Early Irish Law Series Vol. IX. Dublin.

Kenny, C. 1998 *Molaise: abbot of Leighlin and hermit of Holy Island*. Killala, Co. Mayo.

O'Flaherty, R. 1846 [1684] *A chorographical description of west or H-Iar Connaught* (edited with notes and illustrations by J. Hardiman). Dublin.

Pickering, D. 1998 *Dictionary of superstitions*. London.

Webber, C.T. 1841 Untitled note. *Proceedings of the Royal Irish Academy* 2, 65–6.

5

Ice pops, a tent and plaster of Paris: essential requirements for excavation

Rory Sherlock

Sunshine archaeology

'Twenty-four hours in the life of a contract archaeologist.' I could suggest that my experience of excavating a Bronze Age burial in Cork would make a perfect subject for a 24-episode series, with each episode dramatising one hour of the story, if an American television show had not monopolised the motif. But, given that I spent at least six of those 24 hours sound asleep in bed, perhaps some of it would not make for the most compelling viewing. It was, however, an exciting time, and I, together with my colleagues, still remember the excavation for a variety of reasons, some for the technical challenges it presented and others for more subjective reasons—what we might call the experiential discourse if we ever strayed towards the rarefied plateau of theoretical archaeology!

At the beginning of the summer of 2001, I had recently moved to Cork and was settling into my new job as a site director with Sheila Lane and Associates, a growing archaeological consultancy then based in Carrigaline, to the south of 'da real capital', that urban conurbation known to outsiders as 'Cork city'. I was only in the post a few weeks when we began work on the N8 Glanmire–Watergrasshill Road Scheme—a long-awaited dual-carriageway construction project destined to drag at least part of the Cork–Dublin road into the new century. At the time, it was beginning to be commonplace for archaeological test-trenching to precede road construction works by some months so that at least some of the previously unknown sites on the line of the new road could be found and excavated well in advance of engineering works. In the light of an embargo on fieldwork owing to the threat of foot and mouth disease, however, the limited test-trenching on this particular road scheme began just a short few weeks before large-scale topsoil-stripping commenced. Most of the archaeological sites found were therefore

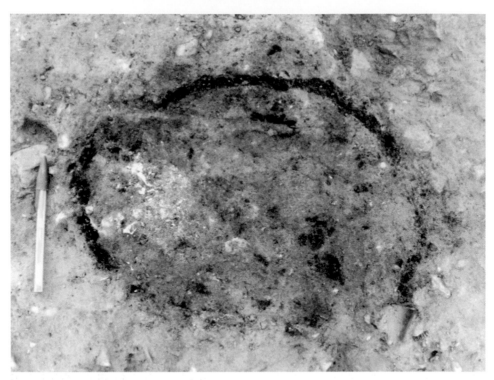

Pl. 18—The charcoal-rich feature as it appeared prior to excavation (photo: R. Sherlock).

discovered through monitoring the many bulldozers and 50-tonne excavators engaged in the topsoil-stripping. These sites were then cordoned off in order to protect them until such time as an archaeological team arrived to begin excavations.

This, essentially, was how I found myself investigating a small charcoal-rich feature in the townland of Killydonoghoe at the southern end of the road corridor on a sunny day in June 2001 (Pl. 18). There was an ongoing need to quickly assess and excavate features in the area, and the weather made working conditions on the site far from ideal. A wonderful spell of sunny weather had dried the exposed subsoil to a degree that made hand-excavation difficult, and the dust generated by the numerous heavy machines working in the area often blew across the site in gusts, engulfing excavators and excavations in a fine orangey-brown silt. It soon became apparent, however, that there was more to this particular feature than first met the eye.

Pieces of cremated bone were embedded in the subsoil, and then pieces of coarse pottery were also noted, some of which were lying on their sides while others were held upright by the soil around them. As the afternoon progressed, the upright pottery fragments were found to form a subcircular shape, and we realised that we were looking at the remains of a large pottery vessel of probable prehistoric date. It had clearly been truncated horizontally by years of tillage, and perhaps inadvertently by the more recent topsoil-stripping programme. The pottery was somewhat fragile, and given the importance of the discovery—a cremation burial associated with the remains of an *in situ* pottery vessel—it was decided (following discussions with Avril Purcell, the archaeological project manager for the road scheme) to seek expert assistance. Cathy Daly, a Dublin-based conservator, agreed to come to the site the very next day to oversee the excavation of the remains of the pottery vessel and gave detailed instructions on how we should proceed.

It was now late afternoon and there was a lot to do in preparation for Cathy's arrival the following day. The plan was to lift the remains of the vessel *in situ*, along with part of its surrounding context, as a single block of earth, and then to remove this block to a conservation laboratory where it could be 'micro-excavated' under more controlled conditions. In order to lift the earthen block, a trench had to be excavated around the vessel, about 10cm out from the visible pottery fragments, with the aim of leaving the pottery embedded in the top of an earthen pedestal which could then be carefully removed. Before the encircling trench could be excavated, the area was drawn, photographed and recorded in detail, and so, almost without our noticing it, the normal end to our working day slipped by. Most of the archaeological team tidied up their areas and paid a cursory visit to 'the burial' before heading for home. At 7.00p.m. the mechanical excavators and bulldozers were shut down for the night and, as the archaeologists on monitoring duty departed, a peaceful silence fell on the site as the dust finally began to settle. Given the small size of the area to be excavated, our excavation team had been rationalised to just two. Niamh O'Rourke, a site assistant on the team who had volunteered to stay on, and I shared the tasks of trowelling, recording and photographing as we gradually deepened the narrow trench around the vessel. Cremated bone was carefully gathered from the excavated material, and soon the next surprise came to light: the burial deposit was associated with not one, but two pottery vessels. This second, smaller, vessel, set adjacent to the first, had probably been broken many years before, perhaps as the burial pit collapsed as a result of agricultural activity. Gradually we unearthed a series of pale red pottery fragments in the soil close to the other vessel. These sherds were very fragile, finely decorated and noticeably thinner, paler in colour and finer in fabric than the first. Trowels were cast aside in favour of thin leafs (thin blades of steel used by masons for fine pointing work), and even a spoon was used when required. The fragments were then photographed *in situ* before they were removed from where they lay. This photographic record proved

Pl. 19—Fragments of the accompanying smaller pottery vessel, a food vessel, as it was revealed in situ *during excavation; note the fine incised decoration (photo: R. Sherlock).*

invaluable, as the fragile fragments never again looked quite as fresh and as well preserved as they did that evening (Pl. 19). During a short break in the evening's work, sustenance, in the form of ice pops, was procured from the nearby shop, which was admittedly more accustomed to supplying the workers on the road scheme with breakfast rolls at 10a.m. rather than ice pops ten or eleven hours later. By the time dusk began to settle on the Cork landscape, the excavation of the encircling trench had been completed and all was ready for the following day. We left the site with a great sense of satisfaction after an exceptional day, secure in the knowledge that such exciting and fulfilling days do not occur very often and are to be savoured whenever they do. The following day also proved to be exceptional, but for very different reasons.

Underwater archaeology

The next morning the blue skies of the previous day had given way to grey clouds, but there was a palpable sense of excitement amongst the excavation crew while we completed various tasks and awaited the arrival of the conservator from Dublin. Cathy Daly arrived before our morning break and quickly got to work

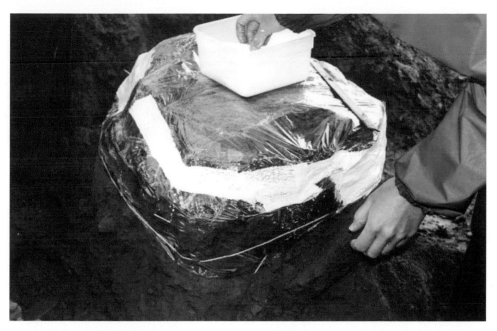

Pl. 20—The earthen pedestal containing the burial deposit and cinerary urn as it was being encased in cling-film and plaster of Paris in preparation for removal (photo: R. Sherlock)

preparing for the delicate operation ahead. She explained that the plan was to wrap the earthen pedestal with cling-film and then encase it in plaster of Paris in order to stabilise it before lifting (Pl. 20). We agreed that the *in situ* vessel was probably a Bronze Age cinerary urn and that it could therefore be over 30cm in height. The inherent difficulties in lifting an earthen block large enough to remove the entire vessel were discussed, but as many mechanical excavators were available in the vicinity this was not considered an insurmountable problem. In any case, as preparatory works were under way it became clear that the *in situ* vessel was not complete and had, in fact, been heavily disturbed by agricultural activity over the years. The relatively common Bronze Age funerary practice whereby urns were inverted over the burial deposits placed in a pit meant that the rim of the vessel had survived undisturbed below the ploughzone (Fig. 3). The body of the vessel, however, had been truncated by ploughing over the years, and so the earthen block that we were required to remove, in order to lift the remaining rim sections as one, measured little more than 10cm high and 40cm square.

As the morning passed, the weather deteriorated. The character of the excavation changed relatively quickly from the memorable sun-drenched,

Fig. 3—Artist's impression of a cinerary urn, inverted to cover the cremation deposit, with an accompanying food vessel in a stone-covered pit (drawing: Rhoda Cronin).

idealised exercise of the previous evening to a near-epic struggle with the elements. Cathy explained that dry conditions were needed in order for the plaster of Paris to set, and so a new plan had to be hastily devised. Heavy-gauge plastic sheeting was spread over a frame of timber uprights to form a makeshift tent to cover the excavation cutting; the flapping plastic was weighed down with large rocks and, at one troublesome corner, the spare wheel from the site Land Rover (Pl. 21). The rain was now falling heavily, to the extent that all the earth-moving equipment was shut down before noon and the drivers were stood down.

Pl. 21—The makeshift tent hastily erected to protect the excavation from the torrential rain (photo: R. Sherlock).

The weather forecast promised no improvement. The area around the excavation quickly became a sea of mud as the rain pooled and flowed across the exposed subsoil. Small drainage trenches had to be rapidly dug by hand on the uphill side of the tent to prevent surface water from flowing under it and flooding the excavation trench. As the rain continued to fall, the various archaeological crews working elsewhere on the road corridor were called off site to the relative comfort of their site huts, from which they occasionally made forays to check on our progress under the tent. Thus our already cramped but tolerably dry working space regularly gave shelter to curious engineers and archaeological colleagues, with those who had been watching the progress of the work for some time giving up their space to dripping newcomers. I generally left the delicate work of encasing the pedestal to Cathy and her new-found assistants, site supervisor Alison McQueen and site assistants Lisa Ennis and Niamh O'Rourke (Pl. 22), and instead tried to keep things going by providing support for their endeavours.

At one stage in the afternoon, with the rain falling steadily and the wind also attempting to make its presence felt, I had to leave the excavation to my colleagues for a while to go on a rescue mission. We had received an urgent phone call from another archaeological crew who, huddled in their site hut, were now in great fear of impending inundation. I arrived in the Land Rover pick-up to find the site hut, a converted steel container located in a slight hollow on an otherwise elevated site, surrounded by rising flood-water. The crew had moved the contents of the hut to the upper shelves and were now waiting to be

47

Pl. 22—(left to right) Alison McQueen, Niamh O'Rourke and Cathy Daly hard at work preparing the earthen pedestal for lifting (photo: R. Sherlock).

Pl. 23—The plaster-encased earthen pedestal ready for lifting, having been neatly decapitated by the wooden board (photo: R. Sherlock).

evacuated. I managed to reverse the pick-up down into the flood-water as far as the site hut, and the crew scrambled aboard over the open tailgate, the last one out shutting the hut door as the rising water lapped the sill. Archaeologists are used to people exclaiming 'Oh, that must be a really exciting job!', and this day, at least, was certainly living up to the reputation.

By mid-afternoon the top of the pedestal was firmly and successfully encased in plaster and a suitable board was found on which to carry the earthen block. The idea was to neatly truncate the earthen pedestal by pushing the board through it, thereby leaving the encased block sitting on the board (Pl. 23), but the practical application of this plan of action proved more problematic than the theory had envisaged. The stony nature of the subsoil made the task of pushing the board through the earthen pedestal very difficult. It was persuaded to comply, however, by the repeated application of a small lump hammer to the rearward edge of the board. By this time the delicate approach of the morning had given way to a more pragmatic attitude, but at least the careful work of the morning had created a secure plaster-encased block that was more than ready for some robust handling. Four or five pairs of hands lifted the board and the earthen block together onto the tailgate of the pick-up, and we slithered a meandering course to the site carpark. With a final cooperative heave, we deposited the precious cargo into the boot of Cathy's car, and soon she was on her way back to Dublin. It was time to call a halt to one of the wettest days on site that anyone could remember.

And then the rain stopped . . .

As Cathy's car left the site, the on-site works were drawn to a close, and soon the next phase of the excavation process began. The remains of the vessel were slowly excavated from its earthen cocoon in the comfort of the conservation laboratory, and we were delighted to hear that the urn rim was found to be decorated with an incised herringbone pattern on both its inner and outer faces and also on its upper edge (Pl. 24). The pottery was eventually passed to Helen Roche, a pottery expert, who classified the larger vessel, of which the rim survived, as an early Bronze Age Encrusted Urn (Fig. 4) and the smaller vessel, of which only fragments were found, as a Vase Food Vessel (Pl. 19). On the basis of the pottery and the form of the burial, Helen suggested that this was a Bronze Age cremation burial dating from between 2300 BC and 1700 BC, but added that it more than likely dated from between 2000 BC and 1700 BC owing to the presence of the accompanying Encrusted Urn (Fig. 3). In time Helen was proved correct, as the two radiocarbon determinations returned by the dating laboratory at the

Pl. 24—A decorated fragment of the cinerary urn.

University of Groningen (one derived from a small sample of oak charcoal and the other from a piece of cremated bone) yielded dates of 1915–1743 BC and 2033–1777 BC respectively (calibrated to 2 sigma).

Linda Lynch, an osteoarchaeologist with Aegis Archaeology Ltd, was also asked to contribute to the post-excavation process. The largest fragment of cremated bone recovered was part of the shaft of a longbone measuring 28.2mm in length. In addition, a number of other elements were identified, including fragments of the skull (including teeth), a vertebra, a number of ribs, longbone fragments (including a portion of the proximal head of a radius and a fragment of the anterior spine of a tibia) and a small number of hand and foot bones. Linda concluded that a portion of the remains of at least one adult individual were deposited in the burial, and that there was evidence for the deliberate pounding or crushing of the bones in the interval between the cremation and the burial.

The wider context of the site is also of considerable interest. Evidence for a continuity of activity throughout the Bronze Age was revealed during other excavations in the townland of Killydonoghoe undertaken as part of the N8 Glanmire–Watergrasshill Road Scheme. The burial we had discovered, dating from between 2033 BC and 1743 BC, was followed by a series of grain-storage pits just 210m away, which were dated to between 1599 BC and 1261 BC. These storage pits were in turn followed by a Bronze Age house, also just 210m from the burial, which was dated to between 1211 BC and 919 BC, and by two other

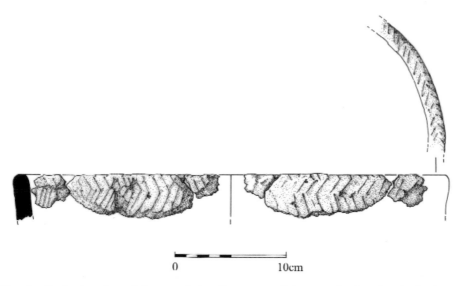

Fig. 4—Scale drawing of the remaining fragments of the urn rim bearing incised herringbone decoration (drawing: Rhoda Cronin).

cremation burials, 260m and 510m away from the site, dating from 1127–905 BC and 1255–941 BC respectively.

In retrospect, the excavation of the burial and associated funerary vessels at Killydonoghoe was the highlight for me (and possibly for others too) of a long summer of enjoyable work in the rolling landscape to the north of Cork city. Thankfully, the pleasant memories of that long sunny evening on site are in no way overshadowed by the memories of the contrasting conditions encountered the following day. The technical challenges of the excavation and the fascinating discoveries merge with memories of the good company on site and the weather (the good, the bad and the ugly!) to leave an overall feeling of satisfaction and wry contentment. If only all sites could be so memorable.

Acknowledgements

The archaeological excavation was funded by the Irish government and part-funded by the European Union under the National Development Plan, 2000–2006. Many thanks are due to Sheila Lane, Avril Purcell and Ken Hanley (NRA Project Archaeologist) for their managerial contributions, which allowed the field archaeologists to focus on the work at hand. A great debt of gratitude is, of course, owed to the excavation team supervised by Alison McQueen,

Niamh O'Rourke and Lisa Ennis, who worked tirelessly throughout the summer of 2001. Thanks are also due to the post-excavation specialists, notably Cathy Daly, Helen Roche, Linda Lynch and Rhoda Cronin, who contributed so much to the project.

Bibliography

Lynch, L.G. 2003 Osteoarchaeological report on cremated skeletal remains excavated at Killydonoghoe, N8 Glanmire–Watergrasshill road scheme, County Cork. Unpublished report for Aegis Archaeology Ltd, Limerick.

Roche, H. 2004 Killydonoghoe, Co. Cork: 01E0494. Unpublished report for Sheila Lane and Associates, Cork.

Sherlock, R. (forthcoming) Archaeological excavation of an Early Bronze Age cremation burial at Killydonoghoe, Co. Cork. In K. Hanley and M. Hurley (eds), *The national roads programme in County Cork (2001–2005): a wealth of archaeological discovery.*

6

Culture materialised: IKEA furniture and other evangelical artefacts

Pauline Garvey

It was at the end of the nineteenth century that the world first became aware of Scandinavian décor, and in 2009 Dublin will rediscover it. In 1899 the book *Ett Hem* ('A home') was published by Carl Larsson. The Swedish artist presented family scenes and idyllic motifs from his house in rural Dalarna. The book became an immediate best-seller. Heavy, mass-produced furniture was in great demand at that time, in Scandinavia as much as elsewhere. By contrast, the rooms in Larsson's house seemed unusually empty. The few pieces of furniture all had different origins and included simple rustic furniture as well as home-made designs by his wife, Karin Larsson. This house was very different from contemporary bourgeois homes, which were traditionally characterised by a horror of vacant spaces and an obsession with ornamentation and ostentation. The Larssons' interior was unique in advocating a simplicity and craftsmanship that departed from contemporary flamboyant fashions. Their home was a uniquely Swedish version of rustic ideals, evoking an aesthetic from hand-woven fabrics, earth colours and wooden furniture.

In 1997 the Victoria and Albert Museum in London presented a Larsson retrospective and called the artistic couple 'creators of the Swedish style'. The exhibition was sponsored by IKEA, a multinational furniture company which sees itself as an informal continuation of that style. The success of the Larssons' approach lies in their show of simplicity and the elimination of the excess that characterised the period. They established simple, airy designs; their approach was avant-garde and international, whilst also being introverted and petit-bourgeois. Thus the Larssons were the founders of a style that was to dominate the post-war furniture market internationally. This style became known on the world stage as 'Swedish Modern'.

Twentieth-century design may seem to have few consequences for our daily lives, but this chapter will challenge this assumption by focusing on some of the neglected nuances of personal possessions. We are, perhaps, familiar with the idea that things can be taken as barometers of individuals' priorities or motives. We have heard enough glib statements regarding fast cars, boys' toys and female 'shopaholics' to be aware that consumption is frequently taken as a prism through which we refract social worries and moralities. When we bemoan the current day we point an accusatory finger at the objects with which we surround ourselves. For the most part, however, the humble consumer durable does not deserve such moral censure. In fact, it is my intention to focus on the complexities involved in consuming household artefacts, and to highlight some of the myriad significances of one type of artefact soon to be found throughout the country: IKEA furniture.

There are countless ways of contemplating the material world. Everything that surrounds us as we pass through each day can be considered, scrutinised and studied. Sometimes, in fact, it is difficult to disentangle the world we inhabit from the world that we study. The material environment is so much a part of our perception of the world and our place in it that we rarely stop to think about the nuts and bolts of our existence. We forget that what we call culture is not just something we read in newspapers or see exhibited in galleries but is a lived quality, a practice and a way of being. Anthropology defines itself as the discipline that studies such an abstract phenomenon as culture. This term is both ambiguous and contested but can be more neatly described as a study of the activities that people engage in: religion, language, death, the body, landscape and bodily practices, for example . In fact, any aspect of life that has been touched by the human hand comes within the radar of anthropological interest. As an anthropologist I am often asked whether I think that Ireland is 'losing' its culture. Culture is not something fossilised at a particular point of time, however. Nor is it a thing that exists only in museums or galleries. Culture changes; it never waxes or wanes. It is the label given to the way people live.

Material culture

If it is true to say that archaeologists try to construct a social context around the artefacts they find, to see the people and relationships behind a burial or an axe, then everyday objects provide anthropologists with a similar material script. Through such a medium we give form to and come to an understanding of ourselves and others, and it is precisely this quality of the everyday object that is significant because it represents the context into which we are born and socialised. It is only when we actively scrutinise the material medium that we realise its effect on our lives. And most of us rarely think about the things with which we surround ourselves. In fact, it is frequently in moments of crisis or comedy that we come to realise how we 'enliven' objects with autonomous will-power. Computers, cars and machines of any kind can become agents of sorts when they shut down and we find ourselves cajoling, caressing and pleading with them to resume operation once more. As the anthropologist Jojada Verrips shows, this capacity for apparent irrationality is occasionally a point of comedy, as the image of John Cleese hitting his car with a tree branch in *Fawlty Towers* calls to mind. But there is a more serious point to be made here. Our material environment not only provides the background to our perception of how things are or should be, but it in turn creates the context that facilitates these expectations. As we reproduce a given material landscape, we simultaneously contribute to the reproduction of the relationships embedded therein. Therefore, if we can rediscover the things around us, we'll also discover a lot about ourselves.

For example, we may know without reflection that household objects have particular gender associations but we tend not to think further about how these nuances inform us about gender roles and activities. A study in south London showed that of all domestic objects it was the power drill that was the most 'gendered'. In part, this association is born out of an increased amount of time spent in the home, a shorter working week and a decline in pub culture (Gershuny 1982). But identifying the Black and Decker drill with masculinity can be taken one step further. If gender roles are considered as a dynamic relationship based on difference—such as the *opposite* sex—these differences may coalesce around traditional definitions of male labour and female domesticity. With a decline in such polar distinctions based on male work outside the home and female work inside, sexual differences are increasingly being played out in new ways. The rise of DIY is one expression of new forms of opposition within the home replacing traditional ones (Miller 1997).

Everyday objects, therefore, are media for thinking about much broader social phenomena. Such things as household implements are particularly interesting because they are overlooked, considered trivial, and therefore not seen as actively telling us about society—class, ethnicity and gender, to name but a few categories. Sometimes trends are only apparent when viewed over time or in patterns. When typewriters switched from being mainly associated with male clerks to being used largely by female secretaries, the keys were enclosed to hide the machine-like element. Likewise, when the motor scooter was developed as a female equivalent to the male motorbike, it not only enclosed the engine but took its lines from the familiar children's scooter (Forty 1986; Hebdige 1988). Both of these examples highlight attitudes regarding particular genders and machines but would be difficult to discern unless viewed over time. The most banal of things may be, and frequently are, ideological. Such objects do not just reflect how people are organised but go some way towards reinforcing these organising principles. That is, our homes, our places of work and our public spaces are not backdrops for the stuff of life but actually create and constitute the distinctions we draw between types of people, gender roles or ways of life. Now, the questions prompted by this recognition are, first, how do we recognise the social life of things, and, second, what do our possessions say about us?

IKEA

In 2009 the giant furniture store IKEA Svenska AB is planned to open in Dublin. Arguably, more than any other furniture store IKEA encapsulates many of the icons of a truly modern trans-national store. It is undoubtedly global, accounting for 235 stores in 31 countries. It is visited by over 583 million people worldwide and has made its reclusive founder, Ingvar Kamprad, one of the world's richest men. In Ireland IKEA's arrival is facilitated only by a change in national legislation that allowed a limited lifting of a size restriction on retail warehouses. Along with this change come the inevitable fears of crowd control. And these fears are well grounded. Judging from experiences abroad, we can expect the flocking of shoppers to store showrooms on its arrival. In north London in 2005 bargain-hunters were 'crushed and suffered heat exhaustion' when up to 6,000 Londoners overran one of the store's sales, while fist-fights in the carpark were also reported. In fact, the superstore was forced to close soon after its special midnight opening as people abandoned their cars on the North Circular Road and made their way on foot, causing severe traffic difficulties (Burkeman, *The Guardian*, 10 February 2005). Just what, one wonders, is so enticing about this one furniture retailer that it can be the focal point of such extreme behaviour? The store is known for inexpensive quality, but it is not the only source of inexpensive furniture and this alone does not fully explain the enormous popularity of the world's largest furniture retailer. As it was argued in the *Guardian* newspaper, despite all its frustrations, regular visitors to the store view it with love/hate reactions: 'It has become something far more emotively substantial—like a football team, or the Church of England or the government'. So how can one account for the sheer enormous popularity of this particular store, or, indeed, the Swedish brand in general? Can we follow a chair from design phase to shop floor to the interiors of people's houses and find there some commentary on society? When is a chair just a chair? The answer to this question in Ireland remains to be seen, but what we can do here is examine the potential nuances of seemingly innocuous furnishings.

When people shop in IKEA they inevitably talk about how much they have saved. In fact, as Daniel Miller makes clear, spending is one of the chief ways in which we save, thrift being universally seen as 'a good thing'. And thrift does not necessarily mean not spending: one can buy vast amounts but conceptualise one's purchases as value for money, good quality or getting what one has paid for. IKEA shopping is ideally suited to this idiom: in 2006 a radio presenter on the nation's airwaves talked of 'saving thousands', whilst spending as much on her recent trip to IKEA in the UK. Undoubtedly, part of the store's success does lie in its promise of modern but inexpensive Scandinavian furniture, and, compared to other retailers, flatpack packaging accounts for considerable gains for the company—and the consumer. Another possible consideration derives from links to the transience of fashion. Stores such as IKEA, and indeed Habitat, are credited with heralding a 'revolution' in attitudes to furniture. Before the mid-twentieth century, furniture was viewed as a much more permanent thing, longevity being particularly valued. With contemporary retailers we find a sea change in popular attitudes, whereby furniture and home décor in general can be transformed, downsized or modernised, depending on one's changing situation. Furniture is no longer for life but for lifestyle. Löfgren illustrates this point nicely with an IKEA advert from France that urges the generation of 1968 to redo their kitchen instead of the world: 'Mai 68, on a refait le monde. Mai 86, on refait la cuisine' ('May '68, we remade the world. May '86, we're redoing the kitchen').

I remember my first visit to IKEA. I was living in London and had seen the advertising campaign contrasting Swedish liberal living with English reserve, the 'Throw out your chintz' slogan, but was still unprepared for the colossal blue warehouse with *IKEA* emblazoned in yellow on the side. It was akin to a giant Swedish flag in the English city, a little oasis of Swedishness in foreign territory. This impression is not coincidental: a crucial selling point in this global empire is a particular play on a local version of the Swedish modern. From the blue and yellow exteriors to imported Swedish meatballs in cross-global cafes, the marketing image of the store links common icons of 'Swedishness' with proffered non-élitist, practical furnishings for the purchasing masses. In terms of brand identity, IKEA has been remarkably effective: few other companies are so intimately associated with their country of origin. So successful has it been that IKEA/Sweden can take its place alongside Coca Cola/US and Sony/Japan. Moreover, not only is there a clear Swedish identity, but alongside flatpacking, rationalisation and efficiency it projects key values associated with the country of origin, such as simplicity, equality, thrift and fashionable design. A key selling point is placed on the particular quality that Swedishness provides: Swedish lifestyles are described on the store homepage as 'fresh' and 'healthy', with 'an international reputation for safety and quality you can rely on'. But added to the inexpensive quality and projections of Swedish lifestyles as aspirational is a projected philosophy or self-proclaimed 'vision' of providing 'a better everyday life for everyone'. This vision takes its line from the store's founder: in 1976 Kamprad wrote 'The Testament of a Furniture Dealer', in which he set out IKEA's 'sacred concept'. Reading the vision one is transported to a realm far beyond furnishings. In fact, as part of the IKEA vision we are seamlessly carried from the realm of furniture production to references to post-war modernism and, more importantly, 'a caring society', 'social equality' and, by implication, the politics of Swedish social democracy.

A recognisable social and ethical theme runs through IKEA's 'vision', such as its claim to deliver non-élitist design at affordable prices. Evocative here are images and ideals based on notions of the modern home. As it states on its homepage, 'In the 1950s the styles of modernism and functionalism developed at the same time as Sweden established a society founded on social equality'. The early twentieth century had a defined aesthetic that is variously described as modernist. What this amounted to in practice was a realisation of the impact of the ordinary, a celebration of clean lines, lack of ornament and machine-like simplicity. Amongst European—particularly Dutch, German and Russian— designers, architects and social planners there was a particular emphasis on the material realities of people's lives, and many treatises of 'good' living were aimed precisely at the interiors of individual homes. Only by changing the domestic environment, it was believed, could one improve living standards and challenge traditional mindsets—create a new classless society without the necessity of revolution. In order to be modern, the environment—from the ordinary domestic to the city space—had to be modern. *Modernism* came to describe this machine aesthetic, based on a utopian fancy that standardisation and abstraction could make a new classless world, devoid of previous ornament and associated hierarchy. Design seemed to provide the scope for a rethinking of everything from chairs and kitchens to bodily exercises, skyscrapers and cities. Radical designs were proposed for common household things. In spring 2006 an exhibition in the Victoria and Albert Museum in London entitled *Modernism: designing for a new life* was sponsored by Habitat, a would-be rival. Now Habitat is owned by IKANO, or in other words, the Kamprad family.

In Scandinavia this style was particularly influential, but was combined in interesting ways with traditional design elements and also with the politics of the day, the Social-Democratic Party. And while all this history of design seems very remote from the IKEA bookshelf named 'Billy', it is something that the store actively plays on. An aspirational convergence between design ethic and a social ethic remains, and Swedish design continues to be described as embodying qualities like equality or social responsibility. Comparing it with other Nordic countries and with Ireland, one finds that, while quality of life is a stated aim of national design policies, Sweden is unusual in stating directly that quality and shared wealth is an objective to be served by better-designed products and services. At the time of writing, national design policy for Ireland by contrast places emphasis on 'Creative Ireland' as part of our national image. In a comparison of such policies among Nordic countries, Sweden's national design objectives are grouped under the headline 'The innovative caring society'. We hear this message echoed in IKEA's webpage when it claims that:

> '[It] . . . was founded when Sweden was fast becoming an example of the caring society, where rich and poor alike were being well looked after. This theme fits well with the IKEA vision. In order to give people a better everyday life, IKEA asks the customer to work as a partner.'

As anyone who has visited a store knows, 'working as a partner' can be translated into hours of frustrating reassembly. In this one statement the efficiency of flatpack is translated into a morality of work. In the 'Testament of a Furniture Dealer' Kamprad writes, 'You can do so much in 10 minutes' time . . . 10 minutes, once gone, are gone for good . . . Divide your life into 10-minute units and sacrifice as few of them as possible in meaningless activity.' As detailed by a visiting *Guardian* journalist to the IKEA headquarters, this moral crusade finds its way into the offices in the form of mid-day gymnastics for the staff and a frugality that insists that even senior executives travel around Europe on budget airlines and stay in cut-price hotels. For the customer it is found in the value of exertion and the hard work necessary to reassemble flatpack furniture. Self-assembly is more than a cost-cutting measure, we are told by the visiting journalist: it is a 'tool of evangelism'.

And where does all of this bring us? In spring 2009 IKEA will come to Ireland, and inevitably thousands of shoppers will flock through its doors. But possibly alongside all this commentary will be the researchers: anthropologists and other social scientists trying to find out just exactly what we see in this Scandinavian chain and whether all the IKEA hyperbole reaches its consumer target. When we purchase a Hensvik storage unit, to what degree, we must ask ourselves, does the image of Swedish lifestyles, the tantalising promise of an ordered modernity, play a part in our choices. While the marketing strategies of the IKEA empire, replete with images of healthy, tidy Swedes, may play a minor part in its popularity, are we aware of the brand vision we are buying into? Within the social sciences it is acknowledged that what we consider individual taste has often very little to do with personal preferences but relates more to upbringing and class allegiance. IKEA claims to go beyond class distinction: 'we do not need fancy cars, posh titles, tailor-made uniforms, or other status symbols. We rely on our own strength and our own will.' Maybe what all this ultimately provides is an awareness that social commentary starts in the least profiled of places—the home. We often talk and think of the house as real estate but neglect this silhouetted space as itself bespeaking volumes on our ideas of society or culture. Forgetting the importance of this institution in favour of the more public spheres leads us to neglect recognition of a deliberately constructed emotional, physical and social environment. After all, it is not happenchance that the home is as it is, and yet, while we labour over our interior décor so attentively, we have still to rediscover its social significance. As G. K. Chesterton so eloquently put it, '. . . of all modern notions generated by mere wealth the worst is this: the notion that domesticity is dull and tame. Inside the home (they say) is dead decorum and routine; outside is adventure and variety.' The truth, he ventures, is that 'the home is not the one tame place in the world of adventure, it is the one wild place in the world of rules and set tasks'.

The writing of this paper was followed by research in Sweden funded by the Irish Research Council for the Humanities and Social Sciences and the Swedish Institute.

Further reading

Burkeman, O. 2004 The miracle of Älmhult. *The Guardian*, 17 June 2004.
Chesterton, G.K. 1910 *What's wrong with the world*. Leipzig.
Forty, A. 1986 *Objects of desire: design and society since 1750*. London.
Gershuny, J. 1982 Livelihood IV: household tasks and the use of time. In S. Wallman (ed.), *Living in south London: perspectives on Battersea 1871–1981*, 149–81. Aldershot.
Hebdige, D. 1988 *Hiding in the light*. London.
Löfgren, O. 1994 Consuming interests. In J. Friedman (ed.), *Consumption and identity*, 47–70. Switzerland.
Miller, D. 1994 Artefacts and the meaning of things. In T. Ingold (ed.), *Companion encyclopaedia of anthropology*, 396–419. London.
Miller, D. 1997 Consumption and its consequences. In H. Macay (ed.), *Consumption and everyday life*, 13–63. London.
Miller, D. 1998 *A theory of shopping*. Cambridge.
Verrips, J. 1994 The thing wouldn't do what I wanted. In J. Verrips (ed.), *Transactions: essays in honour of Jeremy F. Boissevain*. Amsterdam.
Wilk, C. (ed.) 2006 *Modernism 1914–1939: designing a new world*. London.

7

Just how far can you go with a pebble? Taking another look at ploughing in medieval Ireland

Niall Brady

Archaeologists, like people in general, are apt to box things, and among the items to be boxed are inevitably other people. The box in my case is the plough. Of the few in Ireland who may know me or my work, the odds are high that I am associated with the study of medieval ploughing, although there are other facets to my interests. And if there are boxes that stand on top of those tiny character-boxes, then I would have to inhabit the box labelled 'plough pebble'. Professor O'Kelly was the first person in Ireland to be interested in these odd little stones, which he recovered partly among the cultivation furrows excavated at Newgrange. When I chose to consider the plough in medieval Ireland as a master's degree topic, in the halcyon days when the two-year programme allowed postgraduates to sink their teeth into a subject properly, I was inevitably drawn to the pebbles, and I went on to publish a little paper on them in 1982, twelve years after O'Kelly's 'first look'. Today, I find that pebbles are still a strong totem; one has turned up in north Roscommon, quite removed from the 'traditional' eastern distribution, and whenever I have a public opportunity to reflect on the pebble within the context of what the Discovery Programme's Medieval Rural Settlement Project is finding in this part of the world, an audible indulgent snigger and guffaw sounds from the assembly. So I thought that the present volume would be a suitable venue for restating the case for plough pebbles in Ireland. Finding one in Roscommon strikes a chord with comments made about Peter Woodman's departure from Ulster to Cork so many years ago. In double quick time, it seemed, the Mesolithic was discovered in Munster, where before it was not entirely proven. Familiarity with the subject-matter and a scrupulous eye are the key ingredients, and I hope that the new and wider readership associated with the present volume will allow for an unprecedented explosion in plough pebble discoveries in Ireland.

Pl. 25—A quartz plough pebble from Castlemore, Co. Carlow, showing a classic wear pattern of a lightly scratched working surface on the right-hand side. The pebble is 400mm long (source: the Discovery Programme).

Plough pebbles are simple field stones (Pl. 25). In Ireland they are most commonly of quartz, but flint and some other hard stones are used occasionally as well. They are small in size, typically measuring between 300mm and 500mm in length, and are ovoid in shape. What distinguishes the stones is the distinctive wear pattern that develops typically on one surface or sometimes on several surfaces. The worn face is demonstrably smooth, almost flattened, and located on one of the long-axis ends. It retains a slightly convex profile and is usually polished in appearance. Careful inspection will reveal a series of very light scratch-marks across the polished surface. The marks will run parallel with each other and are quite fine indeed. The worn surface may also show different long profiles. The so-called 'leading edge' will be rounded and smooth, while the opposite 'trailing edge' will be very abrupt and possibly fractured.

These features result from wear. The pebbles were inserted into the base of timber plough frames to provide some protection to the wood from the abrasive power of the soils through which the plough was pulled. An alternative view is that the pebbles served to increase the friction of the sole with a view to counterbalancing the drag of the mould-board, but this idea has yet to be developed further. Such pebbles have been found *in situ* in Denmark, where pieces of plough frames have been preserved in bogs. Holes were drilled into the base of the frame on its bottom and along its exposed side to accommodate the pebbles, which were hammered in and secured in place with resin glue. The result would present a timber surface that was studded randomly with small stones that were raised above the wood. They would have served as a hard outer shield to the softer frame on those surfaces that were directly in contact with the topsoil. In time, as the plough was used, the stones would wear back, and the once naturally pointed exposed ends would be smoothed down. This is where the wear patterns develop. The rounded leading edge was where the pebble encountered the soil first and where the clay would be most compressed around the stone; such action would almost grind a pebble's surface smooth. When the clay had passed over the stone, the pressures would be lesser and consequently the progress of wear less, resulting in the abrupt trailing edge. Eventually the pebbles would fall out of the frame and become lost. As O'Kelly discovered at Newgrange, the pebbles would simply fall into the furrows of the working field, where they would become mixed up with the greater topsoil matrix. The astute eye of the modern observer then finds the stones several hundred years later.

On some occasions it is possible to identify a second wear face on pebbles. This must mean that the pebbles were reinserted into the plough, so that another surface was exposed. It also indicates that ploughmen were apt to recycle the stones whenever possible. Ploughing in the Middle Ages was a slow and difficult job; it is hard to imagine the ploughman and his helpers being able to pick up errant pebbles as they fell out of the frame. Perhaps we should consider this opportunity as one that was presented during rudimentary cleaning and fixing of the device, when loosened stones may have been taken out and reinserted, making the plough good before returning to the job that ran endlessly from dawn to dusk. The recent discovery of a plough pebble at Cookstown, Co. Meath, in a context associated with a smithy's workshop has prompted the excavator to suggest that this stone was lost while the plough was undergoing a more thorough outfitting or repair.

Plough pebbles are something of an international phenomenon, and though they are for the most part medieval in date, they are not exclusively so. The Danish contexts are the most remarkable and the best documented. Five plough frame fragments of heavy wheeled ploughs have been recovered with pebbles *in situ*, and these have been dated using the radiocarbon technique. Although the type of plough appears to have been in use since *c*. AD 1225, the earliest piece with pebbles retained is the Andbjerg plough sole, which is dated to cal. AD

1450 (registration K-598), while the latest piece is that from Tømmerby, dated to between cal. AD 1525 and 1630 (K-599). It is also apparent that the pebbles served in a similar capacity to protect the timber axle bars on heavy wheeled ploughs; Lerche suggests that such axles are late in date, extending the tradition of using these ploughs into the early modern period. In France, however, Dauzat notes that pebbles were used on light ploughs, or ards, during the nineteenth century. This context establishes an ethnological time-frame for the pieces and, while it may be a little uncomfortable for those of us who celebrate the medieval pebble, it should also encourage us to try to find them in unambiguously dated contexts whenever we can. Yet this is not easily achieved, since the means by which pebbles may occur on a site in Ireland is typically the direct result of a violent intrusive impact on underlying layers. Plough pebbles have occurred at Knowth, for example, where they were recognised within a 'soft dark earth layer' that is distinguished as a context which contains later medieval pottery and which is cut into pre-existing early medieval levels.

Shortly after my 1988 paper appeared, a group of pebbles was published by Hill and Kucharski from that great early medieval ecclesiastical site at Whithorn in Scotland. The excavator asserts that the 329 pebbles were recovered from within and belong to early levels on the site, and was happy to disagree with the chronological framework that I had suggested based on the stones from Ireland. Whithorn is a site with a thin stratigraphy and many episodes of activity have left their mark on it, ranging from pre-eighth-century levels right through to the seventeenth century. More recently, Martin Carver's excavations at Portmahomack on the Tarbat peninsula in Rosshire have identified a second large assemblage of pebbles and these also appear to be from early contexts. Other finds from Scotland are later. At Jarlshof, Shetland, Hamilton noted that a pebble was found within the midden fill of a Viking Age outhouse that was abandoned in the thirteenth–fourteenth century. The exact provenance of the pebble within the fill was not recorded, and no datable objects were associated. At Coulston, East Lothian, Clarke documents another pebble recovered from a pit that was associated with late thirteenth–early fourteenth-century pottery. Fenton notes a further pebble from Scotland, though in this case it came from an undated context on the monastic site at St Blanes, Bute.

If the Scottish evidence seems to be varied in terms of dating, the Irish data continue to attest to a narrow time-frame of usage that is more or less in keeping with the earlier Danish contexts and the older Scottish finds (Table 1). The pebbles from Knowth were associated with thirteenth-century pottery, and this association was repeated at Ballybarrack, Co. Louth, where an assemblage of seventeen stones was recovered from within midden material that was dated to the same century by copious pottery sherds. More recent finds support this dating framework. The pebble from the smithy in Cookstown, Co. Meath, was from a late thirteenth-century context, associated with Dublin-type ware, Dublin-type cooking ware and Leinster Cooking Ware. A second recent discovery was made in the basal levels of a refuse pit that is adjacent to and contemporary with a medieval potter's yard at McDonagh's Station, Co. Kilkenny. The pebble was associated with classic Kilkenny Ware, dated to *c.* 1250–1350. Contexts for the other pebbles from Ireland are less secure.

In 1988 the distribution of pebbles in Ireland highlighted north Meath and Louth as a focal area. The discovery of pebbles since 1988 has helped to extend the pattern across the country, yet this particular concentration remains (Fig. 5). No doubt the distribution reflects to some extent the location of fieldworkers who know what to look for. But there may be more to it than that. Throughout the latter half of the thirteenth century, during the so-called period of 'high farming', productivity on the Anglo-Norman demesne lands was at an all-time high in Ireland, as it was throughout most of England. The emphasis on arable husbandry is clear. Whether for internal consumption or for export, an enduring feature before the catastrophes of the early–mid-fourteenth century was the growing of grain crops. It is within this milieu that the plough pebble in Ireland appears and disappears. The crops fed growing populations at home and abroad, and the bulk of grain exported from Ireland was through the south-east, via Old Ross and Waterford. Production in the Meath–Louth area was also intensive, and it is possible that 75% of the available land was regularly ploughed. The nature of the documentary record that tells the tale of this productivity is discontinuous over space and time, and this has frustrated attempts, most notably by Down, to observe and discuss regional patterns of production.

The humble plough pebble might provide an opportunity to move forward. If, for argument's sake, the emerging distribution, which is now based on three decades of collecting, reflects more than the perambulations of archaeologists who know what a plough pebble looks like, then the possibility exists that it reflects a regionally distinct aspect of ploughing during the thirteenth century. This is a challenge for fieldworkers to meet. The lack of any indication of an early medieval origin for the use of plough pebbles in Ireland, combined with the absence of any association of early plough-iron types (or, for that matter, later plough-iron types) with pebbles and the consistently thirteenth- to early fourteenth-century context for pebble usage in Ireland, further suggests that the pebbles should be associated with Anglo-Norman period innovations in agrarian practices. The nature and design of new plough types is still an open question. Given the later usage of pebbles in ards as well as ploughs on the Continent, we should perhaps be cautious of assuming the presence of wheeled mould-board ploughs similar to those in Denmark. Equally, the source of any such innovation

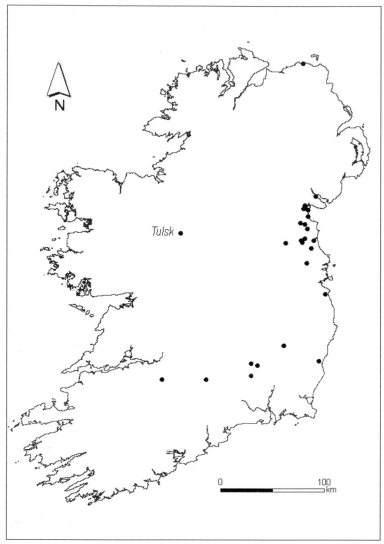

Fig. 5—
Distribution of
plough pebbles
in Ireland, with
the site of Tulsk,
Co. Roscommon,
highlighted
(source: the
Discovery
Programme).

is open for examination. Plough pebbles are not known in England *per se*. Indeed, recent intensive field survey of six parishes in the central midlands area by the Whittlewood Project did not identify a single plough pebble despite extensive field-walking of 997ha. Nor are they reported from the west midlands/south Wales area, which is the likely source of influence for much of the Anglo-Norman cultural assemblage in Ireland. Professor O'Kelly, on the other hand, associated the pebbles at Newgrange with the Cistercians, and indeed the assemblage from Knowth undoubtedly results from ploughing associated with the Cistercian grange there. Could it be that the agricultural innovation came with the arrival of the Continental orders rather than with the secular barons? If this has been a tacit understanding of a previous generation of scholarship, perhaps the opportunity is presented to us to explore and develop this more fully, especially in light of the ever-growing archaeological resource that is especially bountiful today. I do find it odd that plough pebbles are not known in England, and I suspect that it would be useful to examine the landholding contexts of the Danish finds, to see whether the hand of the White Monks can be glimpsed there as well. It seems that there is a longer road to travel with the humble pebble than might at first have been thought possible.

This little essay must, however, conclude with what is perhaps the most intriguing observation in the updated distribution, which is the discovery of plough pebbles west of the Shannon. Rose Cleary recorded pebbles at Lough Gur, Co. Limerick, in the early 1980s, within an Anglo-Norman manor. The discovery of a pebble within a topsoil context during our ongoing excavations of an earthwork site at Tulsk, Co. Roscommon, is an altogether different affair, however. Tulsk lay at the centre of the Gaelic lordship of what became the O'Conor Roe at the end of the fourteenth century. The nature of economic activity within Gaelic areas is not as well understood as it is within Anglo-Norman lands. In part this is because of the absence of manorial accounts and inventories; Gaelic lords, it seems, were not as easily persuaded as their Anglo-Norman counterparts of the need to maintain such written records of their estates. Coupled with narratives of Gaelic lifestyles written by colonial outsiders, such as Giraldus de Barry (or Cambrensis), it has been difficult to move away from the sense that life in Gaelic Ireland was one of instability, impermanence and dominated by cattle. Increasingly this obstacle is being overcome, and a series of new studies are in the offing that may do just that. The Discovery Programme's Medieval Rural Settlement Project's research module that is looking at the O'Conor Roe lordship is one example. The earthwork at Tulsk, technically classified as a raised ringfort, retains a much richer sequence of development than might be expected at first. While only from a topsoil context, the plough pebble nevertheless strikes a chord that is at the heart of the Project's central thesis. Its presence indicates that Gaelic lords were aware of and invested energies in agrarian technologies. North Roscommon was predominantly a livestock region, where sheep and beasts were fattened and where the interest in cattle was immortalised in the epic saga of the *Táin*. Yet the presence of cultivation ridges across the landscape bears witness to arable agriculture as well. The use of plough pebbles suggests further that Gaelic lords, like their Anglo-Norman counterparts, were interested in deploying the latest technologies to maximise returns. Certainly the ethos of cattle-raiding, the exacting of tribute and the bestowing of gifts and rewards to faithful followers was a key aspect of lordship in this warrior society, just as such virtues were praised among the Anglo-Norman barons. So too was the management of the landscape, and the simple plough pebble helps us all to appreciate a more balanced understanding of life and lordship in Gaelic Ireland.

In concluding this short piece, I can feel the supportive smile from those who remain baffled that so much can be retrieved from so simple an artefact. No doubt others will find it beyond the realms of credulity. Yet if there is one truism that is clear it is that there is too little research on basic aspects of rural life in later medieval Ireland. Others might argue that research into the medieval period is too populated by far. I couldn't possibly comment, other than to say that there seems to be a way to go yet with the plough pebble.

Acknowledgements

I am grateful to the following individuals for making available the details of their plough pebble discoveries ahead of publication: Thaddeus Breen and Matthew Seaver for Valerie J. Keeley Ltd; Kieran Campbell; Richard Clutterbuck for CRDS Ltd; Emma Devine and Coilin Ó Drisceoil for Kilkenny Archaeology Ltd; and James Eogan and Sinead Marshall for the NRA Waterford. I would also like to thank Jim Galloway for his views on arable productivity in the Louth/Meath area; Martin Carver, Mark Hall, Strat Halliday and Richard Jones for updated information on the plough pebbles from Scotland and the central midlands; and Grith Lerche for the opportunity to consider once again the data that are retained in Danish wetlands.

Bibliography

Brady, N. 1988 The plough pebbles of Ireland. *Tools and Tillage* **6**, 47–60.

Brady, N. 2006 Personifying the Gael, something of a challenge for archaeologists. *Eolas: Journal of the American Society of Irish Medieval Studies* **1**, 8–26.

Clarke, D. 1972 A plough pebble from Colstoun, East Lothian, Scotland. *Tools and Tillage* **2**, 50–1.

Cleary, R. 1982 Excavations at Lough Gur, Co. Limerick, 1977–1978: Part I. *Journal of the Cork Historical and Archaeological Society* **87**, 3–20.

Cleary, R. 1983 Excavations at Lough Gur, Co. Limerick, 1977–1978: Part III. *Journal of the Cork Historical and Archaeological Society* **88**, 51–80.

Dauzat, A. 1934 Araire et charrue, les anciens instruments aratoire: origine et repartition. *La Nature* **29–30** (I–VIII), 482–6.

Down, K. 1987 Colonial society and economy. In A. Cosgrove (ed.), *A New History of Ireland II. Medieval Ireland 1169–1534*, 439–91. Oxford. Clarendon.

Fenton, A. 1963 Early and traditional cultivation implements in Scotland. *Proceedings of the Society of Antiquaries of Scotland* **96**, 264–317.

Halliday, S. 2003 Rig-and-furrow in Scotland. In S. Govan (ed.), *Conference proceedings. Medieval or later rural settlement 10 years on*, 69–81. Edinburgh.

Hamilton, J. 1956 *Excavations at Jarlshof, Shetland*. Ministry of Works Archaeological Reports No. 1. Edinburgh.

Hill, P. 1997 *Whithorn and St Ninian. The excavation of a monastic town 1984–91*. Sutton.

Hill, P.H. and Kucharski, K. 1990 Early medieval ploughing at Whithorn and the chronology of plough pebbles. *Transactions of the Dumfriesshire and Galloway Natural History and Antiquarian Society* **65**, 73–83.

Lerche, G. 1970 The pebbles from wheelploughs. *Tools and Tillage* **1**, 131–49.

Lerche, G. 1994 *Ploughing implements and tillage practices in Denmark from the Viking period to about 1800, experimentally substantiated*. Royal Danish Academy of Sciences and Letters' Commission for Research on the History of Implements and Field Structures, Publication 8. Herning. Poul Kristensen.

O'Kelly, M. 1976 Plough pebbles from the Boyne Valley. In C. Ó Danachair (ed.), *Folk and farm: essays in honour of A. T. Lucas*, 165–76. Dublin.

Phillips, C. 1938 Pebbles from early ploughs in England. *Proceedings of the Prehistoric Society* **4**, 338–9.

Table 1—Plough pebbles from Ireland.

Site name	County	Registration	Context	Publication/acknowledgement
Ballybarrack	Louth	E166	Excavation; 17 stones, with thirteenth-century pottery.	Brady 1988, 57
Carrickmines/Laughanstown/Glebe	Dublin	None and 00E283, 00E758, 00E133	Stray finds; 36 stones. Private collection. Collection, and excavated assemblage of 45 pebbles from ploughsoil and colluvial levels during Southeastern Motorway excavations project in Laughanstown and Glebe townlands.	Brady 1988, 57
Cashel	Tipperary	E306:133	Associated with topsoil introduced to graveyard.	Brady 1988, 57
Castlemore	Carlow	None	Stray find, field-walking. DP-MRSP. No. 173E. White quartz, fractured. Single worn face, striae visible.	
Castlemore	Carlow	None	Stray find, field-walking. DP-MRSP. No. 485. Coarse brown quartz pebble, complete. Single working surface showing striae.	
Castletown	Louth	1978:118	Stray find. NMI1978:118.	Brady 1988, 57
Clifden or Rathgarvan	Kilkenny	None	Stray find in ploughsoil during walkover for N9/N10 road scheme.	Sinead Marshall and James Eogan
Collierstown	Meath	E31:137–9	Excavations in 1933–4 revealed a multi-period site, Neo.–post-med. No reference to the pebbles occurs in the site notes.	Brady 1988, 57
Colp West	Meath	Not stated	Not stated	Kieran Campbell
Cookstown	Meath	03E1252:3108:0006	White–buff quartz with one polished face displaying fine unidirectional striations. Excavated in the fill of the foundation trench of Structure II, a possible workshop attached to the west side of the forge, which dates from the later thirteenth century. Other artefacts found in this feature include Dublin-type ware, Dublin-type cooking ware and Leinster Cooking Ware.	Richard Clutterbuck, CRDS Ltd
Demesne	Louth	With E166	Stray find.	Brady 1988, 57
Dromin	Louth	None	Stray find, private collection.	Brady 1988, 57
Dromiskin	Louth	None	Stray find, private collection.	Brady 1988, 57
Farrandreg	Louth	None	Stray find, private collection.	Brady 1988, 57
Haggardstown	Louth	1978:272	Stray find.	Brady 1988, 57
Kellsgrange	Kilkenny	None	Stray find in ploughsoil during walkover for N9/N10 road scheme.	Sinead Marshall and James Eogan
Knocknagin	Louth	None	Stray find, private collection.	Brady 1988, 57
Knowth	Meath	E53:12, 15 +	Sixteen stones recovered during excavation, with thirteenth-century pottery.	Brady 1988, 57–8
Lough Gur	Limerick	E174:146, 585, 674a, 1418	Excavation; 4 pebbles found over a wide area of medieval and earlier activity, but all were unassociated topsoil finds.	Cleary 1982, 10–11; 1983, 75; Brady 1988, 58
McDonagh's Station, Highhays	Kilkenny	06E122:555:22	Excavation. Basal fill (555) of a refuse pit that is adjacent to and contemporary with a potter's yard. The pottery associated with C555 is classic wheel-thrown Kilkenny Ware, c. 1250–1350.	Emma Devine and Coilín O Drisceoil, Kilkenny Archaeology Ltd
Newgrange	Meath	E56:1491, :1725; E80:171–2; E126:72	Excavation. Contexts are disturbed but represent ploughing activity, possibly medieval in date. Thirteenth-century pottery as well as seventeenth-century and later wares, all intermixed.	O'Kelly 1976, 169–74; Brady 1988, 58
Raheenagurren	Wexford		Excavation. Found in the backfill of a grain-drying kiln on the N11 road scheme.	Thaddeus Breen, Valerie J. Keeley Ltd
Randalstown	Meath	None	Stray find. Private collection.	Brady 1988, 58
Stickillin	Louth	NMI 1978:260	Stray find.	Brady 1988, 58
Townley Hall	Louth	None	Stray find.	Brady 1988, 58
Tulsk	Roscommon	04E850	Excavation, topsoil. DP-MRSP.	
White Park Bay	Antrim	NMI SA1928:1133	Unknown.	Brady 1988, 58

8

A bridge too far and Blah, Blah, Blah

Ian W. Doyle

My earliest memories of archaeology are of watching a dig in progress on the Roman levels of Bath in 1987. Shortly afterwards, and a little closer to home, I was afforded the opportunity to see the excavation of Viking-age houses in Wexford in 1988. In this latter case, a purpose-built window cut into the site hoarding on Bride Street allowed the public to watch the houses, boundary fences and paths of the Viking town come to life. At the time this struck me as a fascinating way of spending one's career, watching the past reappear from what had previously been a building site. As such, my earliest exposure to archaeology was simply by observing an excavation in progress, and in many ways the public perception of archaeology, or of what archaeologists do generally, centres around the idea of a 'dig'. This association of archaeology with excavation is entirely understandable, although it does tend to ignore the place of surveying, analysis, research and writing as integral parts of archaeological practice. The general identification of archaeology with the physical act of excavation, however, may change in years to come as, sadly, the use of hoarding, site security and safety measures have come to exclude the gaze of the inquisitive public, fascinated by the spectacle as I had been.

Jumping forward to the early years of the new millennium, I became involved as a professional archaeologist in the OPW's River Nore (Kilkenny City) Drainage Scheme, or, as the project was locally known, the 'Flood Scheme'. In looking back on the excavations undertaken at John's Bridge during the summer of 2002, I am often struck by the very open and public nature of the excavation site, which was directly under and around the base of a busy bridge crossing the River Nore in the centre of Kilkenny City (Pl. 26). Every day the public stopped, looked and no doubt wondered what a team of archaeologists were doing below. Large lumps of masonry, massive timbers of oak and pine, noisy water-pumps

Pl. 26—The early twentieth-century John's Bridge, Kilkenny City, viewed in August 2001, with the rubble remains of earlier bridges visible beneath.

Pl. 27—The remains of the pre-1763 bridge visible beneath John's Bridge during July 2002. Each of the three archaeologists is standing on a collapsed late medieval bridge pier.

and a small team of busy people scurrying around in high-visibility vests and life-jackets now occupied the place where formerly the River Nore was to be seen. The concrete bridge of 1910 made for a fine observation point for the public but also doubled as a convenient photographic tower. In the course of taking pictures I would often be asked what we were at, and before I knew it I would be explaining how the work was progressing and pointing out the various remains of the late medieval bridge demolished by the great flood of 1763 or the masonry sections of the later bridge that replaced it (Pl. 27). I would occasionally mention the fact that fourteen people had lost their lives during the collapse of the medieval bridge and that the flood had swept away not just this but both of the city's bridges that spanned the river at the time—in addition to the bridges at Castlecomer, Thomastown, Bennettsbridge, and parts of Inistioge bridge. Revealing something new about the city always excited people, especially those who had spent their lives in Kilkenny or thought they knew the city intimately.

In looking back on this excavation now, what stands out in my mind is not the discoveries made at John's Bridge but the discoveries that happened away from the excavation site. I would never have thought as a kid, observing the archaeologists at work at Bath or at Bride Street, that some of my favourite experiences as an archaeologist would happen in a Carnegie library and in an Italian restaurant.

It all started when in 2001 Margaret Gowen asked whether I would be interested in excavating the medieval bridge remains that had just been identified under John's Bridge in Kilkenny City. I sensed the potential straight away but wondered what this medieval bridge might have looked like. I was soon to find out when I visited the site and talked to Niall Brady and his team of archaeological divers. Their underwater work during 2001 had revealed the remains of a series of bridge foundations on the bed of the Nore under the shadow of the present incarnation of John's Bridge. Remarkably, examples of medieval tombstones were also being found on the riverbed. These included an effigy of a medieval ecclesiastic and a portion of a knight in his armour.

The river was to be widened and deepened at John's Bridge and the success of the flood relief scheme hinged upon this operation. After much discussion it proved impractical to carry out the excavation solely as an underwater exercise and we gradually came up with an alternative strategy. We would examine the bridge remains during the summer months, when lower river levels would allow the construction of a bund or embankment composed of river gravels in order to expose part of the riverbed (Pl. 28). This, combined with the use of large four-inch and six-inch diesel pumps, ensured that this enclosed area remained relatively dry and suitable for standard 'dryland' archaeological works, including drawing scale plans, taking photographs and writing up record sheets like any normal excavation.

Pl. 28—Work in progress on the eastern side of the River Nore at John's Bridge. The two archaeologists at centre right are standing on a late medieval bridge pier that slumped and collapsed during the flood of 1763. A second collapsed late medieval bridge pier can be seen immediately to its left.

It worked. It worked so well that on occasion I had to pinch myself so as not to forget that we were working on the bed of a river. The only difference, however, between this and a dryland excavation was having to grasp a completely different set of site formation processes, such as the lack of formal stratigraphy owing to the scouring effect of the river in spate, as well as getting used to the noise, smell and constant refuelling of diesel water-pumps. So, fortified with daily sandwiches and coffee from a nearby food outlet called 'Blah, Blah, Blah', we set about our task with a small but hard-working crew of ten. The contribution of the crew was immense despite the challenges posed by working in a noisy, smoky and constantly wet environment. While we were surrounded by the detritus and discarded items of other lives, such as swords, guns, door-knockers and mobile phones, what really struck me was the character and quality of the preservation: the sequence of bridges from the late medieval period onwards, the remains of what turned out to be a later prehistoric post-and-wattle fish-trap, or the collection of thirteenth- and fourteenth-century tombstones.

One wet day, when the rain and river levels reminded us that what we were doing was only with the temporary permission of Mother Nature, I slipped away to the local library on John's Quay. In this Carnegie building I discovered that there was a fine series of microfiches of eighteenth- and nineteenth-century newspapers. I started poring over reels of the *Kilkenny Moderator, Finn's Leinster Journal* and the *Kilkenny Journal*. I was searching for something in particular: a document relating to the bridge that I was told still existed. During the late nineteenth century there was considerable debate about the best form of construction and the projected costs of building a new John's Bridge. One enterprising local journalist in the *Kilkenny Moderator* of 26 August 1871 went to the trouble of reprinting a document dating from 1 December 1618. It appears that this document, an agreement between the mayor of Kilkenny and building contractors Conway and O'Hegan, who were to carry out repairs, was originally to be found in the City Archives, but rumours again told me that it had become a victim of a paper shortage in 1916 that saw many documents recycled into new paper.

Fortunately, the *Kilkenny Moderator* reprint preserves the only known complete copy of this document, and it sheds considerable light on the nature of building contracts as well as the building techniques of the period. Interestingly, the document tells us that James Conway and Teige O'Hegan were to erect and repair two broken arches along with the associated piers from which they sprang. This work was to be completed before 1 August 1619 at a price of 115 pounds sterling. To enable this work to be carried out, the contractors were to divert the course of the river. How this was to be done remains unclear, although the text tells us that after the works were completed the workmen were to remove 'all stoanes, stakes, wattle and other stopps'. While the agreement deals with the arches and piers, it also gives details of the finish and overall appearance of the bridge. Parts of the bridge were to be faced with 'astlers' (ashlar stone) and the walking surfaces were to be paved. In addition to the written contract, the bridge specifications were illustrated by a 'plot' or plan drawn up by Edward Shee. It is apparent that the upper part of the bridge was also to be finished with battlements.

Sitting in the library, I was intrigued by the following paragraph:

'Itm.—The said Maior, in the behalf of the said Corporacon, doth agree that the said James and Teige may for their further help towards the said worke, take all wrought astler stones which the Corporacon have now in the black quarry and were formerly bought by them towards the makinge upp of the said bridge, and all the pounched stoane and other stoanes that are now in or under the said decayed arches or decayed Pillers (savinge the tumbes or monumente stoanes that are there).'

It appears that the contractors Conway and O'Hegan were allowed to use ashlar stone stored in the 'black quarry' that the Corporation had been accumulating with bridge repairs in mind. Stone underneath the damaged arches and piers on the bed of the Nore was also to be used, but the agreement specifically stated that the builders could not use the 'tumbes or monumente stoanes that are there'. This is of interest because it states that the gravestones were present on the bed of the river prior to the Cromwellian period and that their presence was acknowledged in the early seventeenth century. This may infer that they were deposited in the Nore at John's Bridge within living memory of the contract being written.

Buoyed by this I returned to the site. In the days that followed, the river levels dropped and we found more pieces of medieval gravestones scattered around the shattered foundations of the bridge destroyed by the flood of 1763. Two of the gravestones were inscribed. One plain and fragmentary slab carried the Norman-French inscription 'AGAT:DE:LEYE . . .', or possibly more fully 'Agatha de Leye rests here'. A second defaced and broken slab read in Latin 'HIC IACET EMMA VXOR THOME DE WAWIL ORATE PRO ANIMA EIUS' or 'Here lies Emma wife of Thomas de Wavil Pray for their souls' (Figs 6–7).

All told, we found twelve additional medieval gravestone fragments, Neil and his team having previously found four. What was odd about this was that the gravestones were distributed across the width of the river and tended to cluster around the pointed upstream side of the former bridge piers. In total the John's Bridge collection represented a good proportion of the total number of such memorial stones known from Kilkenny. Similar medieval gravestones of thirteenth- and fourteenth-century date are known from St Canice's Cathedral, the parish church of St Mary's, St John's Augustinian Priory, the Dominican Black Abbey and St Patrick's churchyard. In many cases in these locations some medieval gravestones had been reused as building material, presumably long after they were originally made and when the memory of the deceased or their family had faded. As a consequence, such stones had a habit of turning up as lintels or doorsteps, reused and recycled, as might be expected of good pieces of well-dressed masonry. So what of the John's Bridge collection of gravestones? Why were they on the bed of a river surrounding the remains of a long-forgotten late medieval bridge? Who had put them there and why? Where had they come from? Were they the result of Reformation iconoclasm or the reforming zeal of a prelate or bishop? Such are the questions that archaeologists faced with such strange discoveries find themselves trying to answer.

Two of the gravestones were found in positions directly underneath one of the collapsed bridge piers, while others were recovered from in or under the

01E980:2274

0   50cm

0   50cm

Fig. 6 (above left)—The early fourteenth-century gravestone of a former resident of Kilkenny City, Agatha de Leye, which was recovered during the excavations under John's Bridge.

Fig. 7 (above right)—The medieval gravestone of Emma, wife of Thomas de Wavil. It was removed from a cemetery, deliberately defaced in order to be reused as building rubble, and subsequently dumped in the Nore at John's Bridge.

collapsed bridge rubble. Some of the gravestones were fragmentary and had been recut, redressed and mortared, clearly for use as building stone. The locations of many of the gravestones around the pointed upstream cutwaters of the late medieval bridge may be of note. In such a fast-flowing river as the Nore at this point, the scouring of poorly founded bridge piers was a constant problem. Good engineering advice, which was clearly available when the post-1763 John's

Pl. 29—The post-1763 bridge was a fine fusion of Georgian engineering and architecture. The eastern pier can be seen here surrounded by a stone and timber casing intended to protect it from the scouring effects of the river. The Kilkenny flag mysteriously appeared in the middle of the river one day.

Bridge was built, recommends that an apron of cobbles, rock fragments or concrete should be placed around bridge piers. The late medieval bridge-builders' knowledge of mortar-mixing was first class, as analysis of their mortars found that they had achieved a very compact hydraulic mix that was as hard, if not harder, than modern concrete. The engineering principles used to provide a foundation for the bridge were technically very poor, however. The post-1763 bridge was founded on a massive pine and stone raft, and other bridges of this period were generally founded on piles (Pl. 29). But the masonry piers of the late medieval bridge had been founded on oak frames laid directly on the river gravels. These oak frames failed to provide adequate resistance against scouring, as proved so dramatically on the evening of 2 October 1763 (Pl. 30).

Clearly the builders knew the limitations of their own bridge engineering techniques. Based on their location, it may be that the medieval gravestones were a good source of rock fragments and were intended to prevent the bridge from being scoured. As such, we may have an early example of what engineers refer to

Pl. 30—A pump sits on a late medieval bridge pier that toppled onto its side during the flood of 2 October 1763. The ashlar stone facing was robbed in antiquity. The remains of the pier's oak frame foundation can be seen behind the two archaeologists where the timbers stick out of the gravels.

as rock armour, or an attempt to prevent the foundation of a bridge from being undermined by the Nore. Although it failed, it does show some appreciation of river engineering, a feature also noted in the archaeological study of the medieval London Bridge, where massive anti-scour constructions called 'starlings' were placed around the bridge piers.

But where did the stones come from? St John's Priory, some 200m to the east of the bridge, is probably the best candidate for the source of the gravestones. In 1541 the priory and part of the property were granted to the mayor and citizens of Kilkenny, and the resulting reorganisation of urban space may have prompted the clearance of a cemetery. The tombstones, dating from the thirteenth and fourteenth centuries, related to the early Anglo-Norman settlement and development of Kilkenny. By the sixteenth and seventeenth centuries Kilkenny was dominated by the leading mercantile and political families of the Shees, Rothes and Archers, and such gravestones may have meant little to the new ascendancy. As a result of a shift in power and a loss of memory and meaning, such grave memorials lost their significance and were perceived merely as useful blocks of building masonry to be quarried, cut and redressed.

Later, after the excavations had concluded, I had lunch with John Bradley, a well-respected medieval scholar from NUI, Maynooth. As we sat in an Italian restaurant on Parliament Street we talked about the discoveries and I showed him drawings of the stones. When he looked at Agatha's gravestone (as it had become known) there was a sudden flash of recognition. John had just published a book on the charters and civic records of Kilkenny, and after a hasty lunch we went straight across to Rothe House to examine a copy. Sure enough, one of the records included in that book concerned one Agatha de Leye, who was party to a deed executed prior to 1299. The deed, from the Kilkenny Borough Council Archives, concerned Johanna and Agatha de Leye, daughters of Martin de Leye, who granted two messuages to Adam le Mercer and his wife. The two properties in question were located near the church of the Friars Minor, a mere stone's throw from where we had eaten. Quite simply, on a human level, it felt immensely rewarding to have added a touch of personal detail to a long-forgotten and discarded gravestone. We had resurrected the stone from the river and the person to whom it belonged from the archive.

Other exciting discoveries were to come later, such as the Groningen radiocarbon laboratory results of late Bronze Age to early Iron Age dates for a post-and-wattle fish-trap, or the discovery of photographs of the concrete bridge under construction in 1910 which explained a series of unusual post alignments we had found. There was also a description in a document housed in the library of Trinity College Dublin of oak frames placed beneath seventeenth-century bridge piers in Dublin, just like the examples from our excavation. The interesting thing was that these 'discoveries' all happened after the excavation had ended. They were made in an office, a library, or at the end of a fax machine—well away from the public gaze, the mud and the noise—and only later communicated locally during a lecture.

Looking back on this experience after four years, I have particularly fond memories of that strange archaeological investigation on the riverbed under John's Bridge. The archaeological remains were unusually well preserved, and so too were the range of artefacts lost or tossed over the side of the various bridges over the centuries. Such evocative artefacts included the tobacco pipe, complete with its motto in support of Home Rule, broken and discarded by someone on their way home in the nineteenth century, the lead-shot musket balls fired by Cromwell's soldiers as they tried to storm the bridge in 1650, and the mid-twentieth-century hand-grenades that failed to explode when dropped in the river by salmon-poachers. Or so a passer-by told me . . .

Further reading

Bradley, J. 2003 *Treasures of Kilkenny: charters and civic records of Kilkenny city.* Kilkenny.

Doyle, I.W. 2003 The lost bridge of Kilkenny city: John's Bridge, 1765–1910. *Archaeology Ireland* 17 (1), 8–12.

Doyle, I.W. and O'Meara, B. 2004 Medieval grave slabs recovered from the River Nore, John's Bridge, Kilkenny City. *Old Kilkenny Review* 56, 6–22.

9

Who was Gormlaith's mother? A detective story

Muireann Ní Bhrolcháin

Gormlaith daughter of Murchad son of Finn, mother of the king of the
foreigners, Sitric, and of Donnchad son of Brian, king of Munster, and of
Conchobar son of Mael Sechlainn king of Tara, died.
                                    —Annals of the Four Masters, 1030

It was May 2004. I was on the Hill of Tara and thinking, not for the first time,
about those kings and queens who had walked this very ground thousands of
years before me, and pondering the goddesses, venerated by many
generations, who have left their names on monuments such as Ráith Meidbe and
Ráith Gráinne. But above all I was thinking about Gormlaith, the woman who
allegedly married the last two men to call themselves kings of Tara: Brian Boru,
killed in the Battle of Clontarf (1014) by a retreating Viking, and Mael
Sechlainn, his sworn enemy (†1022). But Gormlaith's first marriage was to Olaf,
the Viking king of Dublin, who also had a personal involvement with the area,
fighting the Battle of Tara in 980 and remembered in the poem on Achall (the
old name for the modern-day Skryne):

> Amlaíb [Olaf] of Áth Cliath the hundred-strong,
> Who gained the kingship of Benn Étair;
> I bore from him as price of my song
> A horse of the horses of Achall.

My attention had been drawn to her earlier that same year when a first-year
student asked me to give a lecture on her (an unusual event at the best of times).
When I asked him why, he replied, as if it were obvious to all, 'She must have
been some babe'.

Pl. 31—A view looking westwards over the gently undulating rural landscape of the Gabhra Valley towards the Hill of Tara, as seen from the base of Rath Lugh, one of Tara's outer defensive fortifications. The forest clearance in preparation for the construction of the M3 motorway can be seen in the foreground, with the River Gabhra meandering through the landscape in the middle distance (photo: J.F.).

On the hill that day I was surrounded by people involved in the campaign to reroute the M3 motorway away from Tara's Gabhra Valley (Pl. 31), but as it was a particularly beautiful May evening I wandered off alone for a while to contemplate Gormlaith. For that brief moment, whilst treading in her footsteps, I put myself in her shoes and thought of her life and her times—this woman who had sons on both sides of the Battle of Clontarf in 1014 and who sided with her eldest son, Sitric Silkenbeard. For those few moments I felt strangely at one with her.

Some days later the realisation dawned that I did not know who her mother had been, despite the fact that I was working on an edition of a twelfth-century medieval text on famous women called the *Banshenchas* ('The Lore of Women') that listed the women along with their husbands and offspring. Her father was well known, Murchad son of Finn, king of Leinster. Checking the *Banshenchas*, it became obvious why her mother's name would not come to mind: Murchad's wife was never mentioned.

For a number of days I talked of little else, and finally, during a phone conversation with another member of the Tara campaign, I mentioned her again and the fact that I could not find her mother. I was greeted with a curt 'Well, look again', and there the conversation terminated abruptly. That morning I was at home with only a few potentially relevant books, so, almost at random, I took the major collection of genealogies from the shelf and it opened at page 13. There it was, her family's genealogy, the Uí Fhaeláin of Leinster, and her father's name, Murchad son of Finn, along with her brother, Mael Mórda. A little further down the page was Gormlaith, along with the infamous piece of poetry that says of her:

> It is she who made the three leaps of which is said:
> Three leaps Gormlaith made
> that a woman will not ever make again;
> a leap to Dublin, a leap to Tara,
> a leap to Cashel, the rock plain that surpasses all.
> Amlaíb Cuarán her first husband and Mael Sechlainn son of Domnall after that and Brian.

Just above the poem, quoted by anyone who wrote about her, there was the prose section on her family genealogy. I had never paid much attention to it before, being more interested in her marriages and the little poem. It said of her father:

> Four sons by him: Faelán Senior and Mael Mórda and Muiredach from whom the Uí Daimin son of Muiredach and Mael Carmain. **Scirrdech banamas** then his mother and Gormlaith the daughter of Murchad wife of Brian.

I had never noticed the two words *scirrdech banamas* before. *Banamas* did not cause a problem; it meant a female slave or servant. But the first word, on the right-hand side of the page, was strange—*scirrdech*. What was it? Where had it come from? I had never noticed it before; how had I missed it? It certainly was not an Irish word; even to my untutored eye it looked like Norse. I felt a slight shiver running down my spine. What had I found?

Of all the women in the early medieval period, Gormlaith is the one who jumps from the pages of the history books. Like her contemporaries, she is said to have had multiple marriages, three in her case: the first to Olaf, the Viking king of Dublin; the second to Brian Boru, king of Ireland; and a third, less certain, to Mael Sechlainn of Meath, also king of Ireland. Therefore she had been married to the main participants in the Battle of Clontarf, and reputedly sat on the sidelines watching the battle. She definitely had offspring by the first two relationships, including Sitric son of Olaf and Donnchad son of Brian Boru, and they were both involved in this historic conflict. In the accounts, she appears to favour her Norse/Viking son Sitric above the others.

Gormlaith was probably born *c.* 955 and she almost certainly married Olaf in the 970s when she was very young. (This date was suggested to me by my colleague Ailbhe Mac Samhráin. If correct, she was born exactly 1,000 years before me.) In this period girls were married early, probably as soon as they were capable of having children. The average lifespan too was generally shorter than today, although there are some notable exceptions, with certain people living past 80—Brian Boru himself, for example. Her father was killed in 972, and he may have arranged her marriage to the much older Olaf, who died in retirement on the island of Iona in 980/1.

Brian was probably her second husband. This is borne out by the fact that her son by him, Donnchad, king of Munster, was a participant in the Battle of Clontarf and did not die until 1064 (on pilgrimage to Rome). The obit in the Annals of the Four Masters quoted above mentions a third son, Conchobhar son of Mael Sechlainn; this may be proof of her third and final marriage but it is not mentioned in the Lore of Women.

Gormlaith outlived all her husbands, dying in 1030. If born in 955, she would therefore have lived to about 75 years of age and would have been approximately 58 when the Battle of Clontarf took place. But after the battle she disappears from the sources and nothing is heard about her until the death notices in the annals. The entries are sparse: they do not contain any references to donations to the church, repentance or dying quietly, a feature of some notices of other famous women of her age. Sitric survived her by only twelve years, dying in the same year as his daughter, Caillech Finéin, in 1042, with one annalistic entry saying that they died within the same month. Her early marriage is further borne out by the fact that Sitric took over the kingship of Dublin as early as 995 (possibly at the age of 25) when his maternal uncle killed the reigning king. To add to the complexities, Sitric married a daughter of Brian Boru by another wife, not Gormlaith, so this is not incest although it seems slightly distasteful to our modern morality. His wife's name is not mentioned, but Brian had at least three daughters: Dub Esa (†1052) and Sadb (†1048), neither of whom has husbands mentioned in the sources, and Bé Binn (†1073 on pilgrimage to Armagh), who married Flaithbertach son of Muirchertach of Cenél nEogain, Ailech.

We know most about Gormlaith from later twelfth-century sources. There are two accounts of the period directly preceding the Battle of Clontarf: the first is the Irish *Cogad Gaeil re Gallaib* ('The Battle of the Irish and the Foreigners') and the second is a Norse source called the *Brennu-Njál saga*. The Irish text describes the supposed events of 1013: while they are all at Kincora prior to the battle, she taunts her brother, Mael Mórda, for taking a silk tunic as a present from Brian Boru. Mael Mórda has brought pine trees to Kincora to be used for masts, and breaks one of the silver buttons on the tunic given to him by Brian. He asks Gormlaith to mend it, but she throws it in the fire, saying that 'she thought ill that he should yield service and vassalage, and suffer oppression from any one, or yield that which his father or grandfather never yielded', and that Brian's son would exact the same from Mael Mórda's son. It is difficult to explain what they were doing in Kincora at that time and, although explanations have been attempted, this episode is probably pure fiction.

Some modern historians malign Gormlaith as much as these twelfth-century accounts of her behaviour. John Ryan said that the men of Leinster might not have risen against Brian 'were they not nagged into irresponsible fury by a woman's tongue', and again that 'it was Ireland's misfortune that at such a moment this sharp, able and irreconcilable woman was in a position to do untold mischief'. Her place as an 'evil schemer' is repeated by later texts like Keating's seventeenth-century History of Ireland and the Early Modern Irish version of the Battle of Clontarf.

The Norse version of events, the *Brennu-Njál saga*, associates her closely with Sitric, and no mention is made of their presence in Kincora. In fact, it says that she was with Brodir, Brian Boru's murderer, the day before the battle, and that she had a very active role in the lead-up to the battle itself. The text contradicts the Irish sources in saying that she bore Brian no children. According to this account, she urged Sitric to kill Brian and to muster military aid in both the Orkneys and the Isle of Man, where, as part of the agreement, he promises his mother's hand in marriage to both groups. He is also said to have made a pact with Brodir and promised him Gormlaith as well. (Beautiful as she was, at about 58 she was hardly the catch she had been some 25 years earlier.) It continues saying that she wanted Brian dead because she was so angry after their divorce. The fact that Gormlaith is so vehemently set against Brian may indicate that he divorced her rather than she him, if this text is to be believed. The writer casts her in the role of the evil woman in contrast to her saintly husband, who is said to have forgiven a man even when he transgressed three times. He is the best of kings: adopting the son of the enemy as his own (perhaps the writer misunderstood the concept of fosterage), converting a Viking (Ospakr) to Christianity and saving his son Tadc with the blood of his wound when dying. The remarkably beautiful Gormlaith is painted as an evil, vengeful queen, the instigator of the Battle of Clontarf and a much darker personality than her Irish counterpart:

A king from Ireland, called Sigtrygg, was also there. He was the son of Olaf Kvaran. His mother was called Kormlod; she was endowed with great beauty and all those attributes which were outside her own control, but it is said that in all the characteristics for which she herself was responsible, she was utterly wicked. She had been married to a king called Brian, but now they were divorced. He was the noblest of all kings, and lived in Kincora in Ireland.

The historian Alfred Smyth says of her:

In Icelandic tradition she is portrayed as a grim and scheming lady who plays men off against each other in her ruthless quest for vengeance against Brian Boru, and like early Germanic heroines Gormlaith, too, was alleged to have been 'the fairest of all women', even by her Scandinavian enemies. Gormlaith may, or may not, have had good looks, but she did have the royal blood of countless generations of Leinster kings in her veins, and it was this which earned her a place in the beds and counsels of three of the most famous kings of medieval Irish and Scandinavian tradition—Maelsechlainn II, Olaf Cuaran and Brian Boru.

She certainly had Leinster 'royal blood . . . in her veins', but whose blood did it mix with, Gormlaith who excites so much interest in both medieval and modern literature (Table 2)? What about her maternal background? The prose version of the Lore of Women says:

Gormlaith daughter of Murchad son of Finn, mother of Sitric son of Olaf king of the Foreigners and Donnchad son of Brian (Boru) king of Munster.

The metrical version agrees:

Gormlaith offspring of Murchad son of Finn
skilled child of the careful king of Leinster.
Her children (were) wealthy Donnchad son of Brian
and Sitric son of generous Amlaíb.

The genealogies do contain one odd incident about a supposed mother of both Gormlaith and Mael Mórda, but neither the woman nor her father are actually named and the story appears to have no further basis in fact.

It is the mother of Gormlaith daughter of Murchad who saw a vision: that she slept with the king of Leinster and bore a son to him and that he assumed the kingship of Leinster and that she bore a daughter to the same king and that she took the kingship of Ireland. Those were Máel Mórda and Gormlaith. And it is because of that, the king of Leinster i.e. Murchad took her lawfully from the kings of the other provinces who were wooing her. The mother, moreover, was the daughter of the king of Connacht.

This is matched, however, by another unusual incident describing the birth of Bé Binn, mother of Brian Boru. His maternal grandmother is said to be Cianóc, the wife of a hospitaller called Crechán of Connacht, and they are unable to have children. They are helped by St Cairell, who tells her that she will have two daughters called Creise and Osnad. He prophesies that Osnad will become the wife of Erchad, son of Murchad of Connacht. Osnad then will bear him a daughter called Bé Binn, and she in turn will bear Brian Boru, son of Cenn Éitig. There seems to be an attempt here to mythologise Brian by giving his mother a heroic birth as is commonly found in the life cycles of kings and heroes. Both the prose and metrical versions of the Lore of Women agree that Brian's grandmother was Bé Binn, daughter of Erchad son of Murchad, and says:

Bé Binn daughter of Urchad son of Murchad, king of west Connacht, wife of Cenn Éitig son of Lorcán mother of Brian son of Cenn Éitig king of Ireland and of Flann and of Conchobar. [Prose version]

Bé Binn daughter of Erchad, a beautiful woman,
mother of Brian of judgments.
Steady Erchad son of Murchad
king of southern Connacht of the forays. [Metrical version]

To return, then, to that strange word in the original genealogical piece, *scirrdech*: what did this mean? Even I could see that the ending of the word *-ech* was Irish, but with no knowledge of Old Norse where did I begin? The word appears in only one manuscript but a second uses the word *banamas*, agreeing that the woman was a slave or servant. Therefore the genealogies in two of the major manuscripts agree that Gormlaith's mother was a servant/slave.

I looked first at the *Dictionary of the Irish Language*, and the closest word there was *sciggire*, said to be from the Old Norse *skeggiar* 'islanders' used in the saga The Battle of Ros na Ríg on the Boyne, where the phrase 'from Bare of Sciggire' appears when the Ulster king Conchobar mac Nessa is advised by a warrior to send messengers to look for soldiers to various places, including 'Sciggire'. The editor of the text identifies it as the Faroe Islands. Perhaps it meant 'islander', used in the same way as the Modern Irish word *oiléanach* (islander)?

At this point I could no longer keep the news to myself. I rang Edel Bhreathnach, the well-known early Irish historian, and her reaction and support gave me further belief that I had made a major discovery. Eventually, after a number of days, I managed to speak on the phone to my colleague Donncha Ó Corráin, professor of early Irish history in Cork. He had his copy of the genealogies and I directed him to the word. He agreed that it was Norse but was not fully convinced by the Faroe Islands thesis or the general argument. Then I was put in touch with a colleague who is conversant with Old Icelandic and Faroese, and he came up with another alternative: it could derive from the Norse word *skí/rrdh*, 'baptised'. So the word could mean 'the baptised one'.

Armed with this information, I decided to offer a paper to the yearly two-day conference at the School of Celtic Studies in November 2004. In May it seemed like a good idea, but by the end of November it was a terrifying prospect. I was about to throw a bomb into early Irish history. That afternoon the room was full, there was not even standing room; the word was out that my paper would be controversial. My students had turned out in force; their supportive faces, as well as others, made the ordeal a little easier. I delivered the paper at breakneck speed, put the words on the blackboard and stood back, expecting disbelief and annihilation particularly from linguists. To my surprise, with the very odd exception, there was a general consensus that the word was Old Norse and probably came from *skíra* 'to baptise'. This would give the word *skír* 'the baptised (woman)' along with the Old Irish ending *–ech*. I was lucky in the extreme to have present Mark Scowcroft, who was visiting from America and had studied Old Norse. He, along with Professors Kim McCone and Liam Breatnach, agreed that the Old Norse word *skírd* corresponded exactly with the word *scirrd-* from the genealogy.

Apart from the cold historical facts, there is a quiet human drama here. If Gormlaith's mother was a Viking servant or slave, probably taken by an Irish raiding party and perhaps forcibly baptised, it would explain Gormlaith's marriage to Olaf despite the age gap. Both had a similar background and were probably bilingual. He might not see her Viking, albeit slave, pedigree as a disadvantage. On the other hand, perhaps her father felt that it would be difficult to arrange a marriage for a daughter with such parentage? Her mother's ancestry is probably lost forever; a *banamas* in Ireland, she could have been anyone, even of royal descent, at home. It also explains Gormlaith's support for and abiding allegiance to her first-born, half-Viking son, even to the point of sending him overseas for Viking help. I had assumed that she was sending him to his father's relatives for support, but perhaps they were her own maternal relations? We may not know where her mother came from originally, but she herself did and so must Gormlaith. And what of Murchad, Gormlaith's father? No other woman appears in his life at a time when men, and indeed women, married and remarried up to seven or eight times. Did he keep his *scirrdech banamas* as his permanent wife? If this is Gormlaith's background, it goes a long way to explain the animosity towards her in Irish and Norse literature at a period in history when there was great conflict between the two, and within a hundred years the medieval revisionists were out in full force. It appears that her alliance was with the Norse and Sitric rather than with Leinster and her brother.

Table 2—Gormlaith's mother: genealogy.

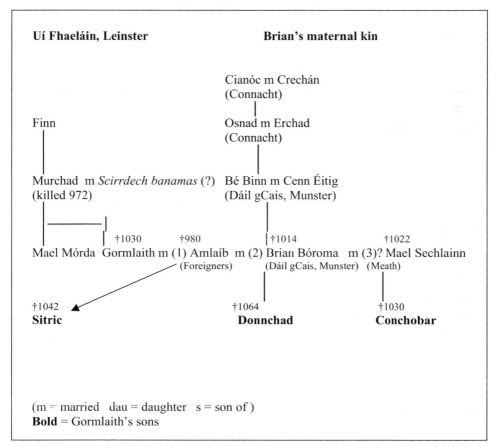

But Gormlaith came closer to home. Looking out of the window of my house in Maynooth, I wondered where Gormlaith had been the night before the Battle of Clontarf. On asking Ailbhe Mac Samhráin the question, his reply sent the now-familiar shiver down my back: 'Right beside you', he said in Irish. Her family had taken over the very land on which I was sitting at the beginning of the eleventh century, and there was quite a battle in the area of the Rye River around Maynooth in 999.

But even this was not the end of Gormlaith's possible connection with my home. A month later, in June 2004, I received a call from a local journalist.

'You must know all about it,' she said mysteriously.

'What are you talking about?' I replied, mystified.

'The bodies they found . . . five of them.'

My blood ran cold.

'What bodies? Where?'

'Right beside you, where they are building the new houses.'

'Have they found the missing women?' I asked, thinking of the large number of young women who had gone missing in the Kildare/Dublin region over the past decade.

'I don't think so,' she laughed. 'Apparently they're about a thousand years old.'

And yes, there was a building site about two fields away from me, outside the very window I had glanced through the month before as I was talking to Ailbhe. Gormlaith's family—outside my window?

We do not know who they are, and perhaps their true identity will forever remain unknown, but these people were certainly contemporaries of Gormlaith, living and buried here on her 'home turf'. With the huge number of archaeological finds in recent years, it may be some time before they are examined in detail. When the dig was completed, the total number of bodies found on the site was 55.

Finally, it was during this voyage of discovery that the enormity of another site at Woodstown, Co. Waterford, came to light: a Viking longfort or town from which thousands of finds have been recovered, including manacles—evidence of an active slave trade. Thoughts again turned to Gormlaith's mother. Somehow I suspect that this story and that of Gormlaith's mother is not yet over. An archaeologist colleague commented that the dead bodies had followed me to my back door. I couldn't help thinking that it was quite the opposite—I had followed Gormlaith to her back door . . .

Further reading

Meyer, K. 1921 Mittelungen aus irischen Handschriften. *Banshenchus sunn. ZCP* **13**, 3–30, 18–19.

Ní Dhonnchadha, M. 2000 On Gormlaith daughter of Flann Sinna and the lure of the sovereignty goddess. In A. P. Smyth (ed.), *Seanchas: studies in early and medieval Irish archaeology, history and literature in honour of Francis J. Byrne*, 225–37. Dublin.

Ní Mhaonaigh, M. 2002 Tales of three Gormlaiths in medieval Irish literature.

Ériu **52**, 1–24.

Ó Corráin, D. 1998 Viking Ireland—afterthoughts. In H. B. Clarke, M. Ní Mhaonaigh and R. Ó Floinn (eds), *Ireland and Scandinavia in the early Viking Age*, 421–52. Dublin.

Ryan, J. 1938 The battle of Clontarf. *Journal of the Royal Society of Antiquaries of Ireland* **68**, 1–50.

Smyth, A. 1982 *Celtic Leinster: towards an historical geography of early Irish civilization A.D. 500–1600*. Dublin.

Sveinsson, E. 1954 *Brennu-Njáls saga*. Islenzk fornrit 12. Reykjavik.

Todd, J.H. 1867 *Cogadh Gaedhel re Gallaibh: the war of the Gaedhil with the Gaill, or the invasions of Ireland by the Danes and other Norsemen*. London.

10

What are the chances? Hints from the tree-ring record

Mike Baillie

Between 1968 and 1982 a team of palaeoecologists at Belfast, including Jon Pilcher and Jennifer Hillam, set out to build a long Irish tree-ring chronology. We realised early on, on the basis of a random scatter of radiocarbon dates obtained from bog oaks and bog pines (dates measured by Gordon Pearson and his team in the Radiocarbon Laboratory at Belfast), that only oak was likely to be available from all periods in the last 7,000 years. Thus we set out pretty systematically to sample large numbers of bog oaks and archaeological samples in order to give ourselves the best chance of successfully piecing together the jigsaw puzzle that lay before us.

As most archaeologists, in Ireland at least, should know, this work resulted, by the early 1980s, in a 7,272-year-long annual record of Irish oak growth. This master chronology allowed us to date samples of wood for radiocarbon calibration purposes, as well as to date individual archaeological specimens. One of the best-known exact dates relates to sample Q1120, the central post of the 'Temple', or 40-Metre Structure, at Navan Fort (Emain Macha, the ancient capital of Ulster). The oak that was used as the central post last grew in 95 BC and was felled sometime between September of 95 BC and April of 94 BC. The reason for this spectacular precision was the presence of the complete ring pattern, right out to the under-bark surface, at one point on the post's circumference.

All of the above is well known, so in this essay I want to make a different excursion. As we were collecting timbers from bogs, riverbeds and lake edges—in fact anywhere they were turning up—the one thing we never knew was what date the timbers would be. Dark brown or black oak samples give no clue as to their age. We could find out the ages of the timbers in two ways, either roughly—within a few centuries—by radiocarbon dating, or precisely by fitting the ring pattern of the sample into the overall tree-ring chronology. This is not the place to discuss the construction of site chronologies, or the linking of long site chronologies, all of which is discussed extensively elsewhere. The point I want to make is that in all this work we could only use 'good' sections of ring pattern. If there were impossibly narrow bands of rings in a sample, or if the pattern was severely distorted in some way, we tended to simply truncate the measured pattern of ring widths. We could afford to do this because Irish oaks are fairly long-lived; leaving off the last 50 rings from a 300-year tree-ring pattern was no great loss.

With that in mind, I want to look at a single sample from the River Blackwater, just to the south of Lough Neagh. The sample, Q1948, was a bog oak that had presumably been pulled from the bed of the river during drainage operations in the late 1960s. It came in with other samples and was of no particular interest at the time of collection. When its ring pattern was examined, along with several other samples from the same location, it was found that samples Q59 (taken many years earlier), Q1942 and Q1948 had all been taken from the same parent tree. Such things could easily happen because dredged trees were often torn to pieces by heavy machinery, or were cut up to facilitate their removal from the site. Somewhat arbitrarily, only the ring patterns of Q59 and Q1942 were measured. The mean ring pattern was found to cross-match with the developing Dark Age chronology, its 302-year pattern dating from the calendar years AD 397–698. All the data relating to this were left residing in the River Blackwater file and archived as computer files with microfiche backup—and there the story could have ended.

It was around the time that the archiving was being undertaken that an interest developed in 'catastrophic events' as recorded in the Irish oak records. Briefly, a fellow dendrochronologist, Val LaMarche from the Tucson Laboratory, had raised the profile of abrupt environmental events by wondering if the frost-damage ring he had observed in his high-altitude bristlecone pine trees from California, in the year 1627 BC, might have been due to the cataclysmic eruption of Thera (Santorini) in the Aegean. LaMarche, by identifying this extreme frost event and suggesting that it might have been due to the eruption of Thera, set a major hare running. Twenty-two years later papers are still being published on this topic, and the very latest independent suggestion—based on multiple stratified radiocarbon determinations on wood from a tree killed by the eruption—is that Thera did indeed erupt somewhere between 1627 and 1603 BC. Personally I always thought that LaMarche would eventually be proved right, if only because his suggestion back in 1984 was such an outrageous 'shot in the dark'.

What LaMarche's work did was prompt me to look through the ring patterns of our Irish oak records. It is worth noting that LaMarche published his suggestion with Kathy Hirschboeck in 1984, which was the same year we agreed with our German colleagues that the Irish chronology was complete, and correct, back to beyond 5000 BC. So we could look at the growth rings for specific dates with full confidence in their calendar accuracy. As it turned out, there was what came to be called a 'narrowest-ring event' in the Irish oaks in the 1620s BC, beginning in 1628 BC. It appeared that LaMarche's frost ring was part of a widespread environmental event. What is meant by a 'narrowest-ring event'? It is a point in time where, in the span of a few years, a number of trees from different sites show the very narrowest growth rings in their long lives. You could interpret this as the trees reporting the worst growth conditions they had ever encountered. By definition such events are bound to be unusual. Overall, this analysis, carried out while visiting the Tree-Ring Laboratory at the University of Arizona, resulted in the identification of a series of what, in the view of Irish oaks, were catastrophic events. Although I didn't realise it at the time, these events at 3195 BC, 2354 BC, 1628 BC, 1159 BC, 207 BC and AD 540 would occupy me for the rest of my research career.

At this point I need to make absolutely clear what this all means. I had effectively asked the Irish oaks, 'What are the dates of the events which you liked least?' In reply, the oaks pointed out to me the dates of a series of catastrophic environmental events. (What I was not aware of at the time, of course, was the fact that by tradition the *oak* has always been regarded as the *oracular* tree; I didn't discover this until the late 1990s.) What the oaks did, however, by pointing out these events was to drop me into an archaeological and historical world in which catastrophes don't happen or, if they do, where they have no effect on the overall progress of human affairs. In these disciplines the concept of 'environmental determinism' is not allowed. In the view of most archaeologists and historians, we live in a post-Darwinian world where catastrophism has no place. Yet it didn't take long to realise that some of these tree-ring events fell very close to effective turning-points in human history. For example, the severe event lasting in the Irish oaks from 1159 to 1141 BC lies right in the middle of the twelfth century BC, which, by tradition, marks the start of the four-centuries-long Greek Dark Age. Similarly, AD 540 sits in the post-Roman Dark Age and coincides very closely with the onset of the major plague named after the Emperor Justinian. Then, just to make life interesting, 3200 BC is widely regarded as the date of the 'start of literate civilisation', and 2349 BC is the traditional—well, according to Archbishop Ussher—date of the biblical Flood. Oh yes, and 207 BC is the year before the traditional start year of the Han dynasty in China, just as 2350 is very close to the traditional date of the first emperor of China, namely Yao. Continuing with China, one could add that 1628 BC is within ten years of one traditional date for the start of the Bronze Age Shang dynasty, while 1141 is within nineteen years of one traditional date for the end of the Shang. So, from quite early on in consideration of the tree-ring events it became clear that some of them might have been global events affecting cultures and regimes around the planet.

All of this was, of course, interesting in itself. Ireland is a little temperate island that doesn't have catastrophic environmental downturns (as far as we know). The worst event in the last two centuries was the potato famine of the 1840s, which was not associated with any environmental catastrophe. What are the oaks doing recording such things in the more distant past? In fact, thinking about it in general terms, how would you produce a catastrophic environmental downturn and, if any had happened, how would they manifest themselves in the available records in Ireland? Well, we could look further back than the 1840s, to the 1740s, for example: 1740 was the coldest, and driest, year on record in the British Isles—by a mile. It has been estimated that in 1740–2, owing to the loss of the stored potatoes in the ground and the failure of planted seed to produce sensible harvests, up to 300,000 people died in Ireland. This 'forgotten' famine gives a pretty strong hint of what a catastrophic environmental event in Ireland could do. At its simplest, such an event wipes out agricultural production and people starve. If it lasts more than three years there simply is no agriculture until it is reintroduced.

Given that last thought, it may not be a coincidence that 3200 BC marks a major archaeological transition in the mid-Neolithic of Ireland and Britain; 2350 BC is around the date of the transition from the Neolithic to the Bronze Age in Ireland and Britain, while, in my view, 1150 BC is as good a date as any for the late Bronze Age phase of hillfort construction in Ireland—again something that implies stress in human populations.

Now, when someone who regards himself as outside the mainstream of Irish archaeology—related to it, but largely independent of it—is presented, by the oaks, with a set of dates for catastrophes, and is presented by his archaeological colleagues with similar dates for archaeological change, it costs little to assume cause and effect: the environmental downturns *caused* the archaeological changes. Consider the following: for ten years, from 2354 to 2345 BC, Irish oaks show a dramatic growth downturn, with some evidence to suggest an inundation of the area around Lough Neagh. To exaggerate only slightly, imagine you have a late Neolithic agricultural population, and in three consecutive years—2353, 2352 and 2351 BC—they lose their harvests. By the fourth year—2350 BC—they have no seed corn left, and they have already consumed their domestic animals. These people—well, the survivors—would have been effectively dumped back into a Mesolithic lifestyle, subsisting by hunting and gathering. But by 2350 BC Ireland had been extensively cleared of forest and probably denuded of significant wild animal populations. These late Neolithic farmers couldn't go back to a Mesolithic lifestyle—the necessary resources would not have been there to sustain a significant population—and therefore most of them would have died and the rest would have become strand-loping foragers. Perhaps it shouldn't be a surprise that we see a significant archaeological change just around this time. Indeed, is there anything to rule out the possibility that the first metal-users arrived into an effectively empty island in the decade of the 2340s? If they did, they would have been unopposed when they arrived, with their new technology, new pottery and fresh seeds and animals.

Now, here is the question: could archaeologists see such an event if it had happened? The answer to this question is interesting. Prehistoric archaeologists can't date things with any precision. How do archaeologists judge the date of the Neolithic to Bronze Age transition? They see it at around 4000–3800 radiocarbon years BP (before present). When they calibrate these dates (the tree-ring chronology was built specifically to calibrate the radiocarbon timescale in Ireland), their best estimate of the date of the transition is 2600–2200 calibrated radiocarbon years BC (2600–2200 cal. BC). Now obviously, given that the tree-ring-dated environmental event fell within the best estimate of the date of the Neolithic–Bronze Age transition, the archaeological community started using the 2340s BC as the notional date for the start of the Bronze Age. No, no, don't make me laugh, of course they didn't. To acknowledge that the 2354–2345 BC environmental event might have had any effect on human affairs would be to admit that 'environmental determinism' might exist in reality. So, although the suggestion is out there, there is no widespread acceptance of the 2340s as the 'working hypothesis' for the date of the Neolithic to early Bronze Age transition. Yet common sense suggests that this *should* be the working hypothesis.

If, however, archaeologists don't accept the 2340s transition as a working hypothesis, there are a couple of ironies. I have already mentioned that Ussher chose 2349 BC as the date of the Flood—a truly catastrophic event involving an inundation. But worse, in some ways, is the curious fact that in early Irish 'history' (or mythology if you like) there are some curious references, written down in the seventeenth century, ostensibly from earlier sources. In the Annals of the Four Masters we find that under the date AM 2820 (i.e. Year of the World 2820 – 2380 BC) it is said:

'2380 BC Nine thousand of Parthalon's people died in one week . . . Ireland was thirty years waste till Neimhidh's arrival',

while under the date AM 2850 (i.e. Year of the World 2850 = 2350 BC) we find:

'2350 BC Neimhidh came to Ireland . . . with his people'.

So, on the basis of the tree-ring evidence I am talking, quite realistically, about an inundation of the area surrounding Lough Neagh in 2354–2345 BC which might possibly have reduced the pre-existing Irish population and aided invading newcomers at some date after 2351 BC, while ancient Irish literature refers to the island being 'waste' for 30 years before the arrival of a new people in 2350 BC. To this can be added the surprising fact that the Annals, under 2341 BC, go on to list:

> 'These were the forts that were erected, the plains that were cleared, and the lakes that sprang forth, in the time of Neimhidh . . . [including] . . . Magh-Lughadh, in Ui-tuirtre . . .'.

O'Donovan, in editing the Annals in the nineteenth century, then proceeded to interpret this place-name as follows: 'Magh-Lughadh: i.e. Lughadh's Plain, a district near Lough Neagh'. How do we explain, in the context of what we now know from the trees about 2354–2345 BC, a pre-existing reference to lakes springing forth in 2341 BC which includes a mention of the plain of Lough Neagh?

So, for some reason (!) there are ancient references, in Ireland, to a catastrophic event in the mid-24th century BC that fit surprisingly well with the dated tree-ring observations. How do archaeologists deal with this? Well, they ignore it. This is largely because there is no paradigm for catastrophe in archaeology, but also because they do not believe that there is any mechanism for the transmission of oral information over long periods of time. Yet in America it has been shown that there are stories told by native tribes in the region around Crater Lake, Oregon, that relate to the eruption of Mount Mazama (the volcano that blew itself away leaving Crater Lake) more than seven millennia ago. So in America oral tradition could, in some cases, survive for over 7,000 years, but in 'enlightened' Ireland catastrophic events couldn't be remembered for 4,000 years or less.

There is another excuse, however, for not believing that a catastrophic event around 2350 BC could have been remembered, or have had any effect on humans. In this 'Plan B' it is suggested that Christian monks simply 'copied' the biblical Flood legend into the Irish records as part of an effort to give Ireland an artificial 'pedigree'. How patronising does that have to be? Apparently, not only were the Irish ancestors incapable of sustaining an oral history, but their descendants felt the need to fabricate a plagiarised early history. It is hard to see, however, how these plagiarising Christian monks could have guessed that the plain of Lough Neagh would be flooded in the 2340s BC, when their Old Testament model would surely have had the entire island submerged. It seems at least as logical to suggest that the Annal reference is a distant memory of a very catastrophic event, specifically an event that may have been associated with the arrival of a new people.

Nothing really prepares one for trying to introduce catastrophism into a non-catastrophic, and non-environmentally-deterministic, world. But, note, this isn't a whim; it is a direct result of observing dated catastrophic effects in tree-ring samples and then finding that some of these tree-derived dates already exist in human records. The logic is that the trees and the humans were both affected by the same events, and both recorded the events; it is just that the human records aren't believed. I believe them, however, because otherwise there are just too many coincidences that would need to be explained away. Take another example. Back in 1937 C. E. Britton published *A meteorological chronology to AD 1450*. Because there are no British records for the pre-Roman period, he used the Irish Annals. Of interest here, Britton picked out 'lakes that broke out' references from the Annals in the decades of the 2340s, 1690s, 1620s and 500s BC. What were the chances of him (or the Annalists) picking a decade that would subsequently be picked out by the oaks as an inundation around Lough Neagh? We could think of it like this: there are 200 decades between 2500 BC and 500 BC. Britton lists 'lakes breaking out' in four of these decades. His chances of picking a reference to lakes breaking out in a decade when lakes actually did break out must be around 1 in 200/4: i.e. 1 in 50. Moreover, the fact that one of his other chosen dates, 1629 BC, falls into the decade of another narrowest-ring event seems also to be intuitively significant. So, their very act of picking 2341 BC and 1629 BC makes it pretty unlikely that Britton/the Annalists had obtained these dates by guesswork. Is there any sensible way they could have got them right? The answer to that is 'yes, by means of an oral record'. If they were transmitted by oral means, were the events probably important? Again, 'yes, common sense tells you that it is important events that will be remembered—years may well be counted from such events'. It looks like there is some truth in the old stories after all.

None of this flood stuff was what I wanted to write about, however. So, let's go back to Q1948 and the fact that its ring pattern runs right across AD 540. When the samples Q59/1942 were dated, it was not known that there was anything special about AD 540. Later, however, after LaMarche's prompting, it was realised that 540 was one of the 'narrowest-ring events'. Subsequently it became clear that it marks a truly global event. The severe growth downturn shows up in tree-ring chronologies from Mongolia to Sweden, across Europe, and in both North and South America. The date coincides remarkably with the start of a major plague—believed to have been as severe as the Black Death—at the time of the Byzantine emperor Justinian. Indeed, a journalist, David Keys, was able to edit a whole book tracing the fact that the event showed up, or had effects, just about everywhere around the world. The story line about AD 540 simply wouldn't stop. For example, if the event was global and environmental, what caused it? Here lay another surprise. While initial thinking was that it was due to a major volcanic eruption—because of descriptions of a dust-veil at AD 536–7—subsequent information from the well-dated ice-core records from Greenland showed that there was no evidence for a volcano at that time. This left the most likely cause of the environmental event to be loading of the atmosphere from space, most probably from a comet. It turned out that Gibbon and Roger of Wendover both refer to terrible comets in the time window AD 539–41. Moreover, in a major subtext to this story, the 540 event also coincides with the death of King Arthur. It didn't take long to discover that King Arthur is cognate with the other Celtic gods, Cúchulainn and Lugh; and it didn't take long to discover that Lugh is described in one text as 'coming up in the west, as bright as the sun, and with a long arm'—a comet description if ever there was one. So, in a short series of steps the 540 tree-ring event turned itself into the possible result of a close brush with a comet, or its debris.

Because archaeologists and historians don't like catastrophism in general, and environmental determinism in particular, I recommend you to try and introduce the idea that human populations have been affected by comets in the not-too-distant past! I've tried, with about as much success as in introducing the 2340s as a working hypothesis for the Neolithic to Bronze Age transition. The reader is probably aware, however, of the fact that, for some reason, humans have for a very long time had a particular dread of comets. Given this little story—with its loading of the atmosphere, reduced tree growth worldwide, famines and plague around AD 540—perhaps the answer is self-evident: people feared comets for perfectly good reasons.

So, when the sample Q1948 was examined, it was noted that the growth rings were clear right up to AD 539. In that year the character of growth changes dramatically; the rings for the remainder of the tree's life are extremely narrow. What had not been realised previously was that this tree had suffered a catastrophic defoliation in 539. That rang a bell, however. It had already been published, back in 1990, that another oak, from Toome, at the extreme north-west of Lough Neagh, showed an almost identical response (the two ring patterns are shown in Fig. 8). Indeed, another oak from south of Portmore Lough, to the east of Lough Neagh, appears to have been pushed over in 539, while a fourth from the same site appears to have been tangentially split at the same time (these were illustrated in *Current Archaeology* in 2001). While the 540 event affected trees around the world, in the whole of Europe these oaks from around Lough Neagh appear to be the *worst* affected—they show the most dramatic damage effects seen anywhere. Obviously the most likely explanation of this set of symptoms is another 'flood event' affecting the Lough Neagh basin (the find of an unfinished dugout boat in the lough, dating from this period, would support

Trees from River Blackwater
and Toomebridge

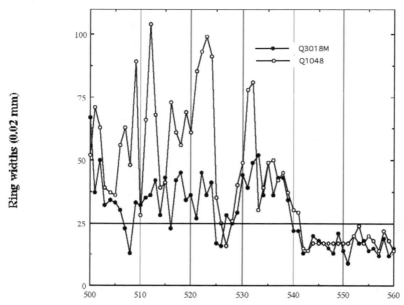

Fig. 8—Tree-ring patterns from the River Blackwater and Toomebridge (from AD 500 to 560).

that possibility). The question is, if the global event was due to a shower of comet debris, was there, locally, a catastrophic airburst somewhere above the Lough Neagh basin? If there was, is the airburst crater represented by the one-mile-diameter, anomalously shallow, near-circular lake called Portmore Lough? But here is the amusing part. The Ballinderry church site beside Portmore Lough is still known locally as Laa Loo. Why? Because, according to the Ordnance Survey Memoirs, the site was founded by St Loo, 'a sixth century B and C'. St Loo is a Christianisation of Lugh, and indeed there was an annual August festival at Portmore up until the late eighteenth century—Lughnasa, no less. Interestingly, if we go back to that reference to the 'lake springing forth' at Magh-Lughadh in 2341 BC, it has to be a little bizarre that this represents the first use of the epithet Lugh in the Annals. Lugh, the comet god, and the plain of Lough Neagh: surely that has to be seen in the light of Newton's (and Halley's) belief that the Flood of 2349 BC was caused by a comet. Thus one is forced to ask whether Newton, Halley and Ussher (who provided the date used by the others) and O'Clery (who compiled the Annals in the early seventeenth century) were all privy to some lost lore about catastrophes which contained at least a core of truth. The lost and found Q1948 thereby plays its part in a story that will one day be recognised as the most important information ever to come out of Irish archaeology, namely the

Irish component of the important story of global catastrophe.

Incidentally, credit where it is due: as early as 1990 it was Richard Warner who was the first to note the possible link between the tree-ring dates and the 'catastrophes' recorded in the Annals.

Note added in proof

Since this article was completed, new ice core evidence has been presented that a previously underestimated, massive equatorial eruption took place in AD 533–4. Given the flexibility in the ice core chronologies, it has been proposed that this eruption took place in 536, causing the extended environmental effects (Larsen *et al.* 2008). It has also been proposed that this new ice core date could be moved to 540–1(Baillie 2008). This new information does not significantly change the main points in the paper. An explanation is still required as to why oaks around Lough Neagh show evidence of physical damage.

Select bibliography

Baillie, M.G.L. 1995 *A slice through time: dendrochronology and precision dating.* London.

Baillie, M.G.L. 1999 *Exodus to Arthur: catastrophic encounters with comets.* London.

Baillie, M.G.L. 2001 The AD 540 event. *Current Archaeology* **15** (6) (No. 174), 266–9.

Baillie, M.G.L. 2008 Proposed re-dating of the European ice core chronology by seven years prior to the 7th century AD. *Geophysical Research Letters* **35**, L15813, doi:10.1029/2008GL034755.

Keys, D. 1999 *Catastrophe: an investigation into the origins of the modern world.* London.

Larsen, L.B., Vinther, B.M., Briffa, K.R. *et al.* 2008 New ice core evidence for a volcanic cause of the A.D. 536 dust veil. *Geophysical Research Letters* **35**, L04708, doi:10.1029/2007GL032450.

McCafferty, P. and Baillie, M.G.L. 2005 *The Celtic gods: comets in Irish mythology.* Stroud.

Warner, R.B. 1990 The 'prehistoric' Irish annals: fable or history? *Archaeology Ireland* **4** (1), 30–3.

11

Dendro-archaeology: of a slightly different kind

Brian Lacey

Owing to the marvellous work carried out in the past few decades at Queen's University, Belfast, particularly by Professor Mike Baillie, as part of our normal archaeological dating apparatus we now have available to us in Ireland the scientific technique known as dendrochronology or 'tree-ring dating', named, of course, from the Greek word for a tree, *dendro*. The system is based, as everyone knows, on the principle that each year a tree adds a new growth ring. Apart from its age, the ring can also tell us other things, as it is indicative of the general environmental conditions in the locality of the tree in that particular year. In the early 1990s I became aware, however, of a form of tree archaeology of a slightly less orthodox, and certainly less scientific, form.

Marko Pogacnik is a Slovenian artist, mainly a sculptor, who was involved with the European conceptual art movement of the 1960s and 1970s. He is a practitioner of what he calls landscape art. He and his wife and daughters, who are also closely involved with him in his various artistic projects, have lived and worked in the village of Sempas in the Vipara region of Slovenia. In his own country he is also well known as the designer of the official flag and coat of arms of the Republic of Slovenia following the breakup of the old Yugoslavia in 1991. Around the same time he was invited by the Orchard Gallery in Derry to research and create an environmental sculpture project in that city and in the surrounding countryside on both sides of the border (Fig. 9).

In his work generally, Marko draws much of his inspiration from the past, especially from archaeological remains as well as from his understanding of ancient religious beliefs. Over time he has developed a distinct philosophy and a method of working that he calls 'lithopuncture', which might be described as a method of 'healing' the land similar to that employed in the concept of healing the human body through acupuncture. As he himself said:

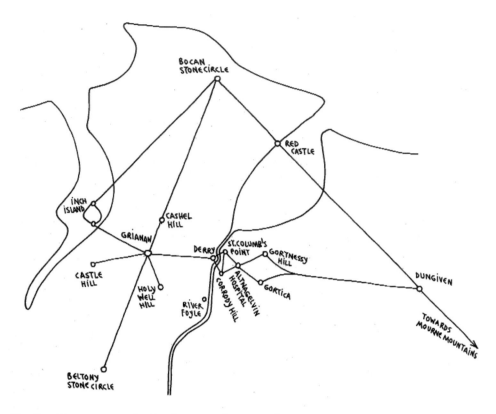

Fig. 9—Concept map for landscape sculpture project.

'My approach to the landscape sculpture is in its first stage similar to acupuncture of the human body. One can imagine a landscape as a vast body of the Earth. Like the human body, the earth is a living organism with energy centres and interconnecting veins of energy—which one can understand as acupuncture meridians. By "touching" permanently the acupuncture points of a landscape through stone sculptures, it should be possible to get some positive and healing effects upon the respective land' (Pogacnik 1992, 4).

He first came to the north-west of Ireland in 1991. Having flown into Aldergrove airport near Belfast, he proceeded westward:

'However when we arrived across the Glenshane [Sperrin] Mountains into the larger area of my future project, I felt at Dungiven a sudden change and my feeling was that the landscape had become, without any outer reason, narrow and uneasy. The same notion came again and again at the same place when I visited during the next few months to work on the lithopuncture project.

Very soon I found manifold reasons for this depressive mood. The landscape I was working in represents a rounded whole with the mighty river Foyle running through its midst. This obvious unity has been split into two halves by the rational fact of the state border between Northern Ireland and the Republic of Ireland cutting through the landscape west of Derry. Secondly the centrally positioned city of Derry has recently experienced severe ecological stress. The former island on the river Foyle had been a sacred oak grove during the Celtic era, hence the Celtic name "Doire". In 546, Saint Columba founded a monastery without destroying the grove. The final destruction of the island came about in the 18th [*recte* 17th] century when the English constructed a walled city in the form of a Roman military camp [plantation Londonderry]. It is still standing in its severe square shape. A painful disharmony exists between the natural features of the hill, with its steep slopes descending to the level of the river, and the severe form of the city.

Another reason for the depressive feeling that I perceived in the Derry/Donegal landscape might be explained by the devastation of the ancient places that I have observed during my travel and exploration of the area. A few of the sites that are of crucial importance for the proper functioning of the energy structure of the landscape were misused, for military purposes, during the middle ages or later (e.g. the Napoleonic era). Examples are Inch pier, Inch Castle and Inch Castle Hill [all in Co. Donegal]. At Burt [Co. Donegal] the Holy Well Hill now carries a huge television tower. There are traces of many megalithic structures that have disappeared in the face of the modern use of the land for agriculture and urbanisation' (*ibid.*, 5).

Marko spent about eighteen months on the project and eventually left behind him a network of stone pillars standing at various points—mainly places with archaeological associations—in the city and the surrounding countryside (Pl. 32). These pillars of granite, quarried in the Mourne Mountains and carved with a variety of 'Celtic-looking' symbols or 'cosmogrammes', as Marko calls them, can still be seen (Fig. 10). There is one near the ancient St Columb's Well in the Bogside in Derry, another in the grounds of Altnagelvin Hospital in the Waterside area of the city, and a third on the hillside running up to the Grianán of Aileach in County Donegal. All of these, as well as several others, are located at what Marko judged to have been significant, aboriginal energy points. He identified these points, as it were, through the medium of experiences that he perceived in his own body, although occasionally he used divining rods to make

Pl. 32—Pillar stone on hillside just below the Grianán of Aileach.

those experiences 'visible' to (undoubtedly more sceptical) others. Where it was inappropriate, or not permitted, to erect a pillar stone, for instance on a footpath, Marko instead positioned eleven similarly marked bronze plaques set flush with the relevant surface (Pl. 33).

In the earlier stages of his project, as he set out to find and explore what he called the energy lines and points in the landscape, I was asked to show him around the area, particularly guiding him to the lesser-known archaeological sites. To say that my own perceptions of the landscape, not to mention my understanding of what constituted 'reality', were challenged by driving him around would be an understatement. I would occasionally find myself suddenly slamming on the brakes in my car at his instant command as, unknown to me, we had just driven across a significant energy line on the road that he wanted to investigate more closely.

COSMOGRAMMES FOR THE THREE HOLY WELLS IN DERRY

Fig. 10—'Cosmogrammes' for individual pillar stones.

Pl. 33—Bronze plaque for insertion in footpath.

Marko was especially excited by my telling him about a group of medieval fortifications strung out, from north to south, along the west shore of Lough Foyle: Greencastle, Redcastle and Whitecastle respectively. Apart from other considerations, apparently that combination of colours (although actually not in that precise geographical order) was of some special cosmological significance. Greencastle is, of course, a major, well-known monument: a fourteenth-century de Burgo—and later an O'Doherty and Chichester—castle that guards the entrance to Lough Foyle. Whitecastle, at the other end of the lough, nearer to Derry, has effectively disappeared, but the original structure may have been on the site now occupied by a house with the same name.

According to Alastair Rowan, the present Redcastle, now a very popular hotel and country club, is basically a possibly seventeenth- or early eighteenth-century house. As we drove down the avenue to the hotel to inspect the site, Marko asked me where the original castle had been. I casually answered that I wasn't sure but that I assumed that it was on the site of the house. He responded by saying that my uncertainty did not matter as he would 'ask' one of the nearby trees! The avenue was, indeed, lined by a fine collection of mature beech trees, which, even if they did not date from medieval times, were at least fairly old. When I stopped the car, Marko went over to one of them, saluted it and apparently struck up a conversation! I was greatly relieved—if a bit surprised—when he returned to the car a few minutes later and told me that the tree had actually confirmed my archaeological opinion!

The main embarrassment, however, was that, at that point, I picked up the 'bible' for that part of the world—the *Archaeological Survey of Donegal*—with which I had some previous acquaintance and which had been lying (I might even add, in this context, 'quietly') on the back seat of the car. According to the short article by Paul Walsh in the *Survey*, the castle had actually been sited on a nearby boss of rock at the shore rather than on the site of the house. I quickly made my apologies to Marko but, to my knowledge, the tree has yet to change its opinion!

Bibliography

Lacy, B. *et al.* 1983 *Archaeological survey of Donegal.* Lifford.
Pocagnik, M. 1992 *Derry/Donegal landscape sculpture.* Derry.
Rowan, A. 1979 *The buildings of Ireland: North West Ulster.* London.

12

Ambergris: a lost link between Connemara and Andalusia?

Michael Gibbons and Myles Gibbons

'Why devil's music do not please?
What sort of thing is Ambergreese?'
—Samuel Colvil, *Whiggs' Supplication: A mock poem in two parts*

During research into the strategically important castle of Bunowen (Pls 34 and 35) in the O'Flaherty maritime lordship, a tantalising early seventeenth-century reference came to light that reveals some previously forgotten links between Gaelic Ireland and the wider world. The O'Flahertys represented one of the last bastions of Gaelic law and custom in Ireland. Once 'lords of Inner Galway Bay' and later of Aran and Connemara, by the beginning of the seventeenth century English power had encroached on their domain. Although they would not lose their lands until after the rebellions of the 1640s, their power had been curtailed by 1607, when an investigation into their old privileges contained the following passage:

'Further that it was customary whenever anyone took any wreck of the sea or ambergresse (i.e. spermaceti) without notice thereof given to O'Flaherty or his sergeants, the person so doing shall pay a fine of seven cows to O'Flaherty' (Inquisition of 1607, quoted in Gibbons 2003, 38–9).

The 'ambergresse' referred to here is ambergris and was clearly greatly valued by the O'Flaherty. The Inquisition of 1607 grants it the same value as a wreck and its cargo. These local monopolies were based on an established principle of early Irish law. The seventh-century *Audacht Morainn* states that 'it is through the justice of the ruler that many creatures and many animals from the deep and

Pl. 34—Aerial photograph of the eighteenth-century Bunowen Castle, built with stone from the original fifteenth-century castle (photo: Michael Gibbons).

Pl. 35—View of the stump of the original Bunowen Castle, home of Donal 'An Cogadh' O'Flaherty and his wife Grace O'Malley (photo: Michael Gibbons).

great seas are cast up on lawful shores'. Since their 'justice' provided it, local lords were entitled to control and distribute whatever came unbidden from the sea.

James Fairley (1981) discusses ambergris in his *Irish whales and whaling*:

'The most highly-prized of all substances obtainable from whales is ambergris, a concretion originating in the intestine of the sperm whale but also sometimes found floating in the sea or thrown upon the shore. Whether it is produced naturally or as the result of some pathological condition is not really known, although it is sometimes suggested that it secreted to the reaction caused by the beaks of squids scraping along the insides of the gut. The beaks are frequently found embedded in it and may act as a sort of nucleus for it to gather upon. When first removed from the whale, ambergris is soft black and malodorous but, on exposure to air, it hardens, lightens to grey and acquires a pleasant, sweet, earthy scent.' (Fairley 1981, 100–1.)

It seems likely that the O'Flahertys' interest in ambergris pre-dates the early seventeenth century. It might be worth reviewing the evidence for Irish involvement in the medieval ambergris trade to see what light this might shed on the country's relationship with the wider world.

The global Islamic trade in ambergris in the Middle Ages

Ambergris was known to classical medicine and valued in the old Mediterranean world as an anti-spasmodic. Greek doctors also held that, if sniffed prior to drinking, it would improve the potency of wine. Medieval Arab doctors used *anbar* (also amber—the origin of the English and French term and used in the Coptic Bible as the name of the great fish that swallowed Jonah) extensively as a medicine for disorders of the heart and brain. Its origins attracted scholarly and artistic interest. In the *Thousand and one nights*, Sinbad is tossed up on an island after a shipwreck and discovers a monstrous spring of unrefined ambergris which flows into the sea. It is eaten by giant fish who later vomit it up in a more fragrant form. This follows the opinion of classical authorities, who held that ambergris originated on land. The great Nestorian Arab pharmacist Ibn Masawayh, writing in the ninth century, noted several different types of ambergris in his book *al-Mushajjar al-Kabir*, and recommended that it be used in combination with other aromatic mixtures. He was aware that it came from sea fish but knew nothing more of its origins.

Ambergris was much sought after by Arab traders. Collected on the coast of the Iberian Peninsula, it often fetched 30 times what it had cost in Andalusia by the time it reached Egypt or Baghdad. Medieval Andalusia was famed for its ambergris, although some preferred the Indian variety. On the east coast of Africa, Arabs traded ambergris, known as 'treasure of the sea', with China through Oman in the twelfth century. The Chinese had known it as *lung sien hiang* (dragon's spittle perfume) since at least AD 1000 and believed it to be a potent aphrodisiac. The Japanese called ambergris *kunsurano fuu* (whale droppings), and it was Japan that first used ambergris as a stabiliser in perfume manufacture. In later years this would be its international commercial application before artificial (and often inferior) substitutes were discovered.

In the Indian Ocean ambergris was considered a prize in the same class as such luxuries as leopard skins, ivory and rhinoceros horns or African slaves. In addition to its use in medicine, a secondary use was also found for ambergris in lamps as an aromatic agent. Chinese–African links developed to such a degree that Arab-African envoys speaking an early form of Swahili visited the emperor with tribute as early as the eleventh century.

Marco Polo was the first western chronicler to discover the connection between ambergris and sperm whales, although he continued to believe that whales vomited up ambergris after eating it somewhere below the surface. He saw sperm whales hunted on Socotra in the Indian Ocean in the thirteenth century and left a memorable description of the technique used. After drugging the whale, the hunters

> 'climb onto it. They have an iron rod, barbed at one end in such wise that, once it has been driven in, it cannot be pulled out again . . . One of the hunters holds the rod over the whale's head, while another, armed with a wooden mallet, strikes the rod, straightway driving it into the whale's head. For, on account of its being drunk, the whale hardly notices the men on its back, so that they can do what they will. To the upper end of the rod is tied a thick rope, quite 300 paces long, and every fifty paces along the rope, a little cask and a plant are lashed' (quoted in Hall 1996, 51–2).

The ambergris trade was intimately connected with Muslim hegemony in the Indian Ocean and remained an important economic factor until previous arrangements were disrupted by the arrival of the Portuguese in the fifteenth century.

Irish trade with the medieval Arab world?

The Viking cities represent the most likely conduit for early medieval trade between Ireland and the Caliphate. Large-scale trade, as distinct from reciprocal gift-giving, was a Viking innovation on the Irish scene. Arab silver was common in Viking Dublin, along with walrus tusks from the north, silk from Byzantium and weaponry from England, which illustrate the extensive cultural and commercial web of which the city was a part. Arab geographers were aware of Ireland as a Viking territory, and also of whaling in Ireland. The Islamic ambassador Ibrahim ibn Ya'qub wrote about Ireland in the mid-tenth century. His information appears to be second-hand, perhaps derived from another Arab, the Andalusian al-Udhri (who wrote an almost identical account). He describes the people as 'Vikings in custom and dress' and claims that 'the Vikings have no more secure base than this Island in all the world', which is ample testimony to the prominence of Viking Dublin, Waterford, Cork and Limerick on the world scene. Ibrahim leaves us an interesting description of whales being hunted off the Irish coast:

> 'It is said that on these shores they hunt the young of the whale, which is a very large fish of which they hunt the young and eat it as a delicacy. It is said that these young ones are born in the month of September and they are caught in October, November, December and January. After that their flesh grows tough and is unfit to eat. As regards the manner of hunting them . . . The hunters assemble on ships, taking with them a large, iron hook with sharp teeth. On the hook there is a large, strong ring and in the ring a stout cord. If they come across a young whale they clap their hands and shout. The young whale is diverted by the clapping, and approaches the ships in a sociable and friendly manner. One of the sailors then leaps onto it and scratches its brow vigorously. This gives pleasure to the young whale. Then the sailor places the hook in the centre of the whale's head, takes a strong iron hammer and with it strikes the hook three times with the utmost vigour. The whale does not feel the first blow, but with the second and third it becomes greatly agitated, and sometimes it hits some of the ships with its tail and shatters them. It goes on struggling until it is overcome with exhaustion. Then the men in the ships help one another drag it along until they reach the shore' (Fairley 1981, 117).

The whalers here are presumably Vikings, who had an established whaling tradition and whose activities are described in the Annals of Ulster for AD 827:

> 'a great slaughter of sea-hogs on the coast of Ard Cianachta [Ferrard Barony, Co. Louth] by foreigners' (Quoted in Fairley 1981, 117).

Fairley interprets the descriptions of whaling in Irish waters by Arab sources as fanciful or humorous, and Buchner (2001) suggests that it may represent a garbled account of organised inshore whaling. The methods described are very similar to those described by Polo some centuries later. Abu Abdallah Muhammad al-Sharif al-Idrisi in his *Book of Roger* of *c.* 1154 describes trade with Ireland, citing the *Book of Wonders*, an earlier Eastern work. This tells us that

> 'there are three cities there, and that they used to be inhabited, and that ships used to call and put in there and buy amber and coloured stones from the natives. Then one of them tried to make himself ruler over them, and he made war against them with his people and they fought back against him. Then an enemy arose amongst them, they exterminated one another and some of them migrated to the mainland. Thus their cities were ruined, and no inhabitants remain in them' (Idrisi, *Opus Geographicum*, quoted in Lewis 2001, 148).

It is not clear whether or not the amber referred to here is ambergris. It is difficult to establish at what point the word 'amber' began to refer to true amber rather than ambergris, but Ibn Yaqub reported that much amber was found on the shore around Bordeaux. This sounds more like a description of ambergris, although amber has been found washed ashore as 'beach pebbles' as far from the Baltic as Norfolk. For the most part, the true amber traded in Ireland was not native, being of 'Baltic type', unlike ambergris, which could be sourced locally. It is clear that the author had no personal knowledge of Ireland. The information in the *Book of Wonders* is clearly at least second-hand and represents hearsay evidence rather than an actual visit by Muslim merchants, but the fact that Ireland was known of as a place with which one traded for luxury goods is significant. It is impossible to pin down the vaguely described events but, given that Arab information about Ireland appears to have been derived from Norse sources, it may be a garbled account of the events leading up to AD 902, when the Annals of Ulster report the

> 'expulsion of the heathens from Ireland, from the longphort of Dublin, by Mael-Finnia son of Flannacán with the Men of Brega and by Cerball son of Muirecán with the Leinstermen so that they abandoned a great number of their ships and escaped half-dead after having been wounded and defeated' (quoted in MacShamhráin 2002, 51).

This occurred after five of the dynasts of Dublin fell in internecine conflict. This facilitated the sack of Dublin, after which 'surviving members of this elite sought refuge in England only to return 15 years later'.

Whales and medieval Ireland

Irish sources amply confirm the Arab observations on the importance of whaling. The medieval Irish law-texts not only provide priceless information on the maritime activities of coastal peoples but also provide hints of the ethical and social context in which they understood these activities. They confirm that whales were an important aspect of Irish economic life in the early medieval period. Whales are well represented in Irish medieval literature, both as economic resources and in the form of sea monsters and magical beasts, and archaeological evidence shows that they have been exploited in Ireland since at least the Neolithic.

Buchner notes that whales were the main species exploited by the Irish rather than seals, which may have been protected by some form of cultural taboo. Whale strandings appear to have been reasonably common, and in a survey of the legal tracts he notes the regulations for distributing them, including arrangements for the bones, teeth and baleen. It was the king's responsibility to organise the collection of stranded whales:

'if whatever thing is cast ashore in a territory, whether a crew of shipwrecked people or a whale, the whole territory is bound to save it from the strand, i.e. the head of the family in whose land it is, goes to the king of the territory and fasts upon him. He (the king) gives notice to the territory that he will take distress, and then they (the whole party) come to save it' (quoted in Buchner 2001, 86).

Adomnan of Iona, writing in the seventh century AD, exempted whale meat from restrictions on carrion-eating. Other forms of meat were forbidden unless it was known how the animal had died, but whales were assumed to be permitted unless decomposition had begun. Buchner suggests that this is because stranded marine mammals were a 'resource too important to be wasted'. Interestingly, whale meat was forbidden to the sick.

Disappointingly, Buchner came across 'no evidence for the knowledge or the use of amber-gris, although the information may be hidden behind some more ambiguous term'. He suggests that the Irish may have favoured shallow-water species rather than the deep-water sperm whale. Tantalisingly, he cites texts in which St Colmcille ascribes meaning to the vomiting of a large sea fish called Rossault:

'a vomiting in the sea, with its tail on high: . . . Foundering of boats, and barques, and ships and destruction to the animals of the sea in that year: a

119

vomiting in the air, with its tail down, while it cast its vomit upwards: . . . destruction to the flying animals of the air in that year. Another vomiting throughout a land, so that the land would stink: . . . destruction to human beings and to cattle this year' *(Dinshennchas of Mag Muireisce,* quoted in Buchner 2001, 89).

This passage indicates that the medieval Irish were familiar with the habits of deep-sea whales such as the sperm whale, as well as with shallow-water species. The description of the whale vomiting, however, would seem to suggest that the writer was unaware of the value of ambergris. Rather than a boon, the whale in question unleashes a string of calamities.

Nevertheless, it seems likely that the early medieval Irish were at least aware of ambergris. The importance given in some law-texts to the rapid exploitation of stranded whales means that it must have been encountered in the bellies of luckless cetaceans over the years. Clearly, however, it was not a major source of revenue at the time, although small-scale exploitation and trade cannot be ruled out. When ambergris became valuable its use was quickly tightly regulated.

If a trade in ambergris had been primarily a Viking activity, it might have been outside the sphere of relations with which the Irish law-texts deal. The principal law-text covering such matters, the *Muirbetha* or 'Sea Judgements', has been lost, and the surviving literary references to trade products within Ireland apparently deal mainly with reciprocal gift exchange among the Irish rather than with items passed on to Norse traders. The Irish–Norse distinction was broken down by succeeding waves of invaders and their law codes, social practices and influences. Irish trade was centred on the large Anglo-Norman port cities and remained so for the duration of the Middle Ages. On the west coast the Anglo-Norman city of Galway would be crucial to this trade.

Post-medieval Irish trade in ambergris

Whether or not trade in ambergris with Islamic Spain was a major factor in Irish/Hiberno-Norse commercial life, such trade certainly became significant after the *Reconquista*. In the west, ambergris was believed to have a similar origin to true amber owing to its similar appearance; indeed, the name amber referred to ambergris before true amber. Theories on its origins included bituminous sea founts, the sperm of fish or whales, the droppings of giant sea birds and of hives of bees living near the sea. It was certainly in use in the British Isles by the fourteenth century as a familiar luxury item and food additive. One recipe dated to the reign of Edward III for a draught known as 'Hypocras' or 'Ypocras for

Lords' claimed that it would do wonders for the digestion when mixed with Aqua Vitae and a variety of other expensive ingredients, including the intriguingly named 'Grains of Paradise'. Irish trade with Britain was, of course, extensive, but the ambergris in question could have come from anywhere.

Medieval communications between the Iberian Peninsula and Ireland had both a commercial and a religious aspect, centred on the cult of St James. Trade in both directions, mainly the exchange of rough cloth for wine or horses, was a feature of Irish relations with all her nearer maritime neighbours, and groups of Basque and Spanish fishing-boats operated in Irish waters. These voyages had a trading aspect and may also have acted as a conduit for ambergris.

Such a trade through Galway is known of from the seventeenth century, and it seems unlikely that this had suddenly sprung into existence in the years immediately preceding the Elizabethan and Stuart conquests. Until central authority was restored in the middle of the seventeenth century, Galway ran its own affairs as a virtually independent maritime city-state. Maintaining a distinct identity as an Anglo-Norman community, Galway passed numerous laws to keep the native Irish outside the walls and to suppress their customs within them, but gave royal edicts little attention and carried on a thriving trade with England, Spain, France and Flanders. The city maintained commercial and political arrangements with the Gaelic lordships around the city and paid protection money to local naval powers such as the O'Briens.

A statute of 1324 stated that 'The King shall have wreck of the sea, whales and great sturgeons in the sea or elsewhere, except in places privileged', which came into direct conflict with the Gaelic order's identical claims for its own local rulers. By the reign of James I the ambergris trade had clearly become large and profitable enough to merit official attention and disgruntled commentators pointed to potential Crown revenue escaping through Galway:

'. . . much ambergrease there had, and gathered on the west and south coasts, and all this usurped by private men which be mere royalties. The Galway merchants and others bring a great quantity yearly into England and Spain of this ambergrease which is held to be as good and perfect as any. In law all the ambergrease and pearl that there hath been gathered all this time past being admitted to be royalties (whereof I doubt not for my part) may be recovered against the usurpers upon an action of account brought against them by the king' (O'Brien, *Advertisements for Ireland* (1923), quoted in Fairley 1981, 101).

The resulting conflict over the right to collect ambergris continued into the 1620s. In a letter to Henry Lynch in 1621 the earl of Clanricarde describes a disagreement with Sir John Bingham over the right to collect ambergris and comments that 'I never yet heard that any vice admiral or other officer made any challenge unto any Amber Greece or any other such commodity (more than a shipwreck) in any of those islands, I will defend no more than I may nor will not forgo what I shall find to be my write.' In spite of the claim that a 'great quantity' was being sent yearly to England, the appearance of ambergris seems to have been irregular. The Connacht trade in ambergris was barely a memory by 1666. When ambergris came ashore in large quantities on the coast of Connemara locals no longer recognised it, although once they realised its value they were quick to exploit it. Roderic O'Flaherty wrote of Galway in 1684:

> 'On these coasts ambergreese is frequently found. In the year 1666 there was a great deal of black amber cast ashore everywhere, and the people, not used to the like, knew it not at first, yet they could get ten shillings an ounce for it, when people understood what it was. The best is of the colour of Castile soap and worth seventy shillings an ounce' (quoted in Fairley 1981, 101).

The political turmoil of the intervening years, with the brutal suppression of the old social and commercial order, may have broken old habits, or perhaps ambergris was found only rarely in the first half of the seventeenth century. Nevertheless, ambergris continued to come ashore to enrich the fortunate:

> 'For as they on the coast of New-England, and the island Bermudas, gather considerable quantities of Ambergreese, so on the western coast of Ireland, along the counties of Sligo, Mayo, Kerry and the isles of Arran, they frequently meet with large parcels of that precious substance, highly valued for its perfume. In the year 1691 Mr Constantine an Apothecary of Dublin, shewed me one piece of Ambergreese found near Sligo, that weigh'd fifty two ounces; he bought it for twenty pound, and sold it in London after-wards for above a hundred' (quoted in Fairley 1981, 102).

Supplies from more distant markets gradually supplanted Irish ambergris on the British or world markets. While some found near Belfast in the 1760s was 'esteemed by the best judges equal to that imported from the East Indies', ambergris continued to decline in importance and probably in quantity. Only one of 68 sperm whales harpooned off Ireland between 1908 and 1922 contained any. The lone example had only fifteen pounds in its carcass, which, considering the masses of 100 pounds or larger of which we have reports, suggests that the population of sperm whales off the Irish coast in times gone by may have been substantially higher than it is today.

Trade in ambergris: the end?

Restorative properties were still being imputed to ambergris into the nineteenth century. The gourmand Brilliat-Savarin, in his *Meditation VI*, writes of the 'chocolat amber' enjoyed in his day as a pick-me-up. Ambergris in the perfume industry was replaced by synthetic substitutes in the twentieth century. A growing concern about declining stocks of sperm whales has since led to the international trade in ambergris being made illegal, and Irish coastal waters have now been declared a 'whale sanctuary'. The invention of the exploding harpoon gun by Thomas Nesbitt, an Ulsterman, in the late eighteenth century massively improved the efficiency of commercial whaling, so perhaps this conservation gesture may go some way towards making amends.

Here and there ambergris retains some of its old mystery. During the Camp David negotiations a senior member of the Egyptian delegation recommended it to a bemused secretary general as a source of vigour. Alternative medicine may someday return to Classical sources and restore ambergris as a picturesque and expensive (if sadly useless) cure-all.

The importance of ambergris for an understanding of Irish maritime trade

The 1607 reference to ambergris in Connemara demonstrates the great importance once placed on a now-obscure product. It provides new insight into the trading contacts and social relations of Irish lordships, and demonstrates that the Gaelic Irish exported a valued luxury item from at least the early modern period and perhaps from the early Middle Ages. There are a number of ambergris artefacts in existence, including 'The Negress', carved from a single block by an anonymous Italian in the sixteenth century, but ambergris has left little trace in the Irish archaeological record and no mention was made of it in the most recent discussion of Galway trade. When discussing native Irish trade (which was technically smuggling) we should be aware that valuable low-bulk products may well have been important while remaining almost invisible.

A number of studies are ongoing into the maritime lordships. It has become clear that coastal lordships sited their fortresses with the exploitation of all available resources in mind and that a complicated structure of customary laws and taxes controlled this exploitation. The study of the ambergris trade, by demonstrating that attention to a little-known substance can open up interesting avenues of research, may aid this process. It seems likely that lordships other than the O'Flahertys may have been involved in sending 'great quantities yearly' to England and Spain. Archives in Spain and the UK may shed some additional light on the matter, and following this up may lead to further discoveries.

'Praise is like ambergris; a little whiff of it, by snatches, is very agreeable; but when a man holds whole lump of it to his nose; it is stink and strikes you down' (Alexander Pope, *Swift's Works* (1841), 837).

Further reading

Blake, M.J. 1902 An account of the castle and manor of Bunowen in the barony of Ballynahinch, Co. of Galway. *Journal of the Galway Archaeological and Historical Society* 2, 39–56.

Buchner, D. 2001 The exploitation of littoral resources in ancient Ireland: mammalian problems. In D. Buchner (ed.), *Studien in Memoriam Wilhelm Schule*, 62–91. Rahden/Westfallen.

Comber, M. 2001 Trade and communication networks in early-historic Ireland. *Journal of Irish Archaeology* 10, 73–91.

Constable, R. 1994 *Trade and traders in Muslim Spain*. Cambridge.

Cunningham, B. 1996 Clanricard Letters. *Journal of the Galway Archaeological and Historical Society* 48, 170.

Cunliffe, B. 2001 *Facing the ocean: the Atlantic and its peoples*. Oxford.

Fairley, J. 1981 *Irish whales and whaling*. Belfast.

Gibbons, M. 2003 Bunowen castle. *O'Malley Journal Centenary Edition* 10, 34–44.

Hall, R. 1996 *Empires of the monsoon*. London.

Hartnett, A. 2004 The port of Galway: infrastructure, trade and commodities. In E. Fitzpatrick, M. O'Brien and P. Walsh (eds), *Archaeological investigations in Galway city, 1987–1998*, 292–308. Bray.

Kelly, F. 1997 *Early Irish farming*. Dublin.

Lewis, B. 2001 *The Muslim discovery of Europe*. New York.

MacShamhráin, A. 2002 *The Vikings: an illustrated history*. Dublin.

O'Connell, J.W. 1994 History and the 'human kingdom'. In J. Waddell, J. W. O'Connell and A. Korff (eds), *The Book of Aran*, 71–94. Kinvarra.

O'Neill, T. 1987 *Merchants and mariners in medieval Ireland*. Dublin.

Shlaim, A. 2001 *The iron wall: Israel and the Arab world 1948–1998*. London.

13

Locked up, locked in, always looking for doorways: the travels of a medieval art-historian

Jenifer Ní Ghrádaigh

Those outside the field of art history often view the study as one pursued only by the wealthy and effete, as witnessed by the cackles of incredulous laughter that greeted Brad Pitt's confession, as the eponymous assassin in *Mr & Mrs Smith*, that he had majored in the subject. Nevertheless, the medieval art-historian is a breed apart, and few perhaps realise the lengths to which many postgraduate students go in their efforts to eyeball at first hand those monuments that are the basis of their research, without the benefits of generous funding for such travel. I intend to start this piece, therefore, with a tale that, while it does not directly bear on any discovery from the past, nevertheless gives an insight into the incidental difficulties of thesis research in the field, with limited cash resources.

Most archaeologists or art-historians embarking on a study of the medieval architecture of Ireland, especially if this study covers a good part of at least two provinces, see fit to beg, borrow or steal a car in which to do their fieldwork. And indeed, given the distribution of early medieval churches in Ireland, nearly always outside urban centres and served not at all or infrequently by public transport, this is the only sensible course of action. Needless to say, it was one that I did not take myself, owing largely to the cash-flow problems alluded to above, which put the straightforward acquisition of a car beyond my means, while my lack of ability in the larcenous line prevented me from acquiring one in the third manner. This was to lead, in the course of time, to various adventures of a less than agreeable nature. Few art-historians or archaeologists, if taxed with a game of word association, would reply with 'Garda drug raid' to 'Ahenny high cross', but this is indeed what springs to my mind when presented with an image of this ninth-century monument (Pl. 36).

In the summer of 2001, my boyfriend Ivan and I embarked on a cycling trip

Pl. 36—Ivan and me and the lengthening shadows at Ahenny, Co. Tipperary, where the crosses cost us a bed.

Pl. 37—The bicycle and I relax after a day's pedalling on another trip, when I more wisely brought a tent. It is now retired from active fieldwork service.

from Dublin to Cork (Pl. 37) that was designed to take in all the more interesting Romanesque sites along the way (the Irish Romanesque being the subject of my thesis), and any other early medieval sites that had previously eluded me. This method of travel has left me with an indelible memory of any sites that were on a high elevation but, apart from imprinting such information on the mind, it is probably not otherwise to be recommended for its practicalities. Determined as I was that nothing should escape me on this trip, I nevertheless combined this passion with an even greater reluctance to tear myself from my bed in the morning (which I like to think was due to the miles I pedalled rather than inherent laziness) with the usual result that we arrived at the last sites at about nine in the evening. The day we left Graiguenamanagh conformed pretty much to the same pattern. Jerpoint, Sheepstown and Aghaviller had engrossed us somewhat, so by the time we reached Kilkieran and stopped to see the high crosses there the shadows were already beginning to lengthen. Prudence would ordinarily dictate what Ivan had attempted to insist on—that we should abandon Ahenny and head straight on to Carrick-on-Suir to get a bed for the night—but prudence failed me on this occasion. The turn-off for Ahenny beckoned promisingly and, crossing a small stream, we began to head upwards, and then further upwards, along a narrow little road. Passing the tiny village, we arrived at the graveyard in time to see the crosses lit truly magnificently by the westering sun. A brief inspection sated me, as my stomach was beginning to press its own claims, and we departed downhill at some speed towards Carrick-on-Suir.

On our arrival in the town, we began our usual scout for B&Bs, only to find they were all full—as was the hostel, and indeed even the hotel. Philosophically, we concluded that we could perhaps make it to Clonmel before it got dark, and rang the B&Bs that lay in that direction, but the conjunction of a music festival, the August bank holiday and some sporting event had left everywhere within a twenty-mile radius well booked up. We were faced with the unpleasant prospect of a night spent on the streets of Carrick-on-Suir, and that the previously unusually hot spell was beginning to break suggested that it would be a chilly experience at best. Cursing our decision to travel light, i.e. without a tent or sleeping-bags, we decided to treat ourselves to a meal and face the consequences later. Indeed, we prolonged our entertainment at the local Chinese to such an extent that it was midnight before we left. At this point I had the genius idea that we could perhaps throw ourselves on the mercy of the gardaí and spend the night (if we were lucky) in a cell! This attempt to emulate the monastic way of life in the 21st century was, however, foiled by government cutbacks: the Garda station closed at nine each night. Prowling the streets like the true vagrants we were, and resigning ourselves to the idea of finding a likely doorway, we finally were taken

Pl. 38—The Nuns' Church at Clonmacnoise, Co. Offaly, finished by Derbforgaill in 1167.

Pl. 39—The Reverend James Graves (by permission of the Royal Society of Antiquaries of Ireland).

pity on by a pair of gardaí, likewise prowling (or, more properly, patrolling). They suggested that, if we liked, we could encamp ourselves in the Garda garage, which at least would be out of the elements. We willingly closed with this offer, which the art-historian in me can't help but note was especially apt, due to its Biblical prefiguration (full inn, nowhere to stay . . . readers may get my drift, though I'm too modest to spell out what role that would place *me* in!). But fancy our surprise to see that the garage already had an occupant, which was no less than a stolen car, crashed after its part as a getaway car during a drugs raid. Peering at it in the gloom, the hospitable gardaí were struck by the same thought as myself and, assuring us that it had already been fingerprinted, suggested that it might prove more comfortable to sleep in than the floor. Thus, for the first and last time on that fieldtrip, I got behind the steering wheel . . .

My inspection of the Ahenny high crosses was not to bear scholastic fruit until many years later. When I was studying the Nuns' Church at Clonmacnoise, they provided the comparison I was looking for in trying to unravel the contemporary foreign influences from those of native antiquity (Pl. 38). It was while attempting to disentangle some of the other intricacies of that church that I made some more interesting discoveries. The Annals of the Four Masters record that the Nuns' Church was finished in 1167 by Derbforgaill, wife of Tigernán Ua Ruairc, daughter of Murchad Ua Maeleachlainn, and supposedly the cause of Ireland's so-called 800 years of oppression owing to her ill-advised elopement with Diarmait Mac Murchada. Though built by such a wicked temptress, it had been rebuilt in 1865, after the collapse of its chancel arch and west doorway, by a man of a very different stamp, the Reverend James Graves (Pl. 39). Graves was one of the founding members of the Kilkenny Archaeological Society (which later became the Royal Society of Antiquaries of Ireland—RSAI) and he combined a dedication to the preservation of Ireland's medieval heritage with an unusual grasp, for the time, of the importance of distinguishing reconstruction from original fabric. His work at the Nuns' Church was undertaken with the remains of a fund that had been raised to help prosecute John Glennon, a member of a pleasure party from Birr visiting Clonmacnoise in 1864 who had decided to spice up their pleasure with a bit of vandalism upon the churches, notably Temple Finghin (Pl. 40). The case fell through but left the Society with enough funds to repair the cap of the round tower of Temple Finghin, as well as clearing the area around its walls. It also allowed for the reconstruction of the chancel arch of the Nuns' Church, which had fallen in 1838, and that of its west doorway, the remains of which were discovered only when clearing the interior of the church.

Graves was careful to record his activities in the reconstruction of the church, accounts of which were published in the Society's journal. His descriptions were

Pl. 40—Temple Finghin, Clonmacnoise, was damaged by vandalism in 1864.

Pl. 41—The 'extra' capital— from the Nuns' Church or Temple Finghin?

Pl. 42—At Bishop Wilton (Yorkshire East Riding), restored for Sir Tatton Sykes in 1858–9 by J. L. Pearson, the paler Victorian replacement stones are easily distinguishable from the original work.

Pl. 43—Graves's sketch (by permission of the Royal Society of Antiquaries of Ireland).

131

Pl. 44—Temple Finghin has an attached round tower.

Pl. 45—The two Romanesque arch stones that caught my eye.

not meticulous enough, however, to account for the appearance of an extra capital (Pl. 41), not currently built into the doorway but so similar in style to one of its other capitals that it certainly seemed to be by the same sculptor. Various other scholars had assumed that this capital really belonged to the Nuns' Church and was perhaps from the inner order, and that it had been found after the reconstruction had taken place and hence could not be included. The very fresh appearance of the stone, in what published photographs I could find of it, made me inclined at first to think that it was a nineteenth-century piece carved in imitation of the other capitals, intended to be included but for some reason abandoned. This was a lamentably common practice in England, where many Romanesque churches contain multitudes of carved replacement stones if the originals were deemed too worn and needed smartening up (Pl. 42). Besides a lack of funds, however, Graves's own standards seemed to argue against this, as for instance in 1872 he had advised on 'a careful conservation (not "restoration")' at Glendalough. I was further convinced that this could not be the case by his invective against Thomas Newenham Deane when appointed first Inspector of National Monuments, precisely because, instead of meticulous study of medieval architecture and sculpture, Deane, as Graves put it, 'merely jotted down pretty bits in his note book for uses without much caring what ages they are'. So I determined on making a more thorough search through Graves's sketches, preserved in the RSAI, as well as going to see the capital itself, then housed in the sacristy of Clonmacnoise cathedral.

In fact, the provenance of the capital was not difficult to establish. Con Manning, then president of the RSAI, told me that he had found a drawing of it amongst Graves's sketch-books (Pl. 43) with, scribbled beside it in Graves's inimitable hand, the information that it had been 'dug up at the base of the south door' of Temple Finghin, and, rather interestingly, on 8 May 1865—leaving Graves more than enough time to include it in his reconstruction of the Nuns' Church had he so wished. This was an exciting discovery indeed, as all that currently remains *in situ* of the doorway are three very worn bases, and more exciting still as the church itself is striking as being one of the very few Irish Romanesque buildings which show any element of architectural innovation. Unlike the plain two-cell plan of the Nuns' Church, Temple Finghin has an attached round tower, entered at ground level through a doorway in the south side of the chancel (Pl. 44). It therefore attracted a good deal of antiquarian and archaeological attention in the nineteenth century as proof of the argument that round towers were indeed Christian belfries rather than pagan fire-temples, gnomons or phallic emblems. Hitherto, however, its more exact date, the circumstances of its construction and its patronage, whether political or ecclesiastic, had all remained obscure. The chancel arch was quite unique in terms of its sculptural decoration, and art-historical deductions based on that were therefore difficult to make—but if more pieces of the elusive south doorway came to light, I felt that some progress on all these issues might be possible.

And here Graves's own words came both to help me and to lead me further towards its rediscovery. Although the Society's own journal was silent on the subject, Graves had written in that same year a longish letter to the *Gentleman's Magazine*, in which he recounted the finding not only of this capital but also of 'one or two arch stones (similar in character with those of the Nunnery Church), and a very singular capital representing a male head with very long hair and moustache, and a greyhound coiled round under the chin'. Alas, the sketches in the RSAI did not contain any drawings of these other pieces, but, armed with this information, I returned to Clonmacnoise, hoping to find these 'one or two arch stones' and the capital so intriguingly described.

Standing in the gloom of the cathedral sacristy, itself dating back to the twelfth century, I scarcely had the patience to let my eyes adjust to the light before I eagerly began to scan the surrounding loose stones for some that might fit Graves's description. The loose capital, which had itself led me so far, was the first to meet my glance, but I searched in vain for another that should display a moustachioed head, and I was forced to conclude that it had gone missing over the course of time. Two other stones, clearly Romanesque, I did soon light upon (Pl. 45). One of these was a clean-shaven human head, the other that of a snarling animal. Hefting these with some difficulty into a better light, a closer inspection convinced me that they also were by the same hand as had carved the loose capital, and that, indeed, I had found two of the arch stones that Graves had so very slightly described. But this was not all. Two further pieces of fire-damaged twisted columns were also among the stones, and measurements soon showed that they would fit the bases still remaining *in situ* at the south doorway itself. Graves had mentioned one further piece, a piece of octagonal pilaster or attached column. While not to be found in the sacristy, I did not have to look far, as it was now built into the west doorway of the cathedral.

I was thrilled with my discovery of these various pieces: never previously properly recorded, they provided the evidence to demonstrate not only that Temple Finghin had had a highly elaborate south doorway but also that that doorway had been the work of the same sculptors who had carved the Nuns' Church. But what was the historical significance of such a point?

On the one hand, by establishing that two churches built in Clonmacnoise in the twelfth century were decorated by the same sculptors, it could suggest that such craftsmen were often based at monastic sites, and that these sites really were an Irish equivalent to the towns of medieval Europe. Another possibility, however, was that these craftsmen were once more working for the same patrons, if not for Derbforgaill then for another member of her family. But where to look? Ironically, considering that Derbforgaill is best known for her elopement, she is also probably the woman with the longest recorded marriage in twelfth-century Ireland. Born in 1108, she was most likely married to Tigernán sometime in the 1120s and, apart from her brief absence with Diarmait Mac Murchada in 1152, there is no reason to suppose that after her return to Tigernán the same year they ever lived asunder until his death in 1172. As with murder mysteries, a process of elimination was required, and it seemed to me that Derbforgaill's husband Tigernán was the most likely suspect behind the patronage of Temple Finghin. To look into this possibility necessitated my removal from the banks of the Shannon to the National Library.

Even in this peaceful environment, however, those in search of adventure can find it—and I'm not among those scholars who would dare to pass off their own research as such. No indeed, but intent as I was on getting to the bottom of this nefarious business—the novel category of the 'who-built-it' rather than the whodunit—I stayed one night in the National Library until closing time and, issuing forth into the dark, discovered that it was raining hard. Shivering beneath the arcades, I rummaged for my raingear, at length found it and drew it on, unlocked my bicycle and resigned myself to getting a thorough wetting. Being otherwise preoccupied, I didn't pay much heed to a library attendant running past me towards the gate and back. When I finally ventured out from under the shelter of the arcade, I found the gate locked. Here was a predicament. Feeling rather ashamed of myself, I went back towards the door, but it was also locked. I rang. No answer. I checked the gate again. Finally, I had to take the demeaning step of flagging down a passing American tourist and asking him to inform the gardaí at the Dáil beside us that I was locked in. A rather incredulous garda soon made his appearance and, peering at me through the bars, told me that they'd have to 'call in the army'! Naturally envisaging helicopters and abseiling commandos, I began to protest that I could probably climb over. But calling in the army, in fact, only meant that the keys to the gate between the Dáil and the National Library are in the custody of a soft-spoken army official, and I slunk out without too much embarrassment.

Despite this episode, my resolve to find the solution to my 'who-built-it' remained firm. While the annals, those records of the year's events that were kept in monasteries from the sixth century onwards, remained resolutely silent on the question of any good deed of Tigernán Ua Ruairc's, I was thrilled to discover another source that suggested he could indeed be the patron. This was the Registry of Clonmacnoise, a thirteenth-century document now preserved only in a seventeenth-century English translation, which records the burial rights of different royal families at Clonmacnoise. It also claims that an O'Rourke king

Pl. 46—*The same sculptors worked on the capitals of the doorway at Kilmore, Co. Cavan.*

Pl. 47—*A capital from Devenish, Co. Fermanagh, shows the same hands at work.*

built both a church and a round tower there. Yet the annals record that the round tower was built in 1124, and by Toirdelbach Ua Conchobair. This seemed to suggest that the tower in question, the one mentioned in the Registry, might be that of Temple Finghin, also the only structure to combine both a church *and* a tower. I was already finding it difficult to eliminate my primary suspect.

But at this point the evidence became a little murky, as historical sources are sometimes apt to do: the name of the king in question was elucidated, 'which was Fergal'. Had my trail come to an end? Was it just a red herring? At first I thought so and, turning to the annals and the genealogies, I looked up all the Fergal O'Rourkes I could find, but none of them seemed promising. Another line of reasoning soon struck me, however. Was it possible that the first name was merely a subsequent addition by a later scribe, a clarifying but mistaken attempt to guess *which* O'Rourke king had been so generous? The various layers of additions or glosses were all ironed out into one smooth narrative in its current form. I turned to look at the other kings mentioned in the document, and here a certain peculiarity struck me: few of them were contemporary with each other. Rather, each seemed to be a particularly important king from a historical point of view. In other words, their identification was very suspect. Since the document in its original form was produced just around the time when Tigernán was active, this left just the bare possibility that the O'Rourke recorded here was originally meant for Tigernán after all, and that it had been 'clarified' to Fergal at a later date.

Of course, the nature of the 'who-built-it' must always be less thrillingly certain than that of the whodunit, and sometimes a bare possibility is all that the art-historian can run with. In the current forgiving political climate, I was anxious to see whether my prime suspect was indeed the man. Was it actually possible to find anything positive on a cultural level to say about the man described by one annalist as 'surpasser of all the Gaels in might and abundance' but abused by Gerald of Wales for his 'treacherous villainy' and laughed at over the centuries as a cuckold? It was time to get on my bicycle again . . .

Bréifne, the kingdom once ruled over by Tigernán Ua Ruairc, stretched from Drumcliffe in Sligo to Kells in Meath, and from the Erne to the Shannon, as described in the twelfth-century Life of St Máedóc. Luckily for my muscles, only one truly splendid Romanesque doorway survives from within the boundaries of the kingdom—that now rebuilt into the nineteenth-century cathedral at Kilmore, Co. Cavan (Pl. 46). Kilmore gained its diocesan status in 1152, during the twelfth-century reforms, and the extent of the diocese was largely the same as Tigernán's kingdom of Bréifne. This was one of two sites that were to clinch my opinion of Tigernán's involvement. Here, over 50 miles as the crow flies from Clonmacnoise, can be seen capitals that were once more carved by the same sculptors who worked on the Nuns' Church and Temple Finghin. It was impossible not to credit Tigernán as patron of this doorway.

Even further north again, in County Fermanagh, on Devenish in Lough Erne, the work of the same sculptors can also be found, in the now-reconstructed doorway of the so-called 'lost church' (Pl. 47). But was there a historical document to link Tigernán with the site? The Erne was certainly one of the boundaries of his kingdom. And indeed, on Devenish in 1147 Gilla Mo-Duta composed the *Banshenchas* or 'Lore of Women', including a short eulogy to Tigernán Ua Ruairc and a tribute to Derbforgaill and her parents, which suggest that it may have been commissioned by Tigernán in his wife's honour. Here, then, was evidence of the same sculptors at work, in such far-flung places that a connection with Tigernán was the only explanation. If Tigernán's involvement was the only thread that linked these sites, then it made sense that his patronage of the same sculptors throughout must also connect him to Temple Finghin. My prime suspect, far from being eliminated in the early stages of my enquiry, had become the hero of my 'who-built-it'.

My journey of discovery began as a Romanesque pilgrimage by bicycle from Dublin to Cork in which doorways figured prominently. While the impending prospect of sleeping in a doorway in Carrick-on-Suir led to my sleeping on the seat of a stolen car, that at Clonmacnoise led me to blocks of carved stone and eventually to something a lot more interesting. I ended by finding a more admirable aspect to a historical figure who had hitherto been remembered largely for his ruthless political scheming and his marital scandal. Thanks to the diggings of an Anglican clergyman in the 1860s, and my own less physical efforts, Tigernán Ua Ruairc can now also be remembered as a patron not merely of the church but of the arts. The art-historian in me can't help but note some interesting parallels . . .

Acknowledgements

I am especially grateful to all the members of the Garda Síochána who rescued me from my various predicaments during the research for my thesis—well beyond the call of duty! Also to Ivan McAvinchey, the unfortunate companion in my Ahenny adventure, who accompanied me to more Romanesque sites than he can ever remember. Finally, my thanks must go to Karen Lundgren, who, upon hearing the above story, nobly undertook to drive me to all the remaining sites on my list, which, lamentably for her, were the most obscure and least interesting, nettle-filled and tide-dependent. And all I could give her in return was an Irish passport—but that's another story!

Further reading

Davies, O. 1948 The churches of County Cavan. *Journal of the Royal Society of Antiquaries of Ireland* **78**, 73–118.

Hamlin, A. and Stalley, R. 2002 A newly-discovered Romanesque church on Devenish, County Fermanagh. *Ulster Journal of Archaeology* **61**, 83–97.

Manning, C. 1994 *Clonmacnoise*. Dublin.

O'Donovan, J. 1856–7 The Registry of Clonmacnoise; with notes and introductory remarks. *Journal of the Royal Society of Antiquaries of Ireland* **4**, 444–60.

Ní Ghrádaigh, J. 2003 'But what exactly did she give?' Derbforgaill and the Nuns' Church. In H. King (ed.), *Clonmacnoise Studies II*, 175–207. Dublin.

Ní Ghrádaigh, J. 2005 Temple Finghin, and two unusual voussoirs from Clonmacnoise. *Archaeology Ireland* **19** (3), 26–31.

Ní Ghrádaigh, J. 2006 'My dear Pickwick': the early sketchbooks of James Graves, and his development as an antiquarian. *Ossory, Laois and Leinster* **2**, 96–122.

Stalley, R. 2000 *Irish round towers*. Dublin.

therefore very glad that Dr Aidan O'Sullivan, who was also on the conference trip, was prepared to seriously exercise his muscles while gingerly carrying the great box around from university to guest-house to airport. Proving too heavy for overhead bins on the aircraft, they were stashed under my feet on the plane. Fortunately they all arrived safely, without incident, back in Ireland. They were then catalogued by Dúlra Ó Riordáin and deposited in the Photographic Section of the National Monuments Service, now in the Department of the Environment, Heritage and Local Government, where the catalogue is available and from where copies of the images can be requested.

The slides date mainly from the later years of the nineteenth century and the early decades of the twentieth century and are a wonderful collection of views of folk life, artefacts and National Monuments from almost every county in Ireland. They are not only a valuable collection for the National Monuments Service and for anyone interested in 'antique' views of National Monuments and life in Ireland but they also have an important historical connection, having been brought to America by the late Myles Dillon (1900–72). He was a son of John Dillon, nationalist politician and MP, and was educated at Belvedere College and University College Dublin. He studied for his Ph.D in Germany and was awarded his degree from Bonn University in 1925, subsequently lecturing in Paris, Dublin, Chicago and Oxford before becoming professor of Irish at the University of Madison, Wisconsin, in 1937. Regarded as a pioneer in the field of Celtic Studies, he published *The Cycles of the Kings* in 1946, *Early Irish literature* in 1948 and *The Celtic realms* in 1967. Following his return to Ireland in 1949 to take up a post in Celtic Studies at the Dublin Institute for Advanced Studies, the slides were left behind in Madison.

Being a Celtic scholar, he clearly used these slides to illustrate his lectures, and one can see how prehistoric Ireland, Early Christian Ireland, Romanesque architecture, early monastic life, high crosses, early manuscripts and many other aspects of life in Ireland could be illuminated, in every sense of the word, by these wonderful black-and-white images. His collection could also have been used to give lectures on folk life as it was at the turn of the twentieth century, and there are some marvellous slides showing, among other things, fishermen using a coracle (Pl. 48), a vernacular house being thatched (Pl. 49), a cattle market (Pl. 50) and a woman spinning (Pl. 51). Views of bogs and bog roads and men cutting turf and carrying home the creels on donkeys are particularly evocative of a lifestyle that has passed and of a period in which he held a special interest. One image that recalled for me a childhood holiday in Clifden, when on one occasion we arrived exceptionally late for Sunday Mass, was that of the men kneeling outside the church door during the consecration (Pl. 52).

In some ways it is strange that the slides were left behind, as Myles Dillon

Pl. 48—Coracle on the River Boyne.

Pl. 49—Vernacular house being thatched.

Pl. 50—Cattle market.

*Pl. 51—Woman
with spinning
wheel.*

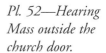

*Pl. 52—Hearing
Mass outside the
church door.*

144

maintained his research interest in Celtic Studies and these lantern-slides were commonly used for teaching purposes in Ireland during the 1950s. The era of the glass slide was passing, however, and was possibly even gone in the United States; much as digital photography has, in the space of the last few years, supplanted the use of 35mm slides, the lantern-slides were probably regarded as antiquated, and their bulk and weight not worth the trouble of bringing back to Ireland.

The slides are almost all labelled as having been produced by T. Mason of 5 Dame Street, Dublin, and date mainly from the latter half of the nineteenth century and the first decades of the twentieth century. According to Doyle, writing in *The Irish Times* in 2003, the Mason family came to Dublin from Liverpool, setting up as tanners in 1712. They later opened a premises in Arran Quay selling telescopes, glasses and microscopes, but by the late nineteenth century Thomas H. Mason had introduced photography to the business and the company offered a developing and printing service to amateur photographers, as well as selling all types of photographic materials, cameras and other equipment, particularly 'magic lantern slide projectors'. Chandler noted that they were one of the few firms in Dublin who offered a slide-making service: one could bring along a photograph, map or print and Mason's would make a lantern-slide for you. This service was most particularly used by academics for the purpose of illustrating lectures. The shop also had a large collection of images; some were copied from other commercial studios but many photographs were taken by Thomas Mason, who had a great interest in archaeology, historical sites and wildlife and travelled the country taking thousands of photographs. He was a member of several societies, including the Royal Society of Antiquaries of Ireland, the Geographical Society of Ireland and the Royal Irish Academy. His combination of interests in wildlife, folk life and heritage is illustrated in a book that he published in 1936 entitled *The islands of Ireland*. Indeed, at least two pictures published in *The islands of Ireland* can be found in the Myles Dillon collection. Thomas Mason died in 1958.

Shortly after his death, the company entered into negotiations with the National Museum of Ireland and about 4,000 lantern-slides were sold to the Museum, with a further 2,866 going to the National Library. Following a disastrous fire in 1963, when Mason's premises in Dame Street were burned to the ground and most of Thomas Mason's photographs were destroyed, a further set of slides were found and given to the National Museum. A guide to the collection in the Museum notes that there are, for instance, 70 views of Irish antique buildings, 22 views of crosses and towers, and 50 views of Clonmacnoise, but these have not been individually identified and catalogued. Neither have the collections in the Photographic Archive in the National Library

Pl. 53a—Temple MacDara, Co. Galway, before restoration.

Pl. 53b—Temple MacDara following restoration.

Pl. 54 (above left)—Kells market cross after 1893 (now moved to a covered location outside the Heritage Centre) (King 2004).

Pl. 55 (above right)—Durrow high cross (now moved into the nearby church).

Pl. 56 (left)—Carndonagh monuments (probably not in their original position and moved twice since this photograph was taken).

Pl. 57—Cross of the Scriptures, Clonmacnoise (now in the Visitor Centre, the surrounding gravestones laid flat on the ground).

of Ireland or the Royal Society of Antiquaries of Ireland (although they have an album of photographs that have been identified), so while many images may be duplicated in all four institutions it is possible that some of the 'Myles Dillon collection' may be unique. Mason slides still turn up very occasionally at auctions and in skips when old houses are being cleared out, so if readers come across these old lantern-slides they should consider donating them to one of the above institutions.

Changes to our landscape and our monuments through neglect and restoration (Pls 53a and 53b), the movement of portable artefacts such as crosses and grave-slabs (Pls 54–57) and the removal of field monuments through development or vandalism are occurring at an alarming rate and with accelerating frequency. These old images, along with the better-known 'Lawrence Collection' of old photographs in the National Library or the 'Welch Collection' in the Ulster Museum, are and will continue to be an increasingly valuable asset for any person interested in the evolution of the culture and heritage of Ireland.

Table 3—Catalogue of the Myles Dillon lantern-slide collection.

Antrim	Fair Head	Crannog	
Antrim		Round tower	
Antrim		Round tower, 1399	Inscriptions
Armagh	Kilnasaggart	Pillar stone	North and east sides
Armagh		St Patrick's Well	
Carlow	Kernanstown	Dolmen or cromlech	
Carlow	Killeshin	Church	West end
Carlow	Tullow	Holed stone	
Cavan	Kilmore	Cathedral	Old door
Clare	Doon Well	Well	People (pilgrims)
Clare	Dysert O'Dea	Doorway	
Clare	Ennis	Abbey	
Clare	Holy Island	Early slabs	
Clare	Holy Island	Ecclesiastical remains	
Clare	Holy Island	St Camin's Church	
Clare	Killaloe	Runic stone	
Clare	Quinn Abbey	Abbey	
Clare	Scattery Island	Round tower	
Clare	St Flannan's	Oratory	
Clare	Tomgraney	Church	West door
Cork	Irish life	Woman in cloak	People
Derry	Dungiven	O'Cahan tombs	
Derry	Maghera	Church	West doorway
Donegal	Ballyshannon	Inis Samer	Island
Donegal	Crolly	Schoolchildren	People
Donegal	Fanan Cross	Cross	
Donegal	Glencolumbkill	Cross	Inscribed
Donegal	Glencolumbkill	Cross	Inscribed
Donegal	Glencolumbkill	Holy well	
Donegal	Inishbofin	Attending a currach	People
Donegal	Inishowen	Inscribed stone	
Donegal	Inishowen	St Patrick's Cross	East face
Donegal	Teelin West	Fishing industry	Industry
Donegal	The Grianan of Aileach	Stone fort	
Donegal	Tory Island		Person
Donegal		A native	Person

Down	Ballynahinch	Farm kitchen	
Down	Downpatrick	General view	
Down	Saul	Stone-roofed cell	
Dublin	Killiney	Church	Doorway
Dublin	Kiltiernan	Cromlech	
Dublin	Rush	An Irish village	People
Dublin	St Doulough's	Church	
Dublin	St Doulough's	Well	
Dublin	Tallaght	Cist	
Dublin	Tallaght	Font	
Dublin (Cabinteely)	Glendruid	Cromlech	
Fermanagh	Lough Erne	Ecclesiastical	
Galway	Aran misc.	'Himself' at the fireside	People
Galway	Aran misc.	Basket-maker	People
Galway	Aran misc.	Basket/crib-making	People
Galway	Aran misc.	Cottage interior	People
Galway	Aran misc.	Gathering seaweed	People
Galway	Aran misc.	Island man on ass	People
Galway	Aran misc.	Islanders	People
Galway	Aran misc.	Islanders on quay	People
Galway	Aran misc.	Launching a currach	People
Galway	Aran misc.	Making land	People
Galway	Aran misc.	Woman and wool at Aran cottage	People
Galway	Aran misc.	Woman at cottage	People
Galway	Clonfert	Ecclesiastical	Doorway
Galway	Clonfert	Ecclesiastical	Doorway, pillars and capitals
Galway	Connemara	Aran Islander	People
Galway	Connemara	Harvesting	People
Galway	Connemara	Market day	People
Galway	Connemara	Pony in habitat	
Galway	Connemara	Weaving a homespun	People
Galway	Inchagoil	Ecclesiastical	Hiberno-Romanesque door
Galway	Inchagoil	Lugnaedon's tombstone	
Galway	Inishere	Gathering kelp	People
Galway	Inishmaan	Cottages	
Galway	Inishmaan	Shipping cattle	People

Galway	Inishmaan	Shipping cattle	People
Galway	Inishmór	Clochan na Carrighe	
Galway	Inishmór	Cloghan na Carrighe	
Galway	Inishmór	Dun Aengus	Interior wall
Galway	Inishmór	Dun Aengus	Rampart from inner wall
Galway	Inishmór	Dun Aengus	Cliff of Inishmór
Galway	Inishmór	Dun Aengus	Man fishing from cliffs
Galway	Inishmór	Dun Aengus	Chevaux de frise
Galway	Inishmór	Islander pony and turf	People
Galway	Inishmór	Killeany Cross	West side
Galway	Inishmór	Teampull Benin	
Galway	Inishmór	Temple Brecan	Stone of the 7 Romans
Galway	Inishmór	Woman weaving a belt	People
Galway	Knockmoy	Abbey	
Galway	McDara's Island	Church	From south-west
Galway	Monasterkieran	Holed stone	
Galway	Monasterkieran, Aran	Church	East window
Galway	Monasterkieran, Aran	Church	East window
Galway	Oughterard	Market day	People
Galway	Spiddal	Cottage	
Galway	Spiddal	Street	
Galway	Tuam	Cathedral	Chancel arch
Galway	Tuam	Cathedral	Chancel arch
Galway	Tuam	Cathedral	Chancel arch
Kerry	Ardfert	Abbey	
Kerry	Ardfert	Cathedral	
Kerry	Blasket Islander	'Tomas O'Crohan'	People
Kerry	Dingle	Pig fair	People
Kerry	Dingle (Ventry)	Kerry dancing	People
Kerry	Dingle, Kilfountain	Inscribed stone	
Kerry	Dingle, Reask	Inscribed stone	
Kerry	Dingle, Reask	The village	
Kerry	Gallarus	Oratory	
Kerry	Gallarus	Oratory	Doorway
Kerry	Killarney	Innisfallen ruins	

151

Kerry	Killarney	Muckross Abbey	
Kerry	Killarney	Muckross Abbey	The cloisters
Kerry	Kilmalkedar	Alphabet stone	
Kerry	Kilmalkedar	Bullaun stone	
Kerry	Kilmalkedar	Church	From south-west
Kerry	Reenconnell	Cross	
Kerry	Skellig Michael	Beehive cell	
Kerry	Skellig Michael	General view	
Kerry	Skellig Michael	Steps to monastery	
Kerry	Skellig Michael	Steps, cell and cross	
Kerry	Skellig Michael	The Great Skellig	
Kerry	Staigue	Doorway	
Kerry	Staigue	Rock markings	
Kerry		Gathering seaweed	People
Kildare	Castledermot	North Cross	North face
Kildare	Castledermot	North Cross	West face
Kildare	Castledermot	South Cross	West face
Kildare	Moone	Cross	North base
Kildare	Moone	Cross	West face
Kildare	Naas	King's Path	
Kildare .	Punchestown	Pillar stone	
Kilkenny	Freshford Church	West doorway	
Kilkenny	Jerpoint Abbey	Cloisters	
Kilkenny	Jerpoint Abbey	Cloisters, arches and nave	
Kilkenny	Jerpoint Abbey		
Kilkenny	Jerpoint Abbey		
Kilkenny	Jerpoint Abbey		
Kilkenny	St Canice's Cathedral		
Kilkenny	St Francis's Abbey		
Limerick	Kilfinnane Moate		
Longford	Edgeworthstown		
Longford	Longford town	Market day	People
Louth	Ballymascanlon	Cromleach or dolmen	
Louth	Mellifont Abbey	St Bernard's Church	
Louth	Monasterboice	Cross of Muirdach	West and north sides
Louth	Monasterboice	Cross of Muirdach	East side
Louth	Monasterboice	Cross of Muirdach	Detail of hand
Louth	Monasterboice	Tall cross	
Louth	Termonfeckin	Cross	West face

Louth	Termonfeckin	Cross	East face
Louth		Fairy mount	
Mayo	Achill	A bog scene near Dooagh	
Mayo	Achill	An Achill road	People
Mayo	Achill	Building the turf stack	People
Mayo	Achill	Dooagh village	People
Mayo	Achill	Milk collectors	People
Mayo	Achill	Modern cottages, Dooagh	
Mayo	Achill	The bog road	People
Mayo	Cong	Baile Moytura	
Mayo	Cong Abbey	Cloisters	
Mayo	Croaghpatrick		
Meath	Dowth	Entrance passage	
Meath	Dowth	Exterior	
Meath	Dowth	Right chamber	
Meath	Duleek	Bronze Age burial	
Meath	Kells	Cross	West base
Meath	Kells	Cross in churchyard	Front
Meath	Kells	Cross in town	
Meath	Kells	Dulane, early church	Cyclopian doorway
Meath	Kells	St Columba's House	
Meath	Kells	St Columba's House	Back and side, front
Meath	Loughcrew	Cairn	
Meath	Loughcrew	Central chamber	Large stone
Meath	Loughcrew	Entrance to cairn	
Meath	Loughcrew	Entrance to cairn	
Meath	Loughcrew	Interior cairn	
Meath	Loughcrew	Stone circle	
Meath	Loughcrew	Western chamber cairn	Roof slab
Meath	Mellifont	Abbey	Interior baptistry
Meath	Mellifont	Abbey	
Meath	Newgrange	Corbelled roof	
Meath	Newgrange	End stone, left chamber	
Meath	Newgrange	Entrance	
Meath	Newgrange	Entrance passage	
Meath	Newgrange	Roof of right chamber	
Meath	Newgrange	Solar ship	

Meath	Newgrange	Stone on left of entrance	
Meath	Newgrange	Triple spiral	
Meath	Rossnaree		
Meath	Tara Hill	Lia Fáil (Stone of Destiny)	Croppy's grave
Meath	Tara Hill	The Farradh	
Meath		Cottages	
Meath		Cottages	
Meath		Gaeltacht colonies	
Offaly	Clonfinloch	Stone	
Offaly	Clonmacnoise	Castle	
Offaly	Clonmacnoise	Cathedral	East window
Offaly	Clonmacnoise	Cathedral	Doorway
Offaly	Clonmacnoise	Nuns' Church	West doorway
Offaly	Clonmacnoise	Nuns' Church	Chancel arch
Offaly	Clonmacnoise	Nuns' Church	Chancel arch
Offaly	Clonmacnoise	Nuns' Church	
Offaly	Clonmacnoise	Slab	
Offaly	Clonmacnoise	Slab	
Offaly	Clonmacnoise	Slab	Sixth/seventh-century
Offaly	Clonmacnoise	South Cross	East face
Offaly	Clonmacnoise	South Cross	
Offaly	Clonmacnoise	St Fingan's Tower	
Offaly	Clonmacnoise	The Cross of the Scriptures	East face
Offaly	Clonmacnoise	The Cross of the Scriptures	West and north sides
Offaly	Durrow	Cross	East face
Offaly	Durrow	Cross	North side
Offaly	Durrow	Cross	Details under circle
Roscommon	Boyle Abbey	Nave and chancel	
Roscommon	Boyle Abbey		
Roscommon	Boyle Abbey		
Sligo	Deerpark	Stone alignments	
Sligo	Drumcliff	Cross	
Sligo	Inishmurray	Beehive cell	
Sligo	Inishmurray	Clocha-Breaca	'Cursing stones'
Sligo	Inishmurray	Holed stone	

Sligo	Inishmurray	Slabs from Teach Molise	
Sligo	Inishmurray	Sweat-house	
Sligo	Inishmurray	Teampul Molaise	'Church of the Men'
Sligo	Sligo Abbey	Cloisters	
Sligo	Tubbernaltha	Holy well	
Sligo		Homestead	
Tipperary	Ahenny	North Cross	West face
Tipperary	Ahenny	North Cross	East face
Tipperary	Ahenny	North Cross	East side
Tipperary	Cahir	Knockgraffon	
Tipperary	Cashel	Cathedral	
Tipperary	Cashel	Cormac's Chapel	Sarcophagus
Tipperary	Cashel	Cormac's Chapel	North door
Tipperary	Cashel	Cormac's Chapel	South front
Tipperary	Cashel	Cormac's Chapel	From south-east
Tipperary	Cashel	Cormac's Chapel	Tympanum of north door
Tipperary	Cashel	Round tower	
Tipperary	Cashel	St Patrick's Cross	North side
Tipperary	Cashel	Teach Molaise	
Tipperary	Cashel	Teampull na Teinidh	
Tipperary	Cashel, Rock of	Cathedral	Interior east window
Tipperary	Cashel, Rock of	From south-east	
Tipperary	Cashel, Rock of	General view	
Tipperary	Holy Cross Abbey	Cloisters	
Tipperary	Holy Cross Abbey	East from weir	
Tipperary	Holy Cross Abbey	Last resting-place of coffin	
Tipperary	Holy Cross Abbey	Sedelia	
Tipperary	Holy Cross Abbey	West end	
Tipperary	Kilcooley	Abbey	From east
Tipperary	Mona Incha	West door	
Tipperary	Mona Incha	West door	
Waterford	Ardmore	Cathedral and round tower	
Waterford	Ardmore	Church	Sculptures at west end
Waterford	Ardmore	Ogham stone in church	
Westmeath	Fore Church	Cyclopian doorway and cross	

Westmeath	Fore Church	From south-west	
Wicklow	Glendalough	Cross and tower	
Wicklow	Glendalough	Cross at back of St Kevin's	
Wicklow	Glendalough	General view	
Wicklow	Glendalough	Great Cross	
Wicklow	Glendalough	King O'Toole's Gravestone	
Wicklow	Glendalough	Lady Chapel	
Wicklow	Glendalough	Monastery	Pillar, arch and window
Wicklow	Glendalough	Rhefert Church	East window and arch and crosses
Wicklow	Glendalough	St Kevin's Kitchen	
Wicklow	Glendalough	St Kevin's Kitchen	
Wicklow	Glendalough	St Saviour's Monastery	East window
Wicklow	Glendalough	St Saviour's Monastery	
Wicklow	Glendalough	Temple Skellig	
Wicklow	Glendalough	Trinity Church	
Wicklow	Glendalough	Trinity Church	Interior
Wicklow	Glendalough	Upper Lake	
	Irish artefacts	Three legs motif	
	Irish artefacts	Ardagh Chalice	
	Irish artefacts	Ardagh Chalice	Interior base
	Irish artefacts	Book of Armagh	Case of
	Irish artefacts	Book of Durrow	Trumpet pattern
	Irish artefacts	Book of Kells	First page of St Mark's Gospel
	Irish artefacts	Book of Kells	Monogram page
	Irish artefacts	Book of Kells	
	Irish artefacts	Book of Kells	Portrait of St Mark or St Luke!
	Irish artefacts	Book of Kells	St Luke
	Irish artefacts	Book of Kells	Evangelical symbols
	Irish artefacts	Book of Kells	The Four Evangelists
	Irish artefacts	Book of Kells	The eight-circled cross
	Irish artefacts	Book of Kells	Detail, St Matthew's Gospel

Irish artefacts	Book of Kells	Page of text
Irish artefacts	Bronze axes	
Irish artefacts	Bronze axes	& attaching handles
Irish artefacts	Bronze ornaments	
Irish artefacts	Bronze shield	
Irish artefacts	Bronze spearheads	
Irish artefacts	Cinerary urn	Found in Co. Meath
Irish artefacts	Coronation chair	
Irish artefacts	Cross of Cong	Back of
Irish artefacts	Cross of Cong	
Irish artefacts	Crozier	From Co. Kilkenny
Irish artefacts	Croziers	
Irish artefacts	Detail of chalice	
Irish artefacts	Domnach Airgid	
Irish artefacts	Domnach Airgid	Back of
Irish artefacts	Flint hatchet	Etching
Irish artefacts	Gold collar and chains	
Irish artefacts	Gold torcs	From Tara, Co. Meath
Irish artefacts	Lismore Crozier	
Irish artefacts	Ogham stone	
Irish artefacts	Ordinary ogham alphabet	
Irish artefacts	St Brigid's crosses	Examples
Irish artefacts	St Lachtan's Arm, shrine of	
Irish artefacts	St Molaise's Gospels, case of	
Irish artefacts	St Molaise, shrine of	
Irish artefacts	St Patrick's Bell	
Irish artefacts	St Patrick's Bell, shrine of	End view
Irish artefacts	St Patrick's Bell, shrine of	Right side
Irish artefacts	Stone implements	
Irish artefacts	Tara Brooch	Back of
Irish artefacts	Tara Brooch	

Irish artefacts	The Cathach	
Irish artefacts	USS manuscripts	St Gall
Irish life	'Fire-starters'	Etching
Irish life	'The mountain road'	People
Irish life	A fair	People
Irish life	An Irish turf bog	People
Irish life	Beehive house and hut	
Irish life	Carrying a currach on shore 1	People
Irish life	Carrying a currach on shore 2	People
Irish life	Carrying hay	People
Irish life	Cave-dwellers	Etching
Irish life	Cottage and rainbow	People
Irish life	Crannog	Etching
Irish life	Cromlech	Plan of (etching)
Irish life	Cromlech	People
Irish life	Donkey and spinner	People
Irish life	Early Irish fort	Etching
Irish life	Great Irish elk	Etching
Irish life	Great Irish elk	Etching
Irish life	Irish spinning-wheel	People
Irish life	Ptolemy's ancient map of Ireland	Etching
Irish life	Primitive village	Etching
Irish life	Salmon-fishing (coracle)	People
Irish life	Thatching	People
Irish life	Thatching a cottage	People
Irish life	Woman with donkey	People
Irish life	Wood canoe	Etching

Acknowledgements

I would like to thank the staff of the Department of Scandinavian Studies in Madison, who took remarkable care of this fragile collection for almost 50 years, and Professor Ringler for repatriating them to Ireland. My thanks also go to Con Brogan and Tony Roche in the Photographic Unit of the National Monuments Service not only for their professional knowledge regarding lantern-slides but also for reproducing the slides digitally for publication. I am indebted to Myles

Dillon's daughter Elizabeth Kelly, Padhraig Clancy in the National Museum of Ireland, Sara Smyth of the National Photographic Archive of the National Library of Ireland, Padhraig O'Brien in the City Archive, Aidan O'Sullivan, Chris Corlett and Elizabeth O'Brien for their helpful information and advice, which contributed to this paper.

Further reading

Anon. 1960 Obituary. *Journal of the Royal Society of Antiquaries of Ireland* **90** (1), 90.

Chandler, E. 2001 *Photography in Ireland: the nineteenth century*. Blackrock.

Doyle, R. 2003 Saga of a scientific family by a seventh generation son. *The Irish Times*, 22 October 2003.

King, H.A. 2004 Excavation of the high cross in the medieval market place of Kells. In H. Roche, E. Grogan, J. Bradley, J. Coles and B. Raftery (eds), *From megaliths to metals: essays in honour of George Eogan*, 233–42. Oxford.

Lalor, B. 2003 *The encyclopaedia of Ireland*. Dublin.

Mason, T.H. 1936 *The islands of Ireland*. London.

15

Harvesting time: digging and living at Raystown, Co. Meath

Matthew Seaver

Archaeological publications, especially those detailed works used as reference documents, are meant to be the end-product of the process of 'finding'. They are productions combed clean of the personal. Only the best photographs, the shiniest special artefacts and the processed data are used in the final report. The excavation usually looks bright, sunny and tidy (hopefully). The process that led to this narrative is mostly squeezed out. The emotion of finding, struggling with the elements, the hard physical work, internal relationships, humour, tensions and camaraderie of the team are usually consigned to memory. These things are not considered an essential part of the scientific story. In a parallel way, our experiences while working on the site were probably not dissimilar to those of the people who lived on the site many generations ago. Their lives, however, are often reduced to a series of archaeological 'phases' of activity in which ditch A replaced ditch B to the detriment of the human element. The subsistence economy of the site may be understood in detail, for instance, but there is often little acknowledgement of the actual people who were part of it. To redress this imbalance, I would like to present here a narrative of my experience while excavating at Raystown, an early medieval site, and combine this with some insights into the physical experiences of those who originally lived and died there.

A large team of archaeologists, under my direction, excavated this fascinating site on behalf of CRDS. It is situated just east of Ratoath and south-west of Ashbourne in County Meath (Fig. 11). Both of these towns are expanding rapidly in the shadow of greater Dublin, and the N2 Finglas–Ashbourne Road Scheme, built to ease traffic congestion along this major artery, led to the discovery of the site at Raystown. The site lies at the end of a bumpy, muddy track just north of the main Ratoath–Swords road. It was found during the

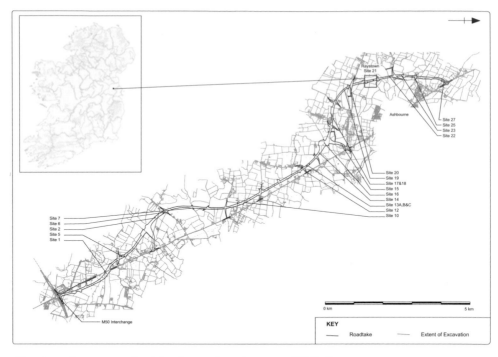

Fig. 11—Raystown, Co. Meath: site location map (CRDS).

course of geophysical survey and test-trenching, and these initial investigations had proved that the site was large and complex, covering an area measuring 250m north–south by 160m east–west. Walking around it on a cold overcast day with Fin O'Carroll (senior site archaeologist) and Stephanie Durning (one of my supervisors), we had little idea of what surprises this wet hillside site would reveal. We knew, however, that the site consisted of both a settlement and an adjacent cemetery.

A relatively small team began the excavation of a cemetery that lay within the road corridor (Pl. 57). This part of the site had distinct advantages in the depths of winter. It was on top of a well-drained stony hillside, some distance upslope from what had become a small lake, and therefore remained relatively dry. It was, however, incredibly exposed. The crew worked throughout the first few months of wintry weather under the relative shelter of a plastic-covered horticultural tunnel, though they often had to struggle with ropes and sandbags to lash it down in the frequent gale-force winds. Kneeling on the penitential rocky boulder clay at close quarters with human skeletons is a strange and unsettling experience and can arouse conflicting emotions. On the one hand it is fascinating and exciting to excavate and analyse the bones of people who had once lived and worked in the adjacent settlement, but on the other hand some

Pl. 57—The excavation crew cleaning the cemetery area (CRDS).

of the burials provoked other emotional responses. We excavated the skeleton of an eight-month-old child buried with a blue glass bead on his/her neck— perhaps threaded as a pendant or amulet to ward off evil. It is easy to imagine the human loss and tragic circumstances but impossible for science to measure the amount of emotion poured into a small piece of ground.

'Why do you have to move them?' This topic is frequently raised at lectures and talks at local societies and schools. The ethics of removing burials is a fraught subject and, while sometimes necessary to make way for national and local infrastructure, it is never undertaken in a piecemeal manner. It is done only if absolutely necessary, with an acknowledged respect for the dead, in a professional manner as part of the overall excavation plan. The careful excavation, cleaning and recording of the burials at Raystown was carried out in consultation with osteoarchaeologist Linda Fibiger, who also carried out the scientific analysis of the remains.

Excavation and subsequent analysis of the burials have revealed interesting information about the people who lived, worked and died at Raystown. Over 93 complete skeletons were excavated, with evidence for many more in the form of

Burial 210841 (Pl. 59; Fig. 12): He died within the time bracket cal. AD 430–600 (Wk16825) at the age of 26–35. His height cannot be estimated as his legs and arms were not present (possibly cut away by subsequent burials). Once again a later burial was laid over him, the head of which rested just below his pelvis. His burial extended south-west/north-east within the confines of the ring-ditch. He had mild wear to his teeth and no major dental disease. Small depressions visible on his lower vertebrae indicated compression of the spine, possibly as a result of heavy lifting. This type of change on the spine was seen more frequently in men than in women. This pattern clearly reflects the differential labour divisions between the sexes at the time, which left tell-tale signatures on their bones. Heavy work involving digging ditches, managing animals, cutting timber, quarrying stone, operating mill mechanisms, harvesting cereals, threshing, tending fires and kilns were all daily tasks that contributed to these wear patterns. This burial, however, is remarkable by being one of only two

Pl. 59—Remains of a man from Raystown, burial 210841 (CRDS).

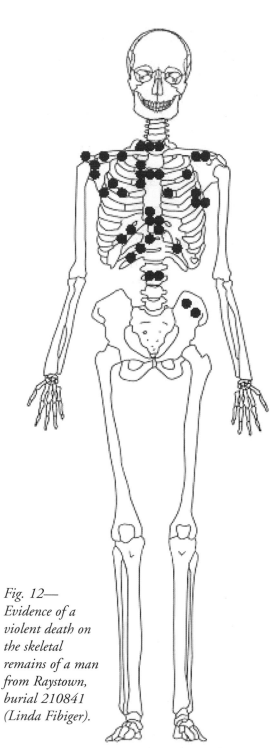

*Fig. 12—
Evidence of a
violent death on
the skeletal
remains of a man
from Raystown,
burial 210841
(Linda Fibiger).*

that showed evidence for a violent death. A total of 110 blade injuries were found on the torso. Assuming that a sword or dagger was used to inflict these injuries, the total number of blows delivered would have been considerably less as each strike is likely to have left multiple marks on a number of bones simultaneously. He obviously died in a frenzied attack, probably during the course of a local battle or skirmish, with his remains returned for burial in his local community. The many annalistic references to raiding and conflict demonstrate that violent death was relatively commonplace at the time. Armed men were usually free men and commonly bound by obligation to wider groups, such as the retinue of a lord or petty king, and as such were duty-bound to avenge or defend him. The people of this community were also bound by the hierarchical class divisions of the time and all were subservient to the nobility. This community was no doubt subject to the vagaries of allegiances, shifting kingdoms and territorial boundaries over the course of its occupation, as a result of the political aspirations of groups such as the Mac Gilla Sechnaill (Clann Chernaig Sotail) and larger kingdoms such as Southern Brega.

Pl. 60—Remains of a child from Raystown, burial 211053 (CRDS).

Burial 211053 (Pl. 60): This child died at between 2.2 and 2.5 years of age around cal. AD 570–660 (Wk16821). Accurate sexing of children is usually not possible on the basis of skeletal remains alone. The child was buried north-west/south-east with hands by the sides. S/he was buried outside the ring-ditch enclosure, or core area, but within the confines of a larger outer enclosure. Many of the children were buried here, in an area that contained a proportionately smaller number of adults, suggesting that this outer area was reserved predominantly for the burial of infants and juveniles. This child was suffering from a chronic, systemic infection at the time of death. It is possible that the infection developed as the result of a weakened immune system during the weaning period. Certain types of food, such as diets rich in animal protein, can leave specific isotopic signatures in the bone that can be measured. This child showed higher levels of nitrogen than other infant burials at the site, indicating that this child, by the time of death, had been introduced to solid food. Most of the children in the cemetery died between one and four years of age, the time when they are most vulnerable to disease. The change in diet, for instance, may result in an increased risk of gastro-intestinal and other pathological conditions.

* * *

By mid-June a team of up to 50 had been assembled on site, with individuals from France, Sweden, Bulgaria, Slovakia, Australia, America, Italy, Poland, Scotland and England. The weather had improved markedly and now the main problem was simply seeing the archaeological features in the sun-baked soil. North of the cemetery two souterrains were being excavated amid a maze of ditches and gullies (Pl. 61). These underground stone, earth and timber-built tunnels with their restricted spaces, blind turns and chambers were clearly designed with refuge and defence in mind, in addition to the storage of goods. A timber-built souterrain with a round chamber was found to have been built around AD 430–650 (Wk18202). At some later stage a larger, stone-built souterrain was constructed nearby.

The job of an archaeological director is quite different on this kind of site than on a small excavation. Dealing with issues such as petrol for water-pumps,

Pl. 61—Aerial photograph of site, showing cemetery enclosures (top left), souterrains to its north (top centre-right) and large, water-filled intersecting ditches (Studiolab).

169

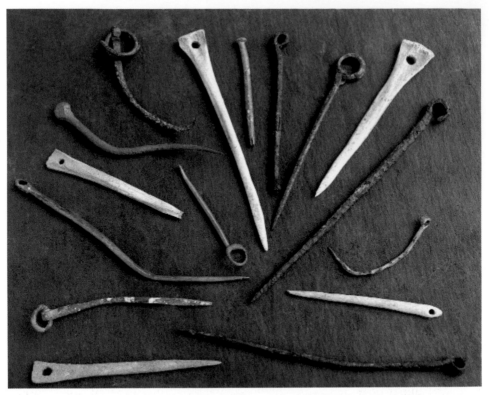

Pl. 62—Assorted pins from Raystown (CRDS).

timesheets, security, toilets, site tours and (most importantly) ensuring adequate water supplies for tea were everyday challenges. I spent the remainder of the day moving between the individual territories of the capable and hard-pressed supervisors—Stephanie Durning, Mairead McLaughlin, Kevin Martin, Alex Southeran, Mandy Stephens and Bernice Watts—taking notes and generally creating spoil with my trowel as I did my daily tour, before walking away, much to the annoyance of the crew.

The dynamics of a long-term site dictate that individual surprise discoveries lift everybody's spirits. While a ditch may be very significant in the overall interpretation of a site, digging it for weeks on end without finding artefacts can really get you down. A lump of dusty, mud-encrusted iron from the enclosure, for example, rapidly became an early seventh-century horse cheek-piece. This horse-bit can be paralleled by an example from excavations at nearby Lagore. This celebrated crannog site was central to kingship in the immediate area and the artefact suggested a cultural link between these two places. A beautiful projecting ring-headed pin found by Alban Verdier and a stick-pin found by Alan Hand proved that the site occupation spanned the period from the fourth to the eleventh century AD (Pl. 62). These artefacts were usually snatched from the startled archaeologist and paraded around the site like trophies before being taken to the finds hut. More commonly recovered artefacts were things such as iron knives, tool fragments and bone pins. The types of artefacts recovered suggest that a high-level display of status was not a major concern of the inhabitants of Raystown, compared to exceptional sites like Lagore, a site connected with feasting, kingship and other military and judicial roles.

The most surprising discovery came on a sunny August day. We had been digging sections through a large ditch that defined the northern edge of the site. It was an unusual feature because it clearly ran directly through the ridge between two low-lying areas. It deepened with the rise of the slope and became wide and shallow at the base of the slope. This type of ditch would be unsuitable for defence, far too elaborate just to keep animals out and too large to be a simple drain. The gradual incline of its base, however, indicated that it was designed to allow for the flow of water, and at one particular point it suddenly began to drop away sharply towards the water-table, where we uncovered the corner of an oak timber. The penny dropped. We were excavating a horizontal watermill! Further excavation revealed a rectangular oak structure that employed sophisticated timber jointing and was overlain by stone walls. A slot in the subsoil indicated the original position of the wooden water-chute or flume, which functioned to direct the water under pressure to turn the horizontal wheel and the millstone above.

Excavation also commenced at the southern end of the site around this time and began to reveal a complicated series of wide and shallow intercutting ditches (Pl. 63). These were defined as a series of linear, dark, silty ditches running east–west. A trench excavated in the centre of this complex revealed a series of oak timbers and, slightly further south, another oak post—the remains of two more mills. This was starting to become surreal!

With the onset of autumn the weather began to turn, bringing endless downpours accompanied by gales that demonstrated, even now, the ability of the ancient mill-races to gather water, and the site rapidly became a mud-bath (Pl. 64). Large ponds of water accumulated at the edge of the road corridor. Each day began with the use of submersible water-pumps operated by a number of hardy individuals, namely Ritchie McGrath and John Harrison, who were often seen with hose-pipes draped around their necks like some strange kind of snake-charmers. Continuing excavation revealed the remains of three mill structures and the position of two others. Further north, another mill undercroft lined with stone was excavated. Raystown was proving to be a truly exceptional and highly unusual site. In the end, a total of eight mill sites were uncovered. Site visitors, among others horizontal watermill aficionado Colin Rynne, were clearly stunned and delighted.

Pl. 63—The assembled crew hard at work excavating the various ditches and mill-races (CRDS).

Pl. 64—Aerial view of large-scale clean-up of Southern Mill area (Hawkeye).

Fig. 13—
Reconstruction of
Southern Mill 1
(Simon Dick for
CRDS).

The complexity of the mill technology revealed on this site is only now being unravelled in the post-excavation process. Mills were designed primarily to facilitate large-scale cereal production and to make this process more efficient, in addition to relieving the hardship of hand-grinding using a rotary quern. Horizontal mills emerged or were introduced into Ireland as part of a package of great agricultural changes before the fifth century AD (Fig. 13). Their construction and operation brought with them a degree of social change. In this instance, the mill-builders channelled water from the Broad Meadow River across the ridge and controlled its course through a series of races and diversion channels to the mills and tail-races before returning it into a stream to the east, which fed directly back into the river.

On digging these features a number of things became clear. First, there was a logical and well-defined plan to the site layout, suggesting that a specialised individual or individuals with authority designed, controlled and managed the construction of these watercourses. A millwright was a high-status craftsman. Only royalty, wealthy lords, groups of cooperating farmers and religious houses owned mills. Digging these long and substantial mill-races would have required agreement with neighbouring landowners or outright ownership of large tracts of land. The construction of a mill also involved managing and directing a large-

Fig. 14—Site reconstruction of Raystown c. AD 900 (Simon Dick for CRDS).

scale specialised workforce. Tasks included the careful surveying and setting out of works prior to digging the mill-race to ensure a steady flow of water; the felling and working of suitable timbers; and the quarrying and gathering of stone for the mill works and buildings. The amount of labour involved in the digging of mill-races was appreciated (if not resented!) by the archaeological team who re-excavated only a relatively small area of the site that fell within the road corridor.

The early medieval inhabitants of Raystown were clearly familiar with the working of mills and the industrial-scale processing of cereals. Their daily lives were undoubtedly an integral part of a complex web of interaction with the wider surrounding community. As Lisa Bitel notes, mills were often considered as meeting-places, and the historical sources relate stories of men, women and children coming from far and wide to wait their turn to process their own cereals. There is no specific word for miller in early medieval Ireland and it is probable that bonded or slave labour was used. Slaves and unfree tenants may also have been involved in the daily operation of mills. In the Life of St Ciarán, for instance, the onerous nature of this work is revealed by the story of a slave woman who had been condemned to a life of mill work but who is set free by the saint. For the lower echelons of society, coercion and brutality were probably part and parcel of life. Many were probably involved with food production and the supply of surplus food supplies to the local lord.

A persistent problem witnessed at Raystown was the silting of tail-races and the occasional flooding of the usually tranquil Broad Meadow River, which could destroy mills and inundate farmland. As a consequence, those controlling the milling were constantly rebuilding, refining and improving mill design, and this was to lead to the profusion of mill buildings on the site. To make the enterprise economically viable, a percentage cut of cereals milled on behalf of individuals would have been retained by the community, and the surplus of this, no doubt, went to the local lord as tribute. The cereals would have been used for a number of purposes, from foodstuffs such as bread and porridge to brewing. Perhaps some of these products were also part of an individual agreed render to the local king or lord, who would provide grants of cattle or land, for example, in exchange.

In parallel with the excavations at Raystown, another 'micro-excavation' was taking place 2km further north in a warehouse unit in Ashbourne. Here an 'X-files'-style bay held stacks of our soil samples, which were being floated for charcoal and charred plant remains. This process, run by Madeleine Murray, ably assisted by Deirdre Walsh, was part of the post-excavation programme. The sieving team also had the monotonous task of weeks of sifting soil, but this monotony was occasionally punctuated by the discovery of an interesting artefact. The flotation process revealed large quantities of charred oats, wheat and barley, with smaller amounts of rye. The soil samples containing these plant remains were mainly taken from the vicinity of corn-drying kilns or ditches close by. The harvesting, drying, threshing and winnowing of grain, along with keeping the kilns supplied with firewood, was hard physical work and must have required considerable labour. The kilns occasionally charred some of their contents, and the wind scattered some of this seed over the wider area. Seven corn-drying kilns found during the course of the excavation were dated to between cal. AD 450 and 900. One of these, a stone-lined kiln, was used for a considerable period of time, and there was evidence that kiln waste was dumped into a nearby ditch, washing down from there to the stream.

As archaeologists on a commercial project, we generally deal with the brown, plant-less horizon that lies beneath the ploughsoil. The plant remains of cereals recovered by 'flotation' and the waterlogged remains of weeds and grasses demonstrate, however, that the site and its environs was a collage of different environments, from open pasture to tillage and from water-meadow to scrubland. Reconstructing and interpreting this past environment is an important and difficult job. This world is shown to great effect in Simon Dick's wonderful illustration (Fig. 14), based on the scientific evidence.

The archaeological work at Raystown concluded on a freezing January day in 2005. The mill remains were recorded and carefully taken apart amid sleet and northern winds. This final day on site, however, was only the beginning of the long task of converting this mass of information into a 'narrative' to interpret and explain the site. Colleagues were slightly concerned about the way I waited in anticipation of the return of radiocarbon and dendro dating results—each one like a Christmas present. The dating of the site is highly significant: AD 400–1150. During this time its inhabitants witnessed a turbulent world and a rapidly changing society. The settlement was established at the very beginning of the early historic period, when agricultural change was followed by a religious and social revolution, an uncertain dynamic that was to transform Irish society. In this time Raystown outlived the ringfort as the dominant settlement type, saw the establishment of towns, the rise of the Hiberno-Norse kingdom of Dublin with its new far-reaching international markets, the founding of foreign religious houses and the growing power of regional Irish kings. The annalistic records for the period encompass the rise of the Southern Uí Neill and the kingdom of Brega, and later the rise of Míde and battles for the high kingship of Ireland. Raiding is recorded at nearby Dunshaughlin and Lagore on numerous occasions. The former was raided in 1026, 1143 and 1152, while the lake fortress was destroyed by the Norse in 935. Despite the chaos and change over the centuries, Raystown had a relatively stable existence, as witnessed by the long-term rhythms of life centred around milling and processing of cereals. It appears, however, through the evidence of radiocarbon samples, that burials in the cemetery tailed off over time. Perhaps the growth of parish churches meant that burial in traditional sites became less popular, or, more probably, the population tending the site was gradually falling before it was eventually abandoned towards the end of the eleventh century.

Conclusion

I have tried in this article to give some sense of the experience of digging this fascinating site and our interpretations of the experiences of those who once lived there. Excavations create a curious dynamic; there is an official record, which becomes the excavation report etc., but, in parallel, each excavator also has their own record, a personal memory of experiences. While we can never know the individual experiences of those who once lived at Raystown, we are in a position to interpret the types of lives and the challenges they encountered in the struggle to harness the elements for milling, in addition to dealing with the everyday issues of life—and death.

We have been given the chance to examine the transition between the late Iron Age and the radically reorganised early medieval world. While this is a difficult horizon to address, regional studies viewed through the lens of excavations like this one could help our understanding of this important time. Raystown has given us fantastic new information on the complexity of early medieval society and has left us with some tantalising questions. Why do these new settlements and burial customs emerge at this time, and were they a result of population movement? What connection does the introduction of Christianity have to these changes? Raystown shows remarkable continuity in purpose and practice over 500 years. Did social life change in the long term over this period? Two thirds of this site still remains unexcavated beneath the Meath countryside. Other sites sharing some similarities to Raystown have also come to light in recent years, so perhaps some of the question may yet be answered. The work of the excavation team and the lives of Raystown's early medieval inhabitants are tied into a narrative that is still emerging. Neither will be forgotten.

Acknowledgements

This article is dedicated to the staff of CRDS. The excavations were carried out for Meath County Council and the National Roads Authority as part of the N2 road realignment. I am indebted to Linda Fibiger for editing and commenting on my non-specialist understanding of her excellent human bone analysis. Many thanks too to Anne-Marie Prizeman, Fin O'Carroll and Maria Fitzgerald for reading and giving incisive feedback on the article. I would also like to thank Maria in her role as project archaeologist for support and encouragement.

Further reading

Bhreathnach, E. 1999 Authority and supremacy in Tara and its hinterland *c.* 950–1200. *Discovery Programme Reports* 5, 1–24.

Bitel, L. 1996 *Land of women: tales of sex and gender from early medieval Ireland.* New York.

Charles-Edwards, T.M. 2000 *Early Christian Ireland.* Cambridge.

Edwards, N. 1996 *The archaeology of early medieval Ireland.* London.

O'Kelly, F. 2000 *Early Irish farming.* Dundalk.

Patterson, N. 1994 *Cattle lords and clansmen: the social structure of early Ireland.* Indiana.

Rynne, C. 2000 Waterpower in medieval Ireland. In P. Squatriti (ed.), *Working with water in medieval Europe,* 1–50. Leiden.

16

In search of medieval sculpture: rockeries, walls and gateposts

Roger Stalley

Most medieval sites in Ireland are now so well recorded that the discovery of new pieces of sculpture might seem a forlorn hope. Nonetheless, unknown carvings still come to light at regular intervals, sometimes in surprising circumstances. The majority are found by accident or chance rather than through archaeological excavation, and scarcely a year goes by without the report of some new piece of sculpture—a Romanesque capital, sections of an ancient cross or fragments of a medieval tomb. Romanesque carvings in particular can turn up almost anywhere. The relatively small blocks of stone used in Romanesque arches were an easy target once a building fell into ruin. In many instances the blocks were used as *spolia*, a convenient quarry for building neighbouring walls; elsewhere they served as convenient grave-markers for the local community, while some of the more glamorous pieces occasionally found their way into the hands of antiquarian collectors. In England Romanesque carvings have been discovered in some very strange places. Examples of the distinctive 'Herefordshire school' of carving turned up, for instance, in a public house, where they decorated the fireplace of the lounge bar (the former Bell Inn at Alveley, Shropshire). A few years ago a superb tympanum carved in the same style was pulled from the walls of a redundant church at Billesley in Warwickshire, where the stone had been reused as a convenient building block, the sculpture set facing into the wall. Medieval fonts have also been known to migrate, some English examples finding their way out of the church and into the vicarage garden, and in some cases even further afield. Are there, I wonder, any Irish fonts unrecognised though now adorned with petunias and geraniums?

Garden rockeries have long been an attraction for anyone with a serious interest in medieval sculpture. In the 1960s scholars investigating the great

65a

65b

Pl. 65—Devenish, Co. Fermanagh: base of an engaged column, probably from a chancel arch. (a) Side showing two entwined beasts, a design that can be paralleled on the Cross of Cong and the Lemanaghan Shrine. It is assumed that the carving was replicated to the left (photo: R. Stalley). (b) Shorter side decorated with foliate scrolls and interlacing snakes (photo: R. Stalley).

twelfth-century castle at Sherborne (Dorset) were compelled to make a pilgrimage to the house of a local historian and antiquary, a man with the (then unremarkable) name of Mr Bean. Sherborne Castle was built by Bishop Roger of Salisbury, for many years the justiciar of Henry I. The bishop was one of the greatest builders of the age and the fabric of his castle was decorated with splendid Romanesque carvings, some of which ended up in the house and garden of Mr Bean. This elderly gentleman regarded callers with suspicion, fearing visits from officials belonging to the Ministry of Works; those untainted by the scent of bureaucracy, however, might be granted permission to explore the rockery, where all sorts of sculptural fragments were quietly decaying amidst the undergrowth.

As far as I know, there are no equivalent rockeries in Ireland, at least none as plentiful as Mr Bean's. Rather it is the demolition of post-medieval walls that have produced the excitement. In the late 1960s and early 1970s, for example, the late Dudley Waterman supervised the reduction in height of a boundary wall that surrounded the monastic ruins at Devenish (Fermanagh). Whether he had an inkling of what he might find is not clear, but as the stones were removed, fine examples of Hiberno-Romanesque sculpture came to light (Pl. 65, a and b). Altogether 33 separate stones embellished with elements of Romanesque ornament were recovered, stones that clearly belonged to one or more ancient churches. In the 1980s Ann Hamlin and I attempted to sort this material as best we could, trying to work out how they might have fitted into a twelfth-century portal or chancel arch. The puzzling thing was that none of the pieces appeared to belong to the ruined churches visible at the site. It seems that an extravagant Romanesque church belonging to the years around 1160 has completely vanished from the landscape. The fragments included monster-head capitals, exquisite panels of animal interlace, and a column base with a superbly delineated example of the Irish Urnes style (Pl. 65a), the sort of thing found on the Cross of Cong or the Lemanaghan Shrine. The best parallels for the sculpture were encountered at sites close to the upper reaches of the River Shannon, suggesting the presence of an atelier active in the north midlands and the basin of the River Erne. One further insight into medieval building methods was gleaned from the material. Many of the stones, especially a group associated with a chancel arch, were furnished with secondary mouldings. In other words, the church from which they came had been dismantled in the later Middle Ages and the stone re-carved for use in a Gothic building. Good stone was too valuable to throw away, and the process of continuous recycling is something encountered with great frequency in all branches of architectural history. Many outlandish examples of recycling can be found in Italy, as for example at Agliate, where a Roman milepost was used as a pier in the church; another notorious example is

Pl. 66—The entrance to the graveyard at Aghalurcher, Co. Fermanagh, as rebuilt in 2004 (photo: R. Stalley).

Pisa Cathedral, where the marble used to cover the exterior was recycled from some Roman monument, the Christian builders being quite content to retain classically inscribed slabs, one of them carved with the imposing letters 'Imperial Caesar'.

Several writers have in the past commented on the lack of Romanesque carving in Ulster, but the discoveries at Devenish suggest that this void may be more apparent than real, a view reinforced within the last few years by a discovery at Aghalurcher (Fermanagh). Here in an ancient graveyard are the ruins of what was once a substantial medieval church. Not much remains of the church itself, though a small collection of carved stones includes some twelfth-century pieces, one carved with the face of a bishop (now in Fermanagh County Museum, Enniskillen). These fragments, however, provided little indication of the surprises in store when workmen arrived to carry out repairs at the site in 2004. Leading into the graveyard is a stone-built archway that had begun to disintegrate (Pl. 66). The arch itself was supported by two large blocks of sandstone, apparently devoid of embellishment (the blocks each measured 55cm by 76cm, with a height of 1.25m/1.2m). As work progressed, it became clear that these great stones, far from being plain, had figures carved on their inner faces, carving that was completely unknown before (Pl. 67, a and b). Following the conservation works, the blocks were rotated so that the sculptures are now clearly visible from within the graveyard.

The block forming the west jamb is carved with a figure of the crucified Christ, set against a solid ringed cross (Pl. 67a). Christ's face is badly damaged, but enough remains to show that he was wearing a crown. The other block is furnished with two superimposed figures, the upper one taller and more elongated (Pl. 67b). Both sculptures are outlined by a curved groove, giving the impression that the carving is set back in a recess. The width between the grooves is 20cm, an arrangement repeated on both blocks, demonstrating that they originally fitted together.

The discovery raises a number of intriguing questions. When was the arch into the graveyard constructed and why were the sculptures deliberately concealed? Did the blocks belong to a free-standing structure or were they fitted into the walls of the Romanesque church? There are also questions of style, in particular the extent to which the work relates to other Irish carving.

As the blocks were evidently intended to be placed one on top of the other, the total height must have been about 2.45m, with the Crucifixion at the top and the two single figures below. The fact that only one face was carved rather suggests that the blocks were set into the walls of the twelfth-century church, though whether inside or out is hard to decide. The fact that the stone is not heavily weathered lends credence to the view that the sculpture belonged inside the building, though exactly where is hard to say. The church at Aghalurcher was rebuilt in the later Middle Ages and it is remarkable that the carvings were retained in the Gothic reconstruction. The gateway into the graveyard is likely to have been erected in relatively modern times, yet somehow the blocks managed to survive.

The placing of figures below a Crucifixion recalls arrangements on the twelfth-century high crosses at Tuam and Glendalough. The analogies with the Market Cross at Tuam are especially close, not least since Christ wears a crown (an indication of triumph and eternal rule). He is also furnished with a triangular loincloth, as at Tuam. The presence of the suppadaneum or footrest gives a strong hint that the Crucifixion was copied from a bronze original; in fact, the carving of the Crucifixion could have been modelled on a processional cross. As for the figure style, the elongated bodies and the character of the faces fit quite comfortably into the context of Irish Romanesque sculpture; there are obvious similarities with the bronze figures on the shrine at Lemanaghan (Offaly) (note in particular the large, rather flattened ears). The style of the figures also recalls the bishop's head already known from Aghalurcher, which may well have been made by the same sculptor.

Pl. 67—Aghalurcher, Co. Fermanagh.
(a) (left) The western jamb of the gate: the crucified Christ is set against a solid ring; the triangular arrangement of the loincloth can just be discerned, thinly incised in the stone (photo: R. Stalley).
(b) (right) The eastern jambs of the gate: the carving shows two superimposed figures, carved in high relief; there are suggestions that the lower figure is holding a sceptre (photo: R. Stalley).

The discoveries are exciting not just because they are fine pieces of carving, though that in itself is cause enough: it is the fact that the function and context of the sculptures remain a mystery, the only known example of Romanesque carving used in this particular way. The identification of the two figures is also a puzzle: were they figures from Christian history or major patrons, perhaps of the church at Aghalurcher?

For someone who has taken a professional interest in medieval sculpture throughout his career, an event that occurred just six weeks after seeing the Aghalurcher sculptures for the first time came as quite a shock. Early in September 2005 the author, frustrated by the miserable appearance of a rockery in his back garden in Sutton (County Dublin), decided that it was time for action. Having dug out the soil, all that was left was a ring of stones, one of which appeared to have a strange geological formation. When extracted from the earth, its true significance turned out to be rather different. The unusual marks in fact represented part of the chasuble of an ecclesiastic or saint. The block was sculpted with a pair of such figures, one on each face, and the general shape suggested that it had formed the shaft of a free-standing cross (Pl. 68, a and b). The style of the carving was late medieval, the closest parallels being with a series of small wayside crosses found in County Meath and other parts of the Pale around 1500.

Excitement soon turned to concern. The chances of a sculptured cross turning up in the garden of someone who has spent a career studying medieval art was surely too much of a coincidence. Who would actually believe that the stone had been there for decades waiting to be discovered? Furthermore, there appeared to be no record of an ancient cross in the Howth or Sutton area.

Sadly, the heads of the two ecclesiastics had long since been broken off, but otherwise the carving is reasonably legible, albeit badly worn. On one face (Pl. 68a) the figure holds a crosier vertically, the right hand raised in blessing; below the chasuble, the triangular ends of a stole are clearly marked. The other figure (Pl. 68b) is more defaced, and this time the crosier is set at an angle. The style of carving is characteristic of the fifteenth century, being similar to that found on the tomb of Christopher St Lawrence (died 1462) in St Mary's Church at Howth. The fragment is cut from grey limestone, measuring 21.5cm by 14cm, the narrower faces being entirely plain. The maximum height of the piece is 42cm.

Mystery surrounds the original location of what must have been quite an impressive monument. Equally mysterious is how a section of it ended up in the author's garden. It was there before 1983 and may have arrived in a consignment of stone used to build the garden walls in the 1890s. Alternatively, it could have been acquired by a previous owner as a garden ornament. While there is no

Pl. 68—Section of a late medieval cross found in Sutton (Dublin) in 2005.
(a) (left) Figure of a bishop or abbot (?) holding a book and crosier. Note the
triangular ends of the stole below the chasuble. (b) (right) Figure of an ecclesiastic with
a crosier (photos: R. Stalley).

certainty, it seems likely that the cross was situated in the Howth area, and perhaps associated with one of the local medieval churches. Given the similarities with late medieval crosses elsewhere in the Pale, it might well have been commissioned by the St Lawrence family of Howth Castle. Since September 2005 every wall in the neighbourhood has been scrutinised but, alas, no further pieces of the cross have come to light. One day perhaps further fragments will reappear. There is also mystery about how the monument came to be lost. One can only assume that the cross itself was smashed, perhaps in the seventeenth century, the pieces being discarded and subsequently used as builders' rubble. While the fragment can hardly be rated as a stunning piece of late Gothic sculpture, it is nonetheless a reminder of the role played by chance. Serendipity is often the scholar's best friend. Stone carvings are not easy to destroy and, even when monuments are broken up, the pieces have to end up somewhere: the most common fate is reuse, and for this reason the dismantling of old walls, rockeries and gateposts will always offer the best chance of extending the corpus of Irish medieval sculpture.

Bibliography

Cone, P. 1978 *Treasures of early Irish art*. New York.

Hamlin, A. and Stalley, R.A. 2004 A newly discovered Romanesque church on Devenish, County Fermanagh. *Ulster Journal of Archaeology* **61**, 83–97.

Harbison, P. 1992 *The high crosses of Ireland: an iconographical and photographic survey*. Bonn.

Hunt, J. 1974 *Irish medieval figure sculpture 1200–1600*. Dublin and London.

Morris, R.K. 1983 The Herefordshire school: recent discoveries. In F. H. Thompson (ed.), *Studies in medieval sculpture*, 198–201. London.

Stalley, R.A. 1971 A twelfth-century patron of architecture: a study of the buildings erected by Roger, Bishop of Salisbury, 1102–39. *Journal of the British Archaeological Association* **34**, 62–83.

Thurlby, M. 1999 *The Herefordshire school of Romanesque sculpture*. Logaston, Herefordshire.

Pl. 69a (above left)—A photograph taken in 1991 of a cutting across an esker deposit to the south-west of Lough Corrib, Co. Galway, which exposed evidence of water layering.

Pl. 69b (above right) —The remnants of the same section of the esker in 2002 (authors' photographic collection).

nature, the roughly stratified layering and the close association with the esker further north suggested that this deposit was in all likelihood a kame. One other aspect of our research carried out on this site in the early 1990s yielded an interesting find—a layer of what was believed to be peat at a depth of 1.3m from the surface, which could imply the existence of possible tundra conditions at one point in its history. Overall, the conclusions reached were that this deposit suggested formation during an interglacial period of the last ice age, when the ice sheets would have temporarily disappeared from the region. In its present state, what we see is a landscape that will yield no further information either to challenge these conclusions or to develop possible alternatives. Again, because of its economic 'value' as a ready source for easily extracted sands and gravels this feature no longer exists. As Pls 70a and 70b clearly illustrate, the landscape we find today is entirely different from the one extant in the early 1990s, and with it we have lost a significant part of the narrative of its past history.

The third and final example is a feature that is a little more unusual and perhaps best illustrates how easily a 'mound of rocks and till' can be dismissed as having little or no intrinsic value. Giving a particular hummocky look to the landscape, the high stoss end and tapering tail of these features—a type of 'crag and tail'-like appearance—lead one to conclude that they have an association with drumlins (albeit very different to the other drumlins found further west in the region). Our research conducted in 1991 suggested that, while this may be

Pl. 70a (top)—A photograph of a cutting across a kame deposit near the village of Moycullen, Co. Galway, taken in 1991, showing evidence of water layering. The type and extent of stratified deposits are clearly visible.

Pl. 70b (above)—A photograph taken in 2002 shows the result of large-scale sand and gravel extraction from the site.

the first impression, a more commonly used term refers to them as cragans. These particular features are quite numerous in the area south of Lough Corrib and north of the previously mentioned esker deposit. They are essentially ice contact features but ones that are very different to the glacially washed sands and gravels in the area further south. The mounds themselves vary in size, averaging 60m long, 35m wide and 7m high, with the materials therein being very angular or sub-angular in content and ranging in size from boulders to sand grains, with

Pl. 71a (top)—The cragan deposit to the south of Lough Corrib as photographed in 1991, displaying the typical debris-strewn mound and the tapering tail of this landform.

Pl. 71b (above)—This photograph, taken in 2002, shows the result of gravel extraction from the same feature, its former existence only apparent from the 'filled' landscape remaining.

no evidence of water layering. It was further suggested that these features may be a type of ablation till, i.e. a till made up of local debris dropped out of the melting ice in knolls or pockets; rather than being dropped down by the ice like other ice contact features, these may have been scooped out of the bedrock and deposited *in situ*. When the particular feature from which this evidence was garnered is revisited some fifteen years later, what one observes leaves an entirely different impression. Where once an imposing mound was found (Pl. 71a), we are now confronted by an entirely flat, featureless landscape (Pl. 71b). Again part of our 'heritage' has been permanently erased with little concern for the narratives of our past landscapes.

Conclusions

It is not our intention here to propose that all changes to the landscape must be prevented. This is neither realistic nor feasible. What this chapter argues, however, is our responsibility and obligation to future generations to preserve our landscape in a sustainable way for their use, enjoyment and interpretation. Furthermore, as stated in an article entitled '(Re)thinking Ireland's attitude to landscape' (McDonagh 2002), if we do not document those features of our landscape which have an important 'story to tell' prior to their removal (should their demise not be preventable), then we are destroying an irreplaceable part of our past history and depriving future generations of a rich well of knowledge.

Landscape is dynamic, and it is inevitable, as a direct result of the increasing levels of economic development taking place in Ireland, that our landscape will also change. The contention here is not against change *per se* but more about the necessity to view the landscape as central to the sustainability debate (which is currently dominant) and to give more significance to landform conservation within this debate.

Landscapes are a continually evolving product of human interaction with nature, and while it may be possible to describe the distinctiveness of one landscape type from another, it may be foolhardy to attempt to determine whether one landscape is better or deserves more protection than any other. There is a narrative within our landscape, however, which is more easily told in some features than in others, and this should be informed by the historical chronology that different features can provide—an element often overlooked owing to a lack of knowledge on the part of the developer, road designer etc. The Irish landscape is probably one of the best 'field sites' of its type in the world in that it still contains numerous examples of features and landforms sculpted by our recent glacial history. The moulding of the Irish landscape during the Pleistocene has left a rich, diverse and irreplaceable landscape with a variety and complexity of deposits, from drumlins and eskers to rocky hillocks and rolling morainic topographies. If we accept that in order to understand what is happening in current processes—be it climate change, mass movements or increased flooding—we must understand our past landscapes and the narrative that they can provide, it is therefore essential that the protection of geomorphological features on our landscape must move from its 'Cinderella'

201

position to a more central focus in the broader conservation debate.

Moreover, there is an urgent need to develop greater awareness among the general public that landscape, once altered, can never be recreated. A more pressing issue, however, is a need for greater awareness by those individuals, institutions and authorities involved in the day-to-day planning, policy and design decisions of the inherent value and narrative that such natural landforms can provide. It is crucial, therefore, that a more integrative framework exists between these decision-makers and the landscape affected by their decisions. As argued by McDonagh (2002), there is also the need to develop a system whereby communities become involved in their landscape. The 'ownership principle' would, we suggest, enable people to appreciate their landscape and associated landforms in a more complete and inclusive way. Consequently, where landscape becomes 'an important part of people's lives, giving individuals and communities a sense of identity and belonging and bestowing a sense of place on our surroundings', as stated in the Draft Convention on Landscape proposed by the Council of Europe, the protection/conservation of a landscape/landform becomes far easier to achieve. In this way landscape becomes viewed not only in terms of topography and terrain but as something which incorporates the local communities that inhabit and manage it.

Finally, what is perhaps of greatest concern is the lack of a landscape policy for Ireland. On one level this lack of policy with regard to landscape may reflect something of the complexity of the term and its multifaceted meanings and the varying ways people view or engage with the landscape; on another level it suggests a complacency, a lack of priority and political will to engage constructively with such environmental issues. While no development can occur without making an impact in some way on the landscape, our respect for the landscape in which we live determines the quality of our economy, culture, heritage and—to an increasing extent—our quality of life. The challenge presented to our contemporary generation is to bring about change in a way that is considerate, creative and, above all, sustainable. To some extent the reactive, *ad hoc* way in which we currently exploit our landscape mirrors the misconceived notions of earlier centuries, which perceived the landscape as an inexhaustible resource to be exploited without restraint or consideration of the future consequences.

Bibliography

Aalen, F.H.A., Whelan, K. and Stout, M. 1997 *Atlas of the Irish rural landscape.* Cork.

Bingham, N., Blowers, A. and Belshaw, C. (eds) 2003 *Contested environments.* Chichester.

Cosgrove, D. and Daniels, S. (eds) 1989 *The iconography of landscape.* Cambridge.

Department of the Environment, Heritage and Local Government (DoEHLG) 2000 *Landscape and landscape assessment—consultation draft of guidelines for planning authorities.* Dublin.

Duncan, J. 1994 Landscape. In R. J. Johnston, D. Gregory and D. M. Smith (eds), *The dictionary of human geography*, 316–17. Cambridge.

Foras Forbartha, An 1976 *Outstanding landscapes.* Dublin.

Goudie, A. 1997 *The human impact on the natural environment.* Oxford.

Gray, M. 2004 *Geodiversity—valuing and conserving abiotic nature.* Chichester.

IUCN 1994 Guidelines for Protected Area Management Categories. http://www.unep-wcmc.org/protected_areas/categories/eng/index.html.

McDonagh, J. 2002 (Re)thinking Ireland's attitude to landscape. In M. A. Parkes (ed.), *Natural and cultural landscapes—the geological foundation*, 165–9. Dublin.

Meinig, D.W. 1979 The beholding eye: ten versions of the same scene. In D. W. Meinig and J. Brinckerhoff Jackson (eds), *The interpretation of ordinary landscapes: geographical essays*, 33–50. Oxford/New York.

Mitchell, F. and Ryan, M. 1997 *Reading the Irish landscape.* Dublin.

Sauer, C.O. 1925 *The morphology of landscape.* University of California Publications in Geography 2.

18

Rathcroghan Mound and other endangered species

Joe Fenwick

There it was, 'as dead as a dodo', on a shelf in the Natural History Museum. Even as a schoolboy I was amazed to see it there—the actual physical remains of a dodo. Unlike the duck, famous for its waddle and quack, the dodo was famous for only one thing: being dead. Worse, it was extinct. Little else is known about the creature, save what can be learned from a few contemporary descriptions and sketches before its ultimate demise—and, of course, the desiccated remains in a handful of privileged institutions. It is unlikely, however, that we will ever learn much more about this comical-looking creature, as its habits can now never be studied in its natural environment. Unlike references to the familiar duck, you will never hear anyone say 'If it hops like a dodo and honks like a dodo it probably is a dodo', because we simply don't know whether it hopped or skipped, honked or squawked. Dead dodos tell no tales.

The study of archaeological monuments in the field shares many similarities with the study of creatures in the wild. Both can be observed, described, measured and examined without necessarily disturbing the subject or, indeed, the integrity of its 'natural habitat'—its landscape context. In some instances, however, a more invasive investigation may be deemed appropriate, in the understanding, of course, that this is done for the greater scientific good. In such cases professional ethical standards will ensure that the welfare of the subject remains paramount and that 'collateral damage' is kept to an absolute minimum.

Excavation is to archaeology what dissection is to zoology. A large-scale excavation leaves no stone unturned, and the archaeologists are working in the knowledge that they are being afforded only one opportunity to record the site (and the stratigraphical context of artefacts and environmental material) as it is being systematically dismantled. Large-scale or total excavations are now largely confined to rescue or salvage digs in advance of major development. As such, these are undertaken not by choice or research design but simply as a matter of necessity (or urgency); if an archaeological site stands in the way of development, a full and thorough excavation is required. Often carried out in less than ideal working conditions and under tight time constraints, it can be a challenging and pressurised job.

Excavation is by definition, therefore, a form of recorded destruction, though 'preservation by record' is now, I believe, the prevailing euphemism preferred by those with a civil service mentality. In the world of zoology the equivalent phrase might be 'conservation by taxidermy'.

By contrast, current trends in archaeological field research afford the archaeologist the relative luxury of selecting an archaeological monument, complex or landscape for sustained scientific investigation within the context of broader, long-term research design. More emphasis tends to be placed on a hierarchical survey strategy, which in turn might inform a series of targeted, small-scale excavations addressing specific research questions. In this way the destruction (and expense) associated with wholesale excavation can be kept to a minimum. Archaeology, after all, is the study of past human society. It attempts to interpret and reconstruct the beliefs, customs and way of life of our ancestors from an examination of the archaeological mounments, the material culture (including, if we are lucky enough, contemporary documents) and the environmental evidence that have survived to the present. Its fundamental purpose is not driven by an overriding requirement to 'preserve by record' or salvage antiquities from the ground, though, sadly, archaeologists are finding that such exceptional circumstances are becoming increasingly commonplace in our development-driven economy (even during recessionary times). But what, you may ask, is archaeology without excavation?

The ArchaeoGeophysical Imaging Project, based at NUI, Galway, adopted a novel research design. It proposed the exclusive use of non-invasive geophysical survey techniques to investigate a select number of archaeological monuments in the Rathcroghan and Carnfree areas of County Roscommon. Such survey techniques allow us to 'see' buried archaeological features below the ground surface by virtue of the fact that these can display contrasting physical properties—primarily electrical or magnetic properties—to those of the surrounding or 'background' soils. This research strategy, however, may seem at odds with the public perception of what archaeologists do. The archaeological profession, after all, is synonymous with digging, but here excavation was not part of the plan. Surely, the idea of an archaeologist without a shovel or trowel is inconceivable? The remarkable results of the pioneering investigations at Rathcroghan, however, would prove such misgivings entirely unfounded.

Pl. 72—(a) (left to right) Michael Kelly (landowner), Yvonne Brennan, Kevin Barton and Professor John Waddell contemplating the results of the GPR survey as it appears in real time on the laptop screen in the field.

(b) Shane Rooney and Kevin Barton conducting a ground-penetrating radar survey on the summit of Rathcroghan Mound using a Pulse Ekko 1000 GPR.

(c) Yvonne Brennan employing a Bartington MS2 with MS2D search loop for the magnetic susceptibility survey.

(d) Finn Delaney conducting the electrical resistance survey using a square array (electrode spacing of 0.5m) with Campus Geopulse electrical resistance meter.

(e) The author using a Geoscan FM36 fluxgate gradiometer (magnetometer survey).

(f) Gerard Healy undertaking a topographical survey using a Sokkia Set 500e total station (Rathcroghan Mound in the background).

The project, directed by Dr John Waddell (Pl. 72a) (now Professor in the Department of Archaeology) and Mr Kevin Barton (Pl. 72b) (formerly of the Applied Geophysics Unit and currently director of Landscape and Geophysical Services Ltd, an integral part of Earthsound Associates), was launched in October 1994 with the generous financial assistance of the Heritage Council. At the time it seemed a natural progression to accept the position of project archaeologist on another major field research project, having cut my field-archaeologist's teeth at Tara as part of the Discovery Programme's Tara Survey (directed by Conor Newman). What clinched it for me, however, was the fact that this project was to investigate another of the major royal sites, Rathcroghan—'the Tara of the west', as Sir William Wilde once described it. About the same time Yvonne Brennan was appointed project geophysicist, and a short time afterwards we were joined by Finn Delaney, a fellow archaeologist (Pl. 72c, d and e).

Over the following months and years we were to get to know each other well, sharing accommodation in Strokestown and Castlerea, and joined on occasion by students from home and abroad keen to assist with the work. This melting-pot of personalities, nationalities and diverse expertise was both an inspiration and an education. The distinction between archaeologist and geophysicist was quickly blurred as everyone, irrespective of experience or background, was expected to pull their weight with the fieldwork, data-processing . . . and household chores. Some volunteers, particularly Vikram Unnithan, Gerard Healy (Pl. 72f) and Maighread Ní Dheasúna, made significant contributions to the field research, but we are no less grateful to all the others, too numerous to name here, who also assisted in our endeavours. Our work, likewise, could not have proceeded without the generous help of the local community, the Tulsk Action Group and the staff of the Cruachan Aí centre. We are particularly indebted to the local landowners, however, who, without exception, permitted unhindered access to their land and facilitated our research in every way possible. Michael Kelly, at that time owner of the land on which Rathcroghan Mound lies, even went so far as to give advance warning of his intention to spread slurry— for which we are eternally grateful.

It was demanding, often exhausting work, but incredibly rewarding. Like a page-turning novel, the excitement of archaeological discoveries—made almost on a daily basis—and our common bond of friendship and enthusiasm generated a wonderful working dynamic.

*   *   *

Rathcroghan has long been recognised as the *Cruachain* of early literature, the ancient royal capital of the province of Connacht. It is situated on the eastern

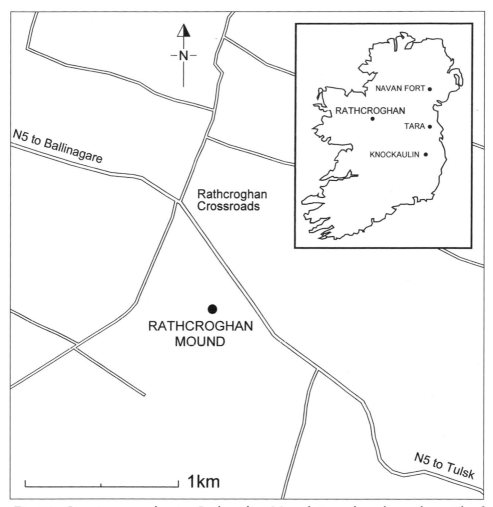

Fig. 15—Location map, showing Rathcroghan Mound situated on the southern side of the N5 between the villages of Tulsk and Ballinagare in County Roscommon.

extremity of a broad elevated plateau known as *Maigh nAí* ('the plains of the sheep'), approximately 5km north-west of the village of Tulsk, Co. Roscommon (Fig. 15). In archaeological terms it can be identified with a concentration of over 60 monuments and related ancient field systems that populate an area of little more than 10km² —the cumulative remains of human activity over a period of several thousand years, from the Neolithic to the later Middle Ages.

As impressive as its archaeological legacy is the wealth of ancient historical, pseudo-historical, mythical and legendary texts associated with this extraordinary place. All of these emphasise its central role as a sacred and royal site long before the arrival of Christianity, and the pivotal political and symbolic role it continued to play in the history of Connacht throughout the early historic and medieval periods. Rathcroghan served as the royal seat, a place of assembly or *óenach*, and a royal cemetery for the kings of Connacht. It was from here, for example, according to the celebrated legend the *Táin Bó Cuailnge* ('Cattle-raid of Cooley'), that Queen Mebd led her armies into the province of Ulster to take by force the Brown Bull of Cooley.

Prior to the commencement of the ArchaeoGeophysical Imaging Project, little—in reality nothing—was known of the internal complexities of Rathcroghan Mound or, indeed, the true significance of the small group of visible monuments surrounding it. On cursory inspection, the monument appeared to be little more than a squat, flat-topped earthen mound (Pl. 72f), its only remarkable attributes being its large size and prominent setting in the landscape. Despite the mound's deceptively plain external appearance, the geophysical survey revealed a wealth of previously unknown archaeological features buried beneath its 'flat', grass-covered summit. Moreover, the dispersed group of satellite monuments surrounding Rathcroghan Mound have also assumed a far greater significance as a direct result of our research.

I intend here to present just a brief interpretative outline of the combined topographical and geophysical survey results – without burdening you with the finer details of the various survey techniques, the scope and limitations of the technology or the inherent challenges of 'reading' the graphical representations of the various datasets. In so doing, I hope to render a degree of transparency to the soils of Rathcroghan and some clarity to the sediments of the great mound, which up until recent years had remained … well … as clear as mud!

An extensive microtopographical survey of Rathcroghan Mound and its environs (Fig. 16) reveals something of the glacial legacy of this undulating landscape, composed, as it is, of a thin veneer of till and sinuous gravel ridges, aligned north-north-west/south-south-east. Rathcroghan Mound, situated in the townland of Toberrory, appears to have been deliberately constructed on the summit of a particularly prominent ridge in order to exploit this naturally elevated and dominant position in the surrounding landscape. The mound itself averages some 88m in basal diameter and 6m in height, with two distinct ramps set into its eastern and western flanks allowing access to its gently domed summit.

Other monuments have been observed in its immediate vicinity. In the townland of Glenballythomas the remains of a trackway can be traced running alongside the townland wall, 40m to the south of the great mound. Possibly pre-dating it are the remains of two low-relief barrows, which, like the trackway, also lie to the immediate south of the townland wall. Some 80m further south again are the faint traces of a broad, arcuate depression, roughly concentric with Rathcroghan Mound.

Fig. 16—Surface-shaded model of Rathcroghan Mound and environs, viewed in perspective from the south (vertical exaggeration 200%).

North of the wall, in the townland of Toberrory, an unusual configuration of two conjoined barrows are situated 70m to the east of Rathcroghan Mound. These monuments are visible only under optimal lighting conditions and are more readily identifiable from the air. More obvious, however, is a squat standing stone, known as 'Milleen Meva', and a now recumbent pillar stone, 'Miosgan Meva', situated 105m to the north-north-west and 100m to the north-north-east of Rathcroghan Mound respectively.

The magnetic susceptibility survey (Fig. 17) has brought to light a long-forgotten agricultural landscape of small subrectangular plots and spade cultivation within the expansive open fields surrounding the great mound. This relic cultivation pattern, which may date from as early as the medieval period, is more readily visible in the magnetic gradiometry survey as parallel bands of positive and negative magnetic gradient representing individual lines of ridge-and-furrow 'fossilised' beneath the surface of the present-day grassland. Though of archaeological interest in its own right, this episode of cultivation will have erased or truncated all near-surface archaeological features that preceded it. Only those relatively deeply buried features will have survived intact beneath this cultivation horizon. Despite this disturbance, a number of important archaeological monuments, displaying little or no surface expression, have come to light.

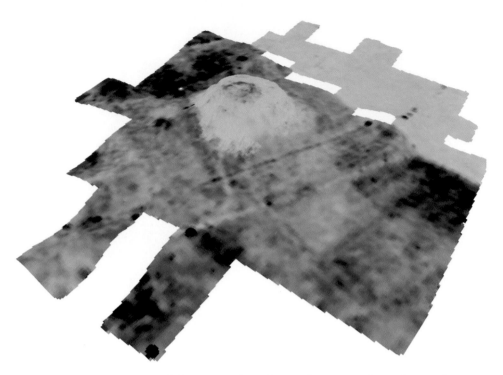

Fig. 17—Magnetic susceptibility image draped over the topography and viewed in perspective from the north-west (vertical exaggeration 400%). Range of values: white (0 SI units x 10E-5) to black (600 SI units x 10E-5).

The broad, low-relief arcuate depression to the south of Rathcroghan Mound was the first evidence of the existence of an enclosure surrounding this complex. Indeed, its presence and extent had remained little more than conjecture as all surface trace of it had entirely disappeared for the greater part of its circumference. The results of the magnetic gradiometry survey (Fig. 18), however, demonstrated conclusively that the limits of its associated ritual complex are neatly contained within a vast circular enclosure some 360m in diameter (i.e. over 1km in circumference). This enclosure consists of a broad ditch—possibly rock-cut—approximately 5m wide. It may be an archaeological equivalent of Ráith na Ríg, the great ritual sanctuary on the Hill of Tara.

The magnetic gradiometry survey also revealed a complex pattern of anomalous features within the 360m enclosure, against the overprint of ancient agricultural activity and modern post-and-wire fences. These may represent the subsurface remains of ancient ditches, drains, palisade trenches and foundation slot-trenches.

Amongst the more remarkable discoveries was evidence of a series of large-

Fig. 18—Fluxgate magnetometry survey of Rathcroghan Mound and environs draped over the topography and viewed in perspective from the north-east (vertical exaggeration 400%). Range of values: -10nT (white) and +10nT (black).

scale circular features on the flat summit of Rathcroghan Mound and the presence of a monumental funnel-shaped avenue approaching it from the east-south-east, and immediately to the north of the great mound, on a spur of elevated ground, the subsurface remains of another large circular enclosure, 28m in diameter, again with an east-facing, elongated, funnel-shaped approach avenue—named accordingly 'the funnelled-enclosure'. The magnetic gradiometry and electrical resistance surveys also revealed that the larger of the conjoined barrows (i.e. the southern one), situated to the east of Rathcroghan Mound, was composed not of a single but of a double set of banks and ditches. These discoveries are of unequivocal archaeological significance, but there are other features, perhaps of no less archaeological importance, also visible in the gradiometry image. These, however, are more difficult to interpret on account of the partial or incomplete nature of their geophysical signature. It has also proved difficult, on the basis of geophysical evidence alone, to establish the relative chronology of individual monuments or features within the 370m enclosure, even in cases where obvious overlaps occur. Many, however, are likely to be broadly contemporary with each other or part of an overall complex of

213

interrelated ritual and ceremonial monuments built and replaced over time.

The relative chronology of certain features and monuments can be inferred in a number of instances. The conjoined nature of the barrows to the east of Rathcroghan Mound, for example, was clearly intentional and undoubtedly had an acknowledged significance and meaning for those who configured them that way. In this instance it is likely that the smaller of the two pre-dates the larger, as the outer ring of the latter appears to flatten slightly to acknowledge the presence of the former.

The funnelled-enclosure by comparison is a much more complex structure and is likely to represent the deep slot-trench and post-pit foundations of a series of large-scale timber structures. Traces of three circles have been identified in the geophysical imagery, two of which are concentric and therefore possibly integral parts of the same building phase. It is likely, therefore, that an elaborate double-penannular structure, 28m in diameter, encircling a number of centrally placed pits or post-pits, was one of at least two large-scale structures, or buildings, that once stood on this conspicuous spur of ground adjoining the northern sector of Rathcroghan Mound.

The axial symmetry of this remarkable monument is readily apparent in the geophysical image. The double-penannular enclosure was entered via a monumental portal at the end of a long funnel-shaped avenue from the east. Despite its large scale, it is possible, on account of its elaborate ground-plan, that this enclosure was roofed, and the avenue leading to it was flanked by a double palisade, perhaps supporting an equally elaborate superstructure. Clearly, those who designed and constructed this structure were well aware of the theatrical backdrop this architectural device would provide in the pageantry of a formal procession leading to the double-penannular enclosure. There is no doubting the importance of this building, the significance of its contents or the gravity and solemnity of the ceremonies that must have taken place within it. It is quite likely to have served as a temple or shrine dedicated to a pre-Christian deity.

It may be significant, too, that this elaborate structure appears to have replaced another that had previously stood on the same spot adjacent to the mound—a motif that is repeated on the summit of Rathcroghan Mound. There is also evidence to support the possibility that one or both of these circular structures actually pre-date some of the later constructional phases of Rathcroghan Mound. The broad band of positive magnetic gradient circumscribing the mound appears to flatten adjacent to the funnelled-enclosure, and in so doing clearly acknowledges its presence. Also of note is the apparent asymmetry of the funnelled eastern approach to Rathcroghan Mound, which is skewed somewhat awkwardly to the south. For this approach to be truly symmetric and facing due east, the northern arm of the funnel would have had

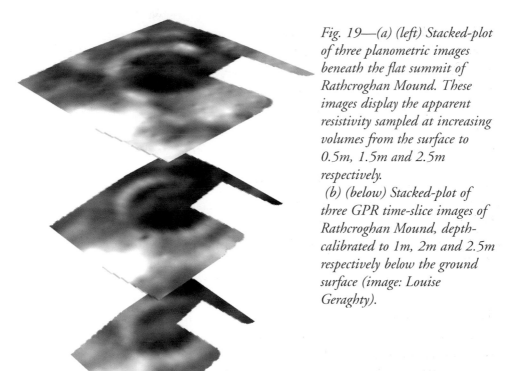

Fig. 19—(a) (left) Stacked-plot of three planometric images beneath the flat summit of Rathcroghan Mound. These images display the apparent resistivity sampled at increasing volumes from the surface to 0.5m, 1.5m and 2.5m respectively.
 (b) (below) Stacked-plot of three GPR time-slice images of Rathcroghan Mound, depth-calibrated to 1m, 2m and 2.5m respectively below the ground surface (image: Louise Geraghty).

to be realigned significantly to the north. In so doing, it would, by necessity, have traversed the southern arm of the funnelled-enclosure, which clearly it does not. It may be the case, therefore, that the funnelled easterly approach to Rathcroghan Mound, possibly flanked by a substantial palisade, was carefully positioned in order to avoid interfering with the pre-existing monument to its north. It may also be significant that the conjoined barrows to the east of Rathcroghan Mound are neatly framed between the arms of the funnel, and this too may have

215

been a deliberate intention on the part of those constructing these monuments.

Though it had been suggested that Rathcroghan Mound was little more than a scarped and sculpted glacial ridge, nothing could have been further from the truth. The detailed scientific investigations of the mound have revealed a monument of exceptional internal complexity, the product of an elaborate and calculated series of constructional phases.

Electrical resistivity tomography and ground-penetrating radar (GPR) have independently detected the presence of two substantial concentric stone walls, *c.* 22m and 34m in diameter, buried deep within the core of Rathcroghan Mound (Fig. 19, a and b), and these features may represent the remains of a large bivallate enclosure or cashel-like structure which was deliberately entombed within the body of the mound. Alternatively, these buried features might just as easily represent some form of internal structural revetment within the mound. It is interesting to note that evidence of what may be a partially rock-cut encircling ditch, 75–80m in diameter, buried beneath the sloping edge of Rathcroghan Mound was also noted in the geophysical survey. This feature may be related to one of the early phases of the mound construction, perhaps a composite element of the perimeter revetment. Alternatively, it may be related to, or contemporary with, the construction of the buried concentric walls. If the latter is the case, it would suggest that Rathcroghan Mound subsumes not a bivallate but a trivallate monument of considerable size. It seems likely, too, that when newly constructed the mound was defined by a vertical or near-vertical sloping façade, perhaps reinforced by a timber-laced retaining palisade. It is probable, therefore, that the great mound may originally have presented a squat, drum-like appearance quite different in profile to the broad, flat-topped mound with sloping edges that survives today.

The internal complexity of the mound, however, is further reflected in the subtle topography of its 'flat' summit. A series of low-relief radiating depressions noted in the detailed topographical survey around the periphery of its summit appear to subdivide its surface into an irregular segmental pattern, like spokes on a great wheel (Fig. 20a). This curious pattern is likely to reflect the deliberate deposition of different materials as part of the mound construction. It may have been done simply to consolidate the mound or to improve drainage, but there is a growing body of evidence to suggest that the surface could have been subdivided for symbolic or ritual purposes. At the centre of the mound a large, low-relief platform can be observed, the sloping edge of which coincides with the inner concentric buried wall. This platform constitutes the central part of a poorly preserved, almost levelled, barrow-like feature, composed of a central low earthen mound encircled by traces of a fosse and external bank. It seems likely that this putative barrow was purposefully positioned with respect to the inner wall buried deep within the mound and therefore is likely to represent one of the

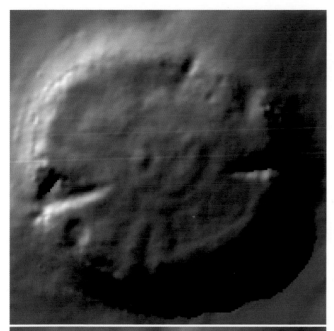

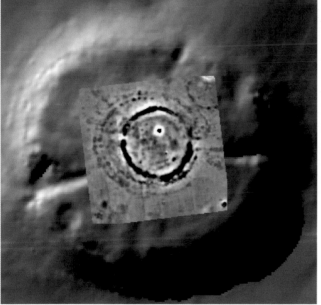

Fig. 20—(a) (top) Surface-shaded model of Rathcroghan Mound, which averages 88m in basal diameter.
(b) (bottom) Fluxgate magnetometry image (40m by 40m) superimposed on a surface-shaded model of Rathcroghan Mound.

first of many phases of construction on the 'flat' summit of the mound (it may also explain why this feature is so poorly preserved).

The largest circular feature identified in the magnetometer survey of the mound's summit is composed of a double ring, 32m and 28m in diameter respectively (Fig. 20b). Each ring appears to be composed of a series of discrete, equi-spaced and radially opposed anomalies of positive magnetic gradient, set

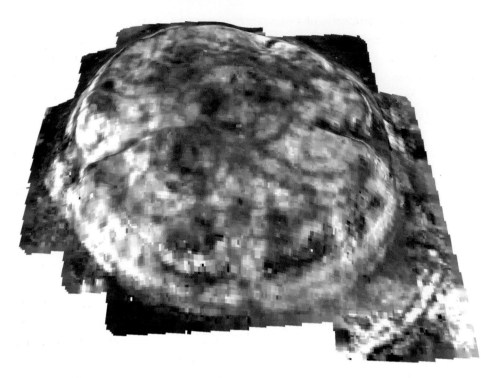

Fig. 21—Electrical resistance image of Rathcroghan Mound draped over the topography and viewed in perspective from the south (vertical exaggeration 300%).

approximately 2m apart centre to centre. These discrete anomalies are likely to represent a series of post-pits dug to support large paired timber uprights, though the nature of the superstructure supported, if not free-standing posts, is a matter of conjecture. It is interesting to note, however, the possibility of at least one smaller internal circle, concentric with the double ring of paired post-pits, which was identified in the electrical resistance survey (Fig. 21). It is also notable that this double ring of post-pits breaks the pattern of concentricity with respect to the buried walls and the barrow-like feature and therefore suggests that it belongs to one of the latest episodes of building on the summit of the mound.

This extraordinary feature is likely to represent the foundation remains of a substantial timber-built structure. The suggestion of at least one internal concentric circle within the double ring of posts raises the intriguing possibility that it has a multi-ring plan. If this proves to be the case, this structure could theoretically have supported a roof (as has been proposed for the 40m multi-ring structure at Navan Fort). At 32m in diameter, such an elaborate construction would have represented a major feat of structural engineering. Roofed or otherwise, this structure was intended to be an imposing and spectacular monument, conspicuously placed, as it is, on the summit of Rathcroghan Mound and elevated above the surrounding landscape. Its function, too, must have had an elevated and central significance to the ritual and ceremonial activities of Rathcroghan and the surrounding region. It would certainly have been visible against the skyline for miles around. In such a central location in this ritual landscape it is likely to have served as a great temple or 'cathedral' to pre-Christian religious belief and royal ceremony. Like the funnelled-enclosure lying immediately to its north, it is likely to have been entered on its eastern side via a formal funnel-like avenue aligned on its eastern ramp. Such formal architectural expression again suggests the enactment of august and stately ceremonial activities.

But this great temple is not the only free-standing structure to have been erected on the summit of Rathcroghan Mound. There is also evidence that a number of other large-scale timber structures once occupied its summit, perhaps intermediate structural phases between the construction of the barrow and the erection of the great temple. Furthermore, several smaller circular features located on the periphery of the mound's 'flat' summit suggest the possibility of conjoined figure-of-eight structures (Figs 20b and 21), though direct associations between individual features are difficult to establish on the basis of geophysical evidence alone. It is clear, however, that these features represent the foundation footings of a succession of large-scale timber buildings and/or enclosures built and replaced over time on the summit of the great mound. The enhanced magnetic susceptibility associated with the central group of large-scale structures or enclosures (Fig. 17) suggests that intensive burning was associated with one or more of these structural phases. This may also explain why the magnetic signatures associated with individual features are, in some cases, particularly well defined. This raises the intriguing possibility, therefore, that some structures were burned down prior to being replaced. It is also possible that a fire or series of fires, perhaps for ritual purposes, was kept burning within one or more of these large, centrally placed structures, the ash from which was unevenly distributed but confined within the encircling perimeter 'walls' of these structures.

Curiously, the very last monument to be superimposed on the summit of Rathcroghan Mound appears to have been a small earthen mound, which is illustrated in a watercolour by Beranger dated to 1779. Though relatively insignificant in archaeological terms, there is a possibility that this feature served as a royal inauguration mound some time after the site was abandoned as a pre-Christian cult centre. During the early historic period this ritual landscape, though in decline, would certainly have been perceived as an appropriate place for such ceremony. Though no longer retaining its religious role, Rathcroghan remained a place of profound symbolic significance for those with political ambition in the province of Connacht and beyond.

On the basis of the research undertaken by the ArchaeoGeophysical Imaging Project, it is now apparent that Rathcroghan Mound not only served as the centrepiece of a pre-Christian ritual sanctuary but was also the focal monument of the entire Rathcroghan landscape—a place of regional significance during the later prehistoric period and of enormous importance to the people who constructed it. Even without the benefit of scientific excavation, stratigraphical sequences, associated material culture and scientific dating techniques, it is now possible to draw compelling archaeological comparisons between the survey results from Rathcroghan (*Cruachain*) and the archaeological remains at the other major pre-Christian royal centres of Navan Fort (*Emain Macha*), Co. Armagh, Knockaulin (*Dún Ailinne*), Co. Kildare, and Tara (*Temhair*), Co. Meath (Fig. 15).

The complexity exhibited in the scientifically excavated monuments at Navan Fort and Knockaulin (and possibly Tara too), in addition to the foundation imprint of a series of large-scale ritual timber structures, bears remarkable similarities to the geophysical picture emerging at Rathcroghan. Chris Lynn has proposed some compelling hypotheses to explain the extraordinary sequence of predetermined building phases leading up to the construction, and subsequent destruction, of the multi-ring structure at Navan Fort, based on early descriptions of Otherworld hostels, cosmological symbolism and parallels with ancient Indo-European kingship and religion. Similarly, Charles Doherty, in Edel Bhreathnach's volume on *The kingship and landscape of Tara*, has interpreted such constructional complexities as the 'physical expression of a sophisticated philosophical reflection of the cosmos', with sun worship (the wheel), creation myths and the concept of a 'world king' as the central driving force and motivation behind this seemingly bizarre series of ceremonial events. There is reason to believe that the rationale behind the construction of Rathcroghan Mound is no different, and it may also be the product of a similar series of predetermined symbolic constructional events associated with sacred kingship.

Our research at Rathcroghan Mound has succeeded in recording this monument in unprecedented detail whilst at the same time preserving it for future generations to visit, study, research and enjoy. In effect, the mound has been tagged and ringed and released unharmed back into the wild. It goes without saying, however, that in order to preserve the future viability of an endangered species it is essential to protect the sustainability of its natural habitat. By the same token, the integrity of an archaeological monument or complex can be irrevocably undermined if its landscape context is compromised. We are fortunate that the plains of *Maigh nAí* are not subject to major development or infrastructural pressures, unlike, sadly, their more famous royal equivalent at Tara. Rathcroghan remains to this day a thriving rural environment, populated by a vibrant farming community justifiably proud of its rich cultural heritage.

As an inquisitive schoolboy I was fascinated by the remarkably lifelike poses of the wonderful creatures in the Natural History Museum, but I could not help my attention being drawn to the carefully plugged bullet-holes, the cross-stitching and the fixed glassy stare of some exhibits, despite the taxidermist's best endeavours. Even in the vivid imagination of a schoolboy, there was no escaping the fact that these magnificent beasts had been stitched up and stuffed.

Select bibliography

Barton, K. and Fenwick, J. 2005 Geophysical investigations at the ancient royal site of Rathcroghan, Co. Roscommon, Ireland. *Archaeological Prospection* **12** (1), 3–18.

Bhreathnach, E. 2005 *The kingship and landscape of Tara.* Dublin.

Cooney, G. and Grogan, E. 1994 *Irish prehistory: a social perspective.* Bray.

Fenwick, J. 2005 The M3 and Tara: gaining the world and losing our soul. *The Word* (September 2005), 10–11.

Fenwick, J. 2008 Driving through history. *Roads Ireland* **5**, 14–17. www.roadsireland.com/RI5.pdf.

Fenwick, J. and Newman, C. 2002 Geomagnetic survey on the Hill of Tara, Co. Meath—1998/99. *Discovery Programme Reports* **6**, 1–18.

Fenwick, J., Geraghty, L., Waddell, J. and Barton, K. 2006 The innermost secrets of Rathcroghan Mound. *Archaeology Ireland* **20** (2), 26–9.

Johnston, S.A. and Wailes, B. 2007 *Dún Ailinne: excavations at an Irish royal site, 1968–1975.* Philadelphia.

Lynn, C.J. 1994 Hostels, heroes and tales: further thoughts on the Navan mound. *Emania* **12**, 5–20.

Lynn, C.[J.] 2003 *Navan Fort: archaeology and myth.* Bray.

Newman, C. 1997 *Tara: an archaeological survey.* Discovery Programme Monographs 2. Dublin.

Waddell, J. 1983 Rathcroghan—a royal site in Connacht. *Journal of Irish Archaeology* **1**, 21–46.

Waddell, J., Fenwick, J. and Barton, K. 2009 *Rathcroghan, Co. Roscommon: archaeological and geophysical survey in a ritual landscape.* Dublin.

Wailes, B. 1990 Dún Ailinne: a summary excavation report. *Emania* **7**, 10–21.

Waterman, D.M. 1997 *Excavations at Navan Fort 1961–71* (ed. C. J. Lynn). Belfast.

www.cruachanai.com

19

Up in the air: 3D modelling of archaeological landscapes from aerial photography

Anthony Corns and Robert Shaw

As surveyors working in archaeology, the opportunity to research and test new technologies is probably the most satisfying part of our job. So you can imagine our excitement when an opportunity presented itself to work on a site as impressive and important as the prehistoric remains at Mullaghfarna, Co. Sligo. The site consists of over 100 circular enclosures clustered on this elevated, karstified, limestone plateau, part of a spectacular prehistoric archaeological landscape containing the Carrowkeel passage tomb cemetery and extending over the neighbouring hilltop ridges of the Bricklieve Mountains (Pl. 73).

Our involvement began with an approach from Dr Stefan Bergh, NUI Galway, who was carrying out extensive research on the site, funded by the Heritage Council. Exploratory excavations of selected enclosure sites had revealed diagnostic artefacts such as flint and chert scrapers, blades and cores, which dated the site to the Neolithic period. In addition, Stefan has carried out a photographic survey from a helicopter in order to plan the site. A short time later we had an opportunity to study these images for the first time during a meeting at the offices of the Discovery Programme. They instantly caught our imagination, but the difficulties posed by the rugged terrain would, in time, compel us to look to new technologies to resolve the surveying challenges that lay ahead.

Stefan was initially hoping that we could collaborate on an accurate three-dimensional ground survey to create a detailed 3D model of the plateau, which would reveal more aspects of the complex interrelationships between archaeological elements and their local geomorphological context. He also hoped to look at the settlement site in its wider landscape context, an approach that we were keen to experiment with as our previous landscape models had tended to

Pl. 73—The Doonaveragh ridge, Bricklieve Mountains, Co. Sligo. The Mullaghfarna prehistoric remains are located on the flat plateau in the centre of the image (reproduced by kind permission of Dr Stefan Bergh).

be left floating in space, divorced from their wider surroundings.

Stefan was aware of the Discovery Programme's history of modelling archaeological landscapes, such as at the Hill of Tara, but was perhaps less aware of just how time-consuming such detailed ground surveys are! Although technology has advanced from total stations to real-time differential GPS systems, ground survey is still a slow, painstaking procedure. Tempting though it would have been to spend six months or more in such a spectacular place surveying thousands of height points, past experience had taught us that such an organic landscape would be poorly recorded by this method. Good 3D models of relatively smoothly contoured earthwork sites can be produced in this way, but here we had a rough and irregular limestone pavement on which every stone and gully could potentially be crucial to the interpretation, and thus the entire surface would need to be carefully modelled. Furthermore, from ground level it was hard to fully appreciate the true morphology and form of the archaeological remains. It proved difficult to distinguish them from the underlying karst in places, so we were forced to look for a different approach.

The photographs Stefan had taken from the helicopter gave us some ideas of how to proceed (Pl. 74). They showed the archaeology in fine detail, but as they were taken from oblique angles with a standard digital camera they lacked the

Pl. 74—A near-vertical photograph showing the complex nature of the archaeology and the background karst geomorphology (reproduced by kind permission of Dr Stefan Bergh).

geometry to enable accurate mapping. To do this properly we would need to apply the science of mapping from aerial photographs, known as photogrammetry. We had both studied this back in our days at university, but remembered it as a complex procedure involving expensive precision optical instruments and a high level of operator skill. Thankfully, developments in computing now allow this to be replicated digitally, but the principles of photogrammetry remain the same. High-resolution vertical aerial photography is taken from an airplane along predetermined parallel runs using a stereo camera mounted on the underside of the fuselage. The results consist of overlapping images known as stereo pairs. The same part of the ground therefore appears on two images, though taken from slightly different angles. By carefully recreating the positions of the photographs at exposure, a model of the ground in the overlap area can be recreated. When viewed in tandem using a stereo viewer, the overlapping area of the imagery is resolved by the brain or computer to produce a 3D model of the landscape scene. This approach is the basis for most of the maps produced by national mapping agencies such as Ordnance Survey Ireland (OSI). The application of this technique can also be used to yield a detailed digital elevation model (DEM).

Our discussions with Stefan quickly turned to whether digital photogrammetry could provide the answer to our problem. Would the digital elevation models produced be detailed enough to show the smallest archaeological features? At what altitude would it be necessary to fly the plane to capture the photography? Could we also model the wider landscape in this way in order to place the plateau in its landscape context? Would we be able to learn how to process the data for ourselves without the need for outside expertise? How much would it all cost?

Obviously neither the Discovery Programme nor the Department of Archaeology at NUI Galway owned an aerial survey plane, so it was necessary for an outside organisation to provide the required digital aerial images. First, we explored the idea of using the OSI to supply orthophotos and DEMs, but it was thought that the photo scale of these images, 1:40,000, was not sufficient to capture the detail of the landscape, never mind the small-scale structural features of the site. Another factor was the prohibitive cost of the annual licensing of OSI data. How many years would these data be required for research? We quickly realised that we needed to be in control of the scale, extent and ownership of the survey imagery in order for it to be successful, but we hadn't the technical ability to carry this out.

After much investigation we turned to BKS Survey Ltd, based in Coleraine, a leading aerial survey company with the capability to deliver client-specific aerial surveys. We were invited along with Stefan to the BKS offices by sales manager John McNally to discuss the project. On our arrival, John took us on a grand tour of the BKS HQ to observe for ourselves the procedures used in a number of aerial survey projects they were working on, and to whet our appetites for its potential use in our proposed venture. Observing all stages of the aerial survey methodology—from the smell of the photographic labs to visualising the 3D model of the island of Bermuda on a computer screen—simply reinforced our enthusiasm and confidence in applying this approach to the survey of Mullaghfarna.

After several cups of strong coffee, an appropriate plan was fleshed out. BKS would provide vertical aerial photography at two different scales. The first would be a low-level survey carried out at 1,800ft, which would provide detailed imagery of the plateau (at 1:1,500 scale) with the aim of capturing, in detail, all archaeological features and structures. This survey would sit within a second, higher-altitude (5,000ft) aerial survey of the surrounding landscape that would position the plateau within its dramatic topographic context. The resulting photo scale of this aerial survey would be 1:7,500. Another detail that needed to be clarified was the appropriate scanning resolution at which to digitise the aerial images. A balance between the extremely large digital files created and the amount of detail captured was needed. A final scan resolution of 14μm was chosen, resulting in digital aerial images in which each pixel represented ground features 16cm in size for the landscape photography (1:7,500 scale) and just 3cm for the plateau photography (1:1,500 scale). The resulting image files were each approximately 500MB in size. With a total of 32 images required to cover the survey area, this was the equivalent to a modest 16GB of data, even at this early stage of the project. It is easy to see how digital photogrammetry has the potential to become an archivist's nightmare!

To fix the true position and orientation of the captured photography it was essential that Irish National Grid coordinates were recorded for suitable ground control points within the survey area using GPS technology. To reduce the costs of the survey, and as the Discovery Programme already had the necessary GPS equipment, we decided that we would do this work ourselves. BKS advised us on the best layout for the ground control points, and an interesting distinction was made between those used for our low- and high-altitude photography. For the low-level, more detailed survey, photographic targets would have to be placed on the ground in predetermined locations in advance of the photography. This was to ensure that the highest accuracy would result from the photogrammetric processing. In contrast, the high-altitude photography would be controlled by identifying features on the photographs which we could also identify on the ground in the real world: these are known as photo points.

As the two sets of aerial photography would be taken in one flight, the ground survey task was neatly split into two stages. We had to get the targets on the ground and surveyed before the low-level photographic survey was flown, and return again when the photographic images had been delivered to survey the 'high-level' ground control.

First things first: we had to make our ground targets. They needed to be big enough to be identified on the vertical photos and yet provide the necessary precision for survey purposes. A trip to the hardware shop saw to the procurement of materials necessary to make the perfect photogrammetric pre-mark target: 50cm by 50cm hardboard, white sticky-backed plastic, and black duct tape for a central cross. The ground survey method used was our standard approach at the time—real-time differential GPS, fixing the base station to the Irish National Grid using rinex data from the OSI geodetic services website. With our base station running, we set off across the landscape to the optimum positions indicated by BKS on a map. A head for heights was needed, as some of these positions proved to be in precarious locations on the edge of the steep rocky slopes. The targets were fixed to the ground using wooden stakes, and the GPS position was then measured (Pl. 75).

Although we had fixed our targets securely in position, using half-metre stakes hammered well into the ground, we had a major scare a few weeks later

Pl. 75—Anthony Corns surveying the GPS position of a pre-mark target, part of the control framework for the low-altitude photography.

when Stefan reported that during a site visit he had found one of them not only blown out of position but lying in an adjacent field. As the photography had now been flown it was too late to check the others. A nervous wait followed until at last we could inspect the photography, which thankfully showed the remaining five targets *in situ*. To compensate for the lost target, extra photo points were surveyed during the second phase of control survey.

This return visit for the wider area ground control presented a different challenge. We now had the photography and knew approximately how the points should be distributed, but we had to identify features on the ground that we could also see in the photographs. In some places this was easy—a wall corner, road markings etc.—but in the more remote areas we had to resort to more subtle features, turns in relict field walls and even junctions on overlapping vehicle tracks. The GPS surveying was the same as before, but some post-processing of data was needed, as the distances from the base station were sometimes too great for the radio corrections to be received. Since this job was completed we have acquired a new GPS system, which has simplified this type of surveying. We can now work with real-time differential corrections received from the OSI via a mobile phone instead of using our own base station. This makes the logistics of surveying control far easier. There is no need to set up a base station or to consider whether radio signals can be received; the only worry is whether the mobile phone network has coverage!

With all the image and survey data captured, it was now time to cut our teeth on the meat of the project: the digital photogrammetry. Would those university lectures from the distant past still be fresh in our memories? The Discovery Programme purchased a copy of Geomatica 9, a professional digital photogrammetry suite available (thankfully) for educational and non-profit organisations at a much-reduced price. After an initial inspection of our hardware requirements, a capital investment was needed to bring our computers up to speed and to process the data efficiently. A peripheral stereo-viewing device was also purchased that enabled the computer-user to visualise the landscape on the computer screen in full 3D. One disadvantage . . . you have to wear a ridiculous pair of polarising glasses that make you look like a '70s TV cop.

Operating the digital photogrammetry software was initially daunting, but after several readings of the software manual, combined with the relatively intuitive nature of the process, progress was rapidly achieved. Digital photogrammetry can be broken down into four stages, each needing to be completed before the following one is initiated.

The first stage is the setting up of the project, which entails importing the aerial survey images and associated capture information. This includes the image resolution and associated map projection system, in this case the Irish National Grid. The focal length and the lens calibration details of the camera used during the flight are also entered. The final phase of the process is the identification of the fiducial marks, or cross-hairs, that surround the aerial photographs. Sequential digitisation of these markers adjusts and rotates the relative position of the images, traditionally known as 'inner orientation'.

The second stage of the digital photogrammetric process is called 'exterior orientation', a procedure that translates and orientates the camera to its real-world position at the point when each image was captured, establishing the relationship between the ground and the aerial image. This is probably the most complex stage of the process, involving the position (x, y, z), pitch (omega), roll (phi) and yawl (kappa) of the plane during its flight. Each image is then correctly scaled using the ground control points established with the GPS. Normally each image would require nine evenly distributed control points but, utilising a process known as aero-triangulation, ground control can be passed along a series of overlapping images, dramatically reducing the number of ground control points needed. By identifying identical features on neighbouring photographs, control can be propagated along the run of images. Once all these values are computed, a mathematical model is created that correctly positions all of the images and enables stereo viewing of the landscape. Huddled around the monitor wearing our groovy specs, the first stereo viewing of the landscape images was no less startling, to say the least. After initial adjustment of our eyes, the terrain of Mullaghfarna jumped out of the monitor screen in all its rugged glory. The clustered enclosures on the plateau and the burial cairns of Carrowkeel could be clearly seen in splendid 3D. The overall effect was similar to looking down upon a model railway, with its tiny sheep, small trees, fields and houses—all that was missing was the railway itself.

The penultimate processing stage was the creation of a digital elevation model (DEM) of the surveyed area. Using a process of image correlation between overlapping images, the software matches pixels that represent the same location on the ground. Each pixel position is subsequently resolved using the mathematical model created previously, and an x, y and z position for each individual pixel is produced. After the creation of separate DEMs for each overlapping stereo pair, subsequent editing is required to stitch together the results into two seamless models: one of the overall landscape (Fig. 22) and the other of the plateau site. The 3D modelling of these data in our GIS software allowed us to visualise the distinctive archaeology and field systems of the area, experimenting with different vertical exaggerations and alternative illumination angles to reveal new features in the landscape. It was evident from the results that the survey was remarkably successful, with the plateau and its associated Neolithic structures displayed in extraordinary clarity. On closer inspection Stefan began to identify new features, including interconnecting passageways, that were simply not possible to see in the field. Looking at the shaded DEM without the distracting noise of colour and textures, it became far easier to differentiate between those structures that had been cut into the plateau and those constructed on its surface (Fig. 23).

The final stage of the photogrammetric process was the production of orthophotos. If one attempts to overlay a standard aerial image over metrically correct mapping data it will quickly be noticed that, no matter how much one

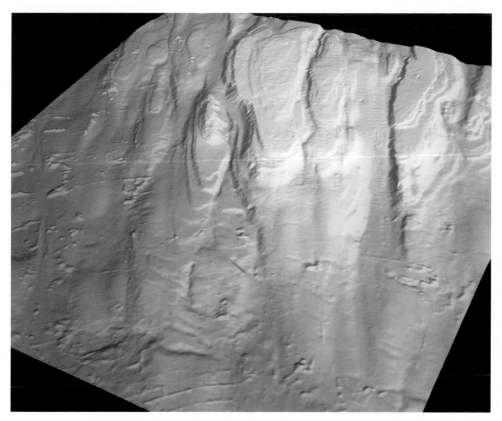

Fig. 22—A 3D view of the DEM created from the higher-altitude photography, showing the overall landscape setting.

shifts and stretches the image, it will never be correctly positioned at every point on the ground. This is caused by several factors, including scale change across the image, distortion owing to the camera lens, and changes in the topography across the ground. Orthophotos, or geometrically accurate images, correct the distortion in the raw aerial image by using the DEM to re-project the image to its true location. The process is akin to stretching the aerial photograph like a rubber sheet over the surface of the underlying topography. The resulting orthophoto images are outstanding in their clarity and detail. Each stone and branch (and unfortunately each sheep) on the plateau was preserved in glorious colour; more importantly, they could all be measured and plotted with a high degree of accuracy (Fig. 23). Using GIS software, we were then able to combine the information from the orthophotos with the DEM surfaces and create a 'draped' image to enhance the visualisation of the landscape in 3D (Fig. 24).

It didn't take long before our colleagues within the Discovery Programme viewed the results from Mullaghfarna with a certain envy and saw the potential

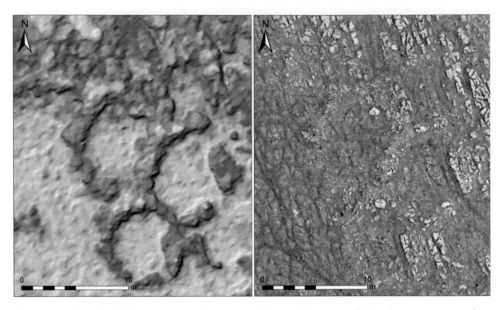

Fig. 23—On the left is a DEM plan view of a small section of the plateau, processed at the highest resolution and assigned a contoured colour-ramp to highlight those features cut into the rock surface. The image on the right is an orthophoto of the same area to aid interpretation.

Fig. 24—The low-level orthophoto draped over the DEM in GIS to give a 3D visualisation of the site.

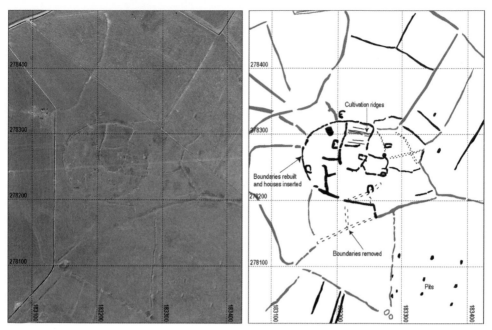

Fig. 25—An orthophoto extract and plan of a deserted settlement and church site at Carns, Co. Roscommon. The relict earthworks visible on the orthophoto were digitised to produce the accompanying metrically accurate plan. This proved ideal for mapping the general form of the settlement and associated field boundaries. The base map was subsequently modified using additional information derived from a combination of oblique aerial photographs, historical maps and fieldwork. Some poorly defined features were confirmed to be house sites, and a relative chronology was established based on evidence for modification and removal of certain earthen boundaries (interpretation and plan by Brian Shanahan, the Discovery Programme).

applications to their own research projects. In particular, the Medieval Rural Settlement team could see the benefit of this approach in their study of field systems in the north Roscommon area. As a result, our second photogrammetric survey was conceived. It consisted of an ambitious 70km² landscape survey, centred on Tulsk and including the renowned archaeological complex at Rathcroghan. The photography was again flown by BKS at 1:7,500 scale; our previous experience suggested that this would give sufficient detail of the landscape features while keeping the amount of processing to a manageable level. Even so, the project was a huge leap forward from the relatively small area surveyed at Mullaghfarna, so we decided to break it down into four quadrants. This meant a few extra ground control points were required, with the results being produced in stages, but it allowed the processing to progress smoothly.

Again the results were met with great excitement and enthusiasm, although this time it was the orthophotos themselves rather than the DEMs that proved most interesting. Viewing these in GIS, the research archaeologists could see clearly the relict field boundaries and other features and could compare them with early map depictions. It was therefore possible to begin to categorise and assign a chronology to the field remains (Fig. 25). For a few sites we increased the resolution of the DEM and then draped the orthophoto image to create effective 3D models (Fig. 26).

One interesting observation from the archaeologists was that, in some cases, it appeared that they could see more detail of archaeological features on the early oblique photography taken by Herity in the 1950s than on our new orthophoto images. This wasn't necessarily a surprise as the obliques would have been deliberately taken in raking sunlight in the hope of maximising the definition of low-relief archaeological features through the use of shadow. Unfortunately, to process images photogrammetrically we need to minimise the effect of shadow to reduce 'no data' areas in the DEMs. This seemed to be a major disadvantage until we tried to fit the early oblique photo to the orthophoto. In normal circumstances such a process is limited by the amount of map control available to carry out a rectification, but in this case the orthophoto provided unlimited reference points. Rectified in GIS, the detail visible on the early oblique photograph could be digitised and the details of this additional information

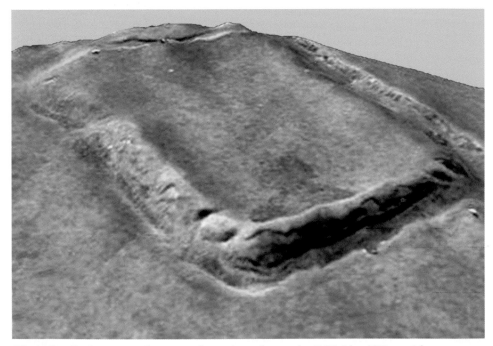

Fig. 26—Orthoimage of a moated site draped over the DEM in GIS to aid visualisation.

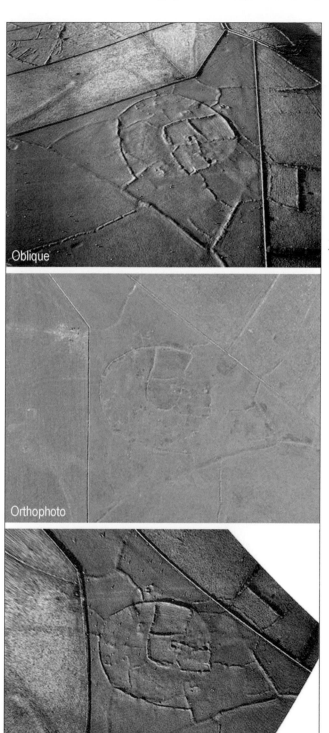

Fig. 27—The oblique image (top) shows the high level of detail visible on aerial photography taken from oblique angles in raking sunlight. Using common features also identifiable on the geospatially correct orthophoto (middle) as control points, the oblique image can be rectified to 'best fit' to the control. This rectified oblique image (bottom) shows that within the selected control, in this case features around the circular enclosure, significantly more detail can be mapped. The extreme distortion beyond the control shows that caution needs to be applied when rectifying images in this way (oblique image: Professor M. Herity).

added to the existing interpretation of archaeological features and field systems (Fig. 27).

From our tentative investigation into its potential use at Mullaghfarna, digital photogrammetry has now become an integral survey method employed by a number of research projects under the umbrella of the Discovery Programme. It is now recognised that for future projects with a landscape component the acquisition of aerial imagery will be a basic requirement. But, as always, technological developments don't stand still. Laser scanning from the air (LiDAR) is advancing and provides exciting possibilities for 3D modelling. Moreover, it has the advantage that it can penetrate vegetation such as bushes and trees. The latest helicopter-mounted systems point to remarkably accurate and detailed modelling, way beyond that achievable from photogrammetric systems. So we can rest assured that the challenge of applying new technology to the field of archaeology will continue for some time yet—with or without the groovy glasses.

Acknowledgements

We wish to express our thanks to the following: Dr Stefan Bergh, whose Mullaghfarna Project pushed us to investigate the potential of digital aerial photogrammetry; John McNally and the team at BKS, who helped enormously with their advice, technical support and patience; and finally all our colleagues at the Discovery Programme, who, as always, enthusiastically supported our research efforts.

Further reading

Bergh, S. 1995 *Landscape of the monuments: a study of the passage tombs in the Cuil Irra region, Co. Sligo.* Stockholm.

Macalister, R.A.S., Armstrong, E.C.R. and Praeger, R.L. 1912 Report on the exploration of Bronze Age cairns on Carrowkeel mountain, Co. Sligo. *Proceedings of the Royal Irish Academy* **29**C, 311–47.

www.discoveryprogramme.ie

20

Boswell's 'ogam'

John Waddell

S trange byways are one of the incidental pleasures of research, and they sometimes take you in peculiar directions. I first encountered Boswell's 'ogam' as I began work on the archaeology of the royal site of Rathcroghan, Co. Roscommon. When I came across a pamphlet entitled *Syllegomena of the antiquities of Killmackumpshaugh, in the county of Roscommon, and kingdom of Ireland, in which it is clearly proved that Ireland was originally peopled by Egyptians*, published in Dublin in 1790, I knew I had to check it out. Kilmacumsey is a parish adjacent to Rathcroghan and there was always the possibility that the writer had something to say about neighbouring antiquities. As it turned out, there was nothing about Rathcroghan there. The title-page declared that the work was printed in Dublin for the author, who is named as Doctor Hastler, M.R.S.P.Q.D.L.M.N.M.A.S.T. and L.L.Z. (a somewhat suspicious set of qualifications); sure enough, Isaac Weld in his *Statistical survey of the county of Roscommon*, published in 1832, indicated that the publication was a joke. Weld remarked: 'A few minutes' reading, however, serves to disclose the nature of the work, a mere production of fancy, written in burlesque of the antiquarian researches of the Academy. I had heard of this book, before, in the County of Roscommon, and that it was written by a clergyman for amusement, during confinement from gout. The sale of it produced well.'

A more detailed and gout-free explanation appeared some years later in *Notes and Queries* (4 November 1854):

'The real author of this work is John Whittley [*sic*] Boswell. We have before us a curious explanation, in his own handwriting, of the object and design of this satirical production, from which we extract a few passages. He states that "the design of the work was to ridicule a false taste which then prevailed for remote antiquarian speculations relative to Ireland, and the weak arguments used to support them, which on many occasions were even more palpably erroneous than those purposely misapplied here; for which purpose an affectation of learning is adopted, and minutely-refined modes of reasoning; of which there may be found many parallel instances in the works published *seriously* on those subjects. To show how easy it is to exhibit an appearance of knowledge on such occasions, which has no real foundation, the author has contrived to make a pompous exhibition of skill in Hebrew and the Irish tongue, with neither of which he had any acquaintance. A friend, Dr Wm Stokes, then studying Hebrew, by searching his Lexicon occasionally at the request of the author, supplied what relates to that language; and the Irish words inserted were acquired by questions directed to those who were well instructed in that ancient tongue, which probably was that of the Gauls in the time of Julius Caesar, as well as of Great Britain and Ireland . . . The name Hastler is fictitious, and was used without any particular design: at the time the work was written, the author was too young to assume the office of censor, having then just taken his degree of B.A. in the University of Dublin. He is well known to the Rev. Dr Burrowes of Enniskillen, Dr Whitley Stokes, Dr Miller, and others, in the university. The number of letters after Hastler, in the title-page, was merely designed to imitate the affected style of those who use this species of foppery." The work contains two folded engravings.'

Little is known about John Whitley Boswell. Though he is very briefly and quite appropriately noted in Rolf and Magda Loeber's recent *Guide to Irish fiction 1650–1900,* he does not figure in any of the usual dictionaries of biography. As *Alumni Dublinenses* records, he did indeed graduate from Trinity College, Dublin, in 1788, having entered, aged 17, in 1784. He was born in Dublin and was the son of a merchant also named John. A youthful William Stokes evidently helped him in this precocious prank, which must have offended some of the eminent members of the Royal Irish Academy. It may even have been encouraged by articles in the very first two volumes of the Academy's *Transactions.* The first volume, in 1787, contained an article entitled 'An Account of an Antient Inscription in Ogam Character on the Sepulchral Monument of an Irish Chief', by a student contemporary in Trinity College, Theophilus O'Flanagan. This was a description of a supposedly ancient ogam inscription found on Slievecallan, near Milltown Malbay, Co. Clare. While the Mount Callan ogam, as it became known, was the first stone of its kind to be published, it was not the memorial of 'Conan the fierce', a contemporary of Fionn mac Cumhaill, as O'Flanagan claimed. Its authenticity was debated for over a century and today it is believed to have been carved in all probability shortly before 1780.

The second issue of the *Transactions*, in 1788, contained a paper by Charles Vallancey on a very ordinary sixteenth-century grave-slab found at Lusk, Co. Dublin, that, in his usual fashion, was full of Egyptian, Persian and other exotic parallels. This was typical of his antiquarian work, and his belief in an eastern, Mediterranean or even Asiatic origin for the ancient Irish was often supported by wild linguistic speculation. It was this sort of antiquarianism that prompted Boswell's 53-page satirical pamphlet and its elaborate dedication to the members of the Royal Irish Academy:

> 'To you Gentlemen, permit me to dedicate the important discoveries contained in this little tract. You alone are adequate to comprehend their utility in its full force . . . Pardon my presumption in confessing, that I once had thoughts of soliciting a place for this work, in your yearly volume; but I soon gave over such vain thoughts, when I reflected how it would be lost in the splendour of the surrounding publications.'

The description of the antiquities of 'Killmackumpshaugh' follows, ostensibly the results of an exploration in 1786. Boswell and a friend first explore a cave, evidently a man-made souterrain, and then examine 'an antique building' some 50 paces to the south. In describing the souterrain he is struck by the resemblance to the passages in Egyptian pyramids, and a reference to 'Letters from Egypt, published in 1784', may be an allusion to Claude-Étienne Savary's influential *Letters on Egypt*, of which a Dublin edition appeared in 1787 and which contained a plan of the inside of the Great Pyramid. Boswell found some bones in the cave, and after lengthy study and with the aid of an ingenious invention of his own, 'a kind of micrometer, or instrument for measuring an imperceptible decay in bones', he is able to prove that they are nearly 2,600 years old.

After this analysis of the bones, involving complex mathematical calculations and the use of the 'multiplying wheels' on his micrometer, he turns his attention to the nearby building, which, since it has no altar at its eastern end, cannot be a Christian chapel. Because, he claims, there is a large stone within bearing ancient inscriptions, it has to be a place of heathen worship. The stone bears the figure of a bird, the representation of several nails, an ogam inscription 'but six inches long' and a Latin inscription. Boswell pretended to read the very short ogam inscription as 'The shrine of Belus, who is an eternal oracle, sacrifice to him'. A glance at the illustration he provides in his plate I shows that he has horizontally split the IHS inscription common on eighteenth-century gravestones to provide the spurious ogam, and the other figures such as the cock

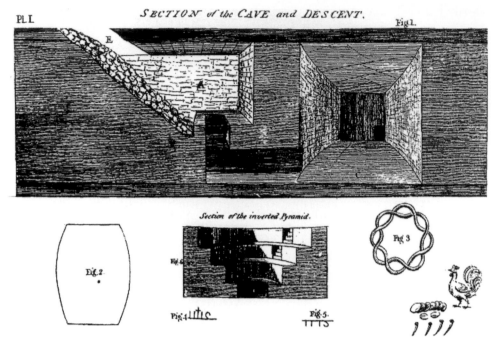

Fig. 28—A section of a souterrain supposedly at Kilmacumsey with vertical trapdoor or creep-hole is depicted in Boswell's plate 1. The 'ogham' (shown in his figs 4 and 5, bottom centre) is an IHS inscription (with the usual cross on the bar of the H) split horizontally. The items on the lower right (his fig. 3) comprise a crown of thorns, a cock, pieces of silver and nails, emblems of the Passion sometimes found on eighteenth- and early nineteenth-century grave-slabs.

and the nails are some of the emblems of the Passion occasionally carved on such stones (Fig. 28). He goes on to assert that there is a Latin inscription engraved lower down on the same limestone slab, which he claims to read with some difficulty. It supposedly begins with the words 'Praetores fortes Gracchus . . .' and is, he suggests, a reference to two Romans separated from Caesar's fleet who eventually settled in Ireland. His plate II (Fig. 29) reveals how he has deliberately and mischievously misrepresented an inscription that clearly reads 'Pray for the soul of father hugh flin'!

He also offers a brief description and a sketch of the 'antique building', which of course for him is not a church but a temple dedicated to the worship of Belus or Baal. His sketch lacks detail and bears little resemblance to the church remains at Kilmacumsey today, where just part of the western gable end and the lower parts of the south and north walls survive. According to Boswell, the structure measured 30ft by 16ft, but in fact the featureless remains at Kilmacumsey are about 15m (50ft) in length and about 5.5m (17ft) wide. There are no

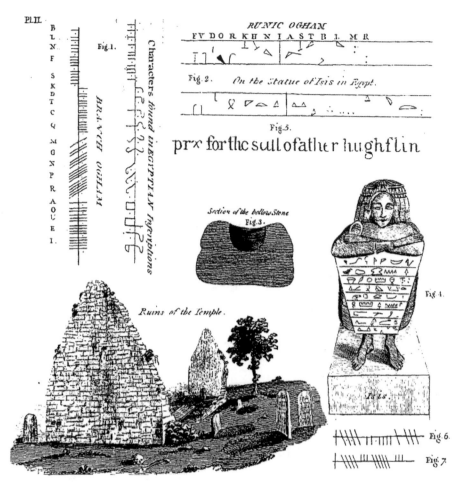

Fig. 29—Boswell's plate 2 includes a sketch of a church site and a section of a bullaun stone, neither of which bear comparison to the remains at Kilmacumsey today. His deliberately clumsy depiction of the alleged Latin inscription (his fig. 5) is clearly legible as 'Pray for the soul of father hugh flin'.

tombstones in the church or in its vicinity, and here Boswell's sketch must be taken as an imaginative exercise, if not entirely fictitious. Intriguingly, there is a large bullaun-like stone lying in the church. An unusual large circular perforation extends through the stone at the bottom of the hollow. Boswell does illustrate a 'hollow stone' (which he calls 'a well known emblem of Baal or Vulcan') in cross-section but without the basal hole so evident in the Kilmacumsey object. Today there is no trace of the souterrain, which is supposed to lie 50 paces north of the church, and it is impossible to know to what extent, if any, the section of the 'cave' he illustrates is an accurate depiction of an actual monument. A reference to 'a hole of about two feet square' through which he descends to a second chamber suggests a vertical creep-hole or trapdoor and some acquaintance with this sort of feature. There was also another small hole at the end of this chamber but it was blocked with earth and stones.

Wherever this souterrain was, it is not the one at Oweynagat in Rathcroghan, as suggested by Joseph Lennon in his recent *Irish Orientalism* (2004), and Boswell's invented ogam is of course not the genuine ogam inscription recorded at that famous site by Samuel Ferguson in 1867.

John Whitley Boswell deserves to be remembered for more than his ingenious nonsense on the antiquities of Kilmacumsey and his satire on the Vallancey school of Oriental antiquarianism. As his daft micrometer for assessing the age of bones might suggest, he had an interest in mechanics and mathematics. He figures briefly in the diaries of Theobald Wolfe Tone, who, in 1792 in Dublin, records:

> 'Breakfast in college. Boswell shows us a loom of his invention for weaving fishing nets which executes it completely with the fisherman's knot. He sent a sample to the Society for Encouraging the Arts in London, who had offered 60 guineas premium for such an invention. Several others put in their claim but his was the only one which answered. He would in consequence have got the award, only it was luckily discovered in time to prevent it that he was an *Irishman*, for which reason only did they refuse him. Wise and liberal! Boswell gives us a yard of his net which he wove before us.'

According to H. T. Wood in his *History of the Royal Society of Arts* (1913), Boswell was later given an award of some twenty guineas for his net-making machine.

In 1807 Boswell applied unsuccessfully for a position in London in the Royal Society of Arts and gave some details of his interests:

'My Lords and Gentlemen

Having been informed that the under Secretaryship of your Institution was vacant, I beg permission to propose myself for that situation; and hope my not doing so sooner will not be considered to be caused by any neglect, as in reality I knew nothing of the vacancy before last Wednesday; and applied next day to Dr. Taylor relative to it.

On an occasion, where it is to be expected that proper qualifications for an employment would be much more attended to than personal solicitation, I hope my not have been able to make use of the latter, will not be imputed to any want of attention, and that my mentioning my pretensions to the former will be considered as alone proceeding from its being absolutely necessary to enable the honourable Society to form a judgement on the subject.

I beg leave therefore to state, that for upwards of twenty years I have had my mind engaged in studying the usefull Arts, Mechanics, and the various branches of natural philosophy which apply to them; and that in that time I brought forward several useful mechanical inventions before the public; for two of which I have had the honour of the highest remunerations given by the honourable Society, having been voted a premium of fifty guineas for one Invention, and the Gold medal for the other; and two more of which remain in your repository, which you have done me the favour to accept.

I have also for the last four years been engaged in endeavours to bring forward a branch of the Arts, the most useful to the greatest commercial nation in the universe, consisting of a method of building ships with smaller timber, and possessing superior strength; (which would demonstrably facilitate the supply of timber for the Navy, so as effectually to remove the great difficulties that department labours under in this respect;) the strength and efficacy of which I have proved in the most compleat manner at a very heavy expense to my friends and myself, by a ship built on this construction; whose good properties in every way have been, in the most trying weather, in the fullest manner demonstrated. For my information on other subjects, which engage the attention of the honourable society, I have to refer to various papers, which I have published in the Philosophical Journal, and in the Repertory of Arts.

My qualifications for the literary part of the employment, are I hope much as would be deemed sufficient; I several years ago graduated in that university which was formed after the model of Cambridge, and where the sciences are equally attended to; and in the last two years, during the intervals of my attention to the ship before mentioned, have edited and prepared for publication some hundred papers, on Arts Manufactures and, for various periodical works, to the proprietors of which I can refer if necessary.

For personal recommendation and other qualifications, I can refer to Mr. Bonnycastle mathematical Professor of the Royal Academy at Woolwich, and to Wm. Lushington Esq. formerly representative for the City, and to Revd. Dr. Rees and to other gentlemen of respectability and learning.

Should I be so fortunate to meet the approbation of the honourable society, I will endeavour to the best of my power to discharge my duty so as to give satisfaction; and also to promote the views of the society; which I hope might in some degree be advanced by the appointment, as it would enable me to bring forward to publick notice several useful inventions that I have already perfected; and some others of considerable importance, that want of time and opportunity cause to remain still unproved.

My Lords and Gentlemen your most humble and respectfull obedient servant.

John Whitley Boswell.

Feb. 12 1807'

The inventive Boswell had indeed published various articles. His 'Description of a machine for netting' appeared in Vol. 14 of the *Transactions of the Society for the Encouragement of the Arts*, and his 'Description of a Capstan, which works without requiring the Messenger or Cable coiled round it to be ever surged' was published in Vol. 31 of the *Philosophical Magazine* in 1808. Other publications included 'A description of a new instrument called the Blast Ventilator'; 'Improvements in the Hydraulic Engine at Schemnitz, and that of Mr Goodwyn's, with comparative remarks on the most useful applications of each, and some facts relative to the invention of the pressure Engine'; 'Observations on the different degrees of facility with which masses of the same material admit of changes in their temperature; with applications of the facts to the construction of Pendulums, and speculations upon various new forms of pendulous Regulators of Time'; 'Construction of a line in a circle equal to the side of a square of the same superficies as that of the circle itself; with Remarks on Pendulums and other objects'; and 'Description of a new Parallel Rule exempt from lateral deviation'. These all appeared in *Nicholson's Journal* in 1801, 1802, 1805 and 1806. *Nicholson's Journal*—or, more accurately, the *Journal of Natural Philosophy, Chemistry and the Arts* (1797–1814)—is famous as the first journal of its kind in Britain and an important step in the history of science and engineering. Whatever about the antiquities of 'Killmackumpshaugh', it does seem that John Whitley Boswell himself is worthy of more research.

Acknowledgements

My thanks to Michelle Comber for inspecting Kilmacumsey with me, and the RSA (the Royal Society for the Encouragement of Arts, Manufactures and Commerce, London) for providing me with a copy of Boswell's letter (AD.MA/100/10/81). Linde Lunney (Dictionary of Irish Biography) kindly drew my attention to the reference to Boswell in T. W. Moody *et al.*, *The writings of Theobald Wolfe Tone*, Vol. 1 (1998), 233.

21

'Chalices have wings'

Małgorzata Krasnodębska-D'Aughton

'Chalices have wings', said Father Ignatius knowingly, when I spoke to him in the wonderful library of Dún Mhúire in Killiney. That chalices have wings was one of the first and most important lessons I learned as I embarked on this project in March 2004.

The project, which is being carried out by the UCD Mícheál Ó Cléirigh Institute, aims at making an inventory of portable ecclesiastical artefacts associated with the mendicant orders in Ireland pre-dating Catholic Emancipation. Originally the focus was solely on artefacts within Irish Franciscan houses. Later, with funding from the IRCHSS, the scope was extended to other mendicant orders.

So for more than four years I have been trotting through the country, visiting various religious houses, meeting wonderful people, sharing their meals and occasionally availing of their baby-sitting skills, as well as discovering some truly wonderful treasures. Each place has left a particular imprint on my memory, and each has been marked by a particular sense of discovery: the discovery of previously unrecorded treasures, of vast collections, or indeed the discovery of a story enclosed within those very treasures. Ornate and simple chalices, crucifixes and crosses of all shapes, numerous patens, pyxes, monstrances and sculptural pieces have become my daily bread: each of them carefully photographed, measured, described and subsequently researched. While each object is interesting in its own right, it is the chalices that I find especially appealing.

The first port of call was the Franciscan library in Killiney, where Fr Ignatius Fennessy, OFM, with his usual graciousness shared his knowledge on the subject with me. His notes, paper cuttings, books, letters, old photographs, drawings and rubbings of artefacts all proved invaluable. He himself had already started to make an inventory of Franciscan altar plate. In Killiney I came across lists of altar

Pl. 76—The Crucifixion: detail of the Malachy O'Queely chalice, 1640.

plate made by other friars, such as Fr Cathaldus Giblin, Fr Kevin McGrath and Fr Patrick Conlan. When I visited the Franciscan friary at Merchants' Quay in Dublin, Fr Patrick told me more about the chalices in various Franciscan houses that he had noted in the 1990s.

Examining page after page of Buckley's invaluable book on Irish altar plate, comparing it with notes taken in Killiney, I made a provisional list of objects that I expected to see in different places. Later, when I visited the Augustinians in Ballyboden, Dublin, I got to read the notes on their altar plate written by Fr F. X. Martin. Daphne Pochin Mould provided me with more information on the Dominican artworks. It was at once exciting and challenging to be following in the footsteps of these scholars.

Of course, Fr Ignatius was right: chalices have wings, they fly away, and they are not always where you expect to find them. I remember my disappointment at not seeing the Malachy O'Queely chalice where I thought it would be. I knew this chalice from photographs and descriptions, and I knew of its 'supposed' whereabouts. The chalice was made for Malachy O'Queely, archbishop of Tuam, and given to the convent of Friars Minor in Rosserrilly in 1640. O'Queely, a native of County Clare, received the degree of doctor of divinity in Paris. On his return to Ireland he was appointed vicar apostolic of Killaloe in 1622, and in 1631 became archbishop of Tuam. In 1643 he attended the National Synod in Kilkenny, where the Catholic Confederation was organised, and was elected to the Supreme Council. In 1645 he sought to recover the port of Sligo from the Scots. Unfortunately, the archbishop was killed during the Scottish attack on the Confederate camp at Ballysodare. I read speedily about him, thinking about his eventful life as an ecclesiastic, a politician and a patriot. It took two further visits to other Franciscan houses to 'find' the chalice. Finally, there it was: a richly decorated piece of high-quality workmanship with beautiful floral decorations delicately engraved on the bowl, and on its foot a great Crucifixion image (Pl. 76) and the archbishop's coat of arms.

Each object has its own story to tell. Looking at the object I admire its beauty, but it is the story behind that object which makes it really sparkle. There is the chalice donated by Francis Guiffe to the Franciscan convent of Kilconnell on 27 July 1638, as declared by an inscription running around its foot. The knop is made with great finesse from openwork ovals and circles, filled with openwork crosses (Pl. 77). The Crucifixion image on its foot, depicting Christ's body, is well modelled, the sun and the moon witnessing the event. Francis Guiffe was made guardian of the Franciscan friary of Kilconnell at the provincial chapter on 9 October 1658. The friary, founded around 1414 for Conventual Franciscans, was suppressed in the Cromwellian period. F. J. Bigger, in his paper published in 1900, paints a gloomy picture of the friary's fate at that period: 'Then the end came and the friars were driven to the bogs; the bells had sounded their last angelus and the roofs had fallen in, exposing to time's devastation some of the richest and rarest of man's handiwork dedicated to God's glory . . .' (p. 146). It was at that time that a certain Brian O'Flaherty fled to Brussels, taking with him other chalices and vestments belonging to the monastery of Kilconnell. The Guiffe chalice remained in Ireland, but was given for safekeeping to a local family in 1698 following the act of banishment. In 1901 it came to the friary at Merchant's Quay, Dublin.

Many chalices left Ireland and returned here through circuitous routes, in themselves telling stories about the nation. A simple Franciscan chalice made for the chapel of Claregalway in 1687 travelled the world for a century and a half

Pl. 77—The knop: detail of the Francis Guiffe chalice, 1638.

before returning to Galway in 1998. It was used by the friars until 1847. In that year, during the Famine, Fr James Hughes used it while ministering to the sick in the parish of Oranmore, Co. Galway. When he himself fell sick he returned to Galway, leaving the chalice behind him. He died a few days later. It is not clear what happened next to the chalice. It was eventually entrusted to Anne Laracey 'during the time of anti-Catholic trouble', as stated in the family's correspondence with the friars, copies of which are kept in Killiney. She passed the chalice to her son, Joseph Michael Finnerty. It travelled with him when he fought with the First Connaught Rangers in the Boer War, and later when he was stationed at the Tower of London with the Irish Guards. Joseph Michael took the chalice to New York in 1926. He gave it to his daughter, Mary Dorothea, in about 1937. The chalice then travelled with her and her husband, Clarence

Pl. 78—The James FitzSymon
monstrance, 1664.

Pl. 79—Detail of the James FitzSymon
monstrance, 1664.

Appleby, when they moved from New York to Illinois, to California and to Oregon, before returning once again to California. Mary Dorothea tried over the years to return the chalice to the Galway friars. Finally, she entrusted the chalice to her son, John J. Appleby. He contacted his cousin, Canon Hilary Wakeman of the Church of Ireland in West Cork, who subsequently returned the chalice to the Galway Franciscans. Thus the chalice went from Ireland to Africa, to England and America and back to Ireland within the space of 150 years.

The troubled seventeenth century also produced a magnificent silver monstrance decorated with numerous angelic faces. It was commissioned for the Friars Minor by James FitzSymon in 1664, when he was guardian of Dublin (Pls 78–9). Once again, research unveils the story behind an object. James FitzSymon went under the name of Don Jaime Nochera, doing espionage work in London for Irish interests in the 1640s. In 1646 he became confessor to the Poor Clares in Galway. In 1647 he acted as army chaplain. He became guardian of Multyfarnham in 1647 and 1649, and army chaplain again in 1650. In 1661 he was guardian of Dublin. He must have been a colourful character: an Irish Franciscan pretending to be a Spaniard in London!

It is a real privilege to be allowed to see these treasures, to feel a tangible connection with the past and with the people whose names are carefully recorded in neat engravings. Turning the chalice slowly and reading word after word of an inscription feels like turning the pages of a history book. Many chalices were reused in later centuries; they bear nineteenth-century inscriptions, but their shape and style betray a much earlier craftsmanship. Some are connected with the history of more than one mendicant order. For example, a 1641 chalice displaying an image of St Francis receiving the stigmata was offered to the Dominicans. Another inscription shows that a chalice depicting SS Dominic, Thomas Aquinas, Catherine of Siena and Peter Martyr, all Dominican saints, was offered to the Augustinians in and around the 1630s by a Jacobus Kennedy. Some chalices continue to be used liturgically to the present day: in 2004 the Sinan chalice, made in 1600, was used to celebrate the requiem Mass of Jack Sinan.

Apart from the precious silverware, I have come across more modest artefacts that have been recorded only sporadically in secondary literature. Among the simpler works are the pewter chalices, known more frequently as penal chalices. These are plain chalices, often lopsided and chipped, at times accompanied by an equally worn paten. They were used by Irish Catholics to celebrate Mass secretly during the era of the Penal Laws. They consist of three parts: a bowl, a stem and a foot that could be detached, and each part could then easily slip into the other (Pl. 80). In that ingenious way, a chalice could be neatly hidden in one's pocket.

Pl. 80—Pewter chalice.

Not so long ago, during a working trip to Cork I made a brief visit to one of the friaries outside Cork city. I did not know of any artefacts of any historical importance preserved in that church. It was to be a routine check, a 'just-in-case' visit. The prior presented me with a lovely silver chalice bearing an 1847 inscription on its bowl. It seemed too late for the current project, whose terminus is 1829. Nevertheless, the style of the chalice, its shape and the script of the engraving recording the name of Fr Mahony on the foot all seemed to point to the 1780s. The prior, accompanied by another friar, told me that the chalice is known as the 'penal chalice'. I mentioned to them that pewter penal chalices can be easily unscrewed and split into three parts. After a careful examination of the chalice, we removed the bowl from the stem. Under the mid-nineteenth-century bowl was hidden an original eighteenth-century top! All three of us looked at it with excitement and disbelief. This discovery made our day. And it would not have been possible without the accommodating attitude of the two friars.

The project is ongoing. An ever-growing inventory of the Franciscan, Dominican, Augustinian, Capuchin and Carmelite artefacts is showing a wealth of artwork associated with the respective orders. I hope that in time it will allow for a more in-depth comparative work between the artwork of various orders, as well as a more detailed study on various artefacts. There are, of course, artefacts held in museums around the country, there are artefacts in parish churches, in

Pl. 81—The houses of 'Tarant Street'.

contrast there were a number of outstandingly ambitious projects, including the establishment of entirely new settlements. These were often industrial schemes, for example Prosperous, Co. Kildare, which attempted cotton production. A fishing station in the Rosses would also be built as an entirely new settlement, with facilities to process and transport fish, as well as houses for workers and a dockyard for ship repairs. Burton Conyngham chose the small island of Inismacduirn, largely for its sheltered, deep-water harbour. He renamed it Rutland, in honour of the lord lieutenant, and construction work on the settlement began in 1783. Other infrastructural improvements included the establishment of a mainland harbour at Burtonport and the upgrading of the road from it to Mount Charles in the south of the county.

As I left Burtonport for my first visit to Rutland, the island presented itself as a low, undulating body with grass broken by occasional granite outcrops. The shores on the eastern side are rocky; the west side is a long sandy beach. Breaking the skyline towards the centre of the island was a sight that remains out of place in rural Donegal to this day: a street of terraced houses (Pl. 81). This was the first indication that something might remain of the Rutland settlement. My confidence in this clue was provided by one of the great advantages in carrying out historical archaeology—an accurate map and a series of documentary

Pl. 82—'Union Store' and quay.

references. The map evidence was a series of plans depicting the island before, during and after the construction of the settlement. These provided an insight into the location of native settlement pre-dating the station, the planned extent of the station and the actual finished build. The planned fishing station was to have extensive quays and storehouses connected by a road network. There were also three planned residential streets for workers. As the island is approached, the channel between it and neighbouring Edernish comes into view. Here was the harbour where 300–400 vessels anchored 'perfectly secure' in the winter of 1786. According to the plans for the station, most of the facilities should be located along its rocky shores. Spying a sheltered baylet on the coast of the island, I steered the boat carefully through the rocks and tied up at a new quay below a holiday home. Above me stood a large, unroofed warehouse. Known as Union Store (Pl. 82), the building was part of the eighteenth-century fishery and is depicted on a contemporary plan. It was built on a flat area between the main island and a small islet and featured quays to the north and south. Examination of the rock faces of the island and islet revealed many tubular quarry marks, and it became obvious that the quarrying had provided the flat surface of the quays and the stone for the store. One historian, on examining the maps of the planned settlement, had noted that some of the streets and buildings were in the water and so considered the document unreliable. In fact the lines in the sea were quays, and the area behind them provided space for the fishery buildings—the maps were impressively accurate. The enclosed baylet, flat quay and walls of the store provided fine shelter for me to pitch my tent on the uninhabited island. I

257

would spend the next two weeks identifying and recording the remains of the fishing station, with only Rutland's foxes for company.

The remaining monuments to the fishing enterprise did not disappoint. Towards the north of the island another massive reclamation project overlooking the deepest part of the harbour had created Conyngham Quay—100m long and incorporating another small, quarried islet that provided building stone. Set on the quay were the main processing centres: three massive gables protruded from the sand-dunes that had migrated across the island during early nineteenth-century storms. Three storeys high, they extended west towards the main street, where they were connected by a long north–south spine. These buildings would have housed the cooper's stores and salt for preserving and barrelling the fish for export. They also contained a 'Sailor's Inn' for visiting crews, and a custom house. Rutland was not the only island to feature remains of the enterprise, as nearby Edernish and Inishcoo also border the Rutland channel. On Edernish the map evidence was to prove crucial in locating the cork stores among the thick bracken undergrowth. These two buildings had originally extended onto the beach, although erosion had reduced part of the site to its foundations. A small quay was also located conveniently to the site. Further north were the remains of the saltworks, a vital component of the scheme. Located at sea level for ease of saltwater extraction, they had also suffered from erosion. A central building, which would have housed the evaporating pans, could be discerned, as well as the outline of a rough landing-stage. On Inishcoo a dockyard was constructed for the building and repair of fishing vessels. This comprised a large quay overlooking a sandy basin where vessels could be laid up for cleaning. The low remains of a shipbuilder's house and forge could also be detected.

Archaeological survey had shown that Burton Conyngham's fishing station was designed to suit the requirements of a modern, improved fishing fleet. Ships arriving in the deep-water anchorage of Rutland harbour could offload their catches on Conyngham Quay. The herring would be gutted and salted using locally produced salt from the pans on Edernish. They would then be packed in barrels, ready for transhipment. Eventually exports could be carried out directly from Rutland owing to the establishment of a customs office (Pl. 83). Meanwhile, ships' captains could have their vessels inspected and repaired at the Inishcoo dockyard, where fittings or lost anchors and chain could be replaced in the forge by the resident shipbuilder. Other equipment, such as nets, rope and cork, could be purchased from the stores. Crew could be refreshed in the Sailor's Inn and then load barrels of fish back onto their vessel while their master settled his bill with customs and the fishing station bookkeeper. Rutland also had its own fishing crews, and timber was imported to build suitable vessels on site. Thus the station not only profited from efficient processing of catches for export

Pl. 83—The interior of the large customs house and stores, now partially inundated by blown sand.

but also pocketed the direct proceeds of its own fishing activities. In the 1780s the catches continued to be enormous. In 1784–5 the fishery was worth £40,000; it employed 3,300 men and 339 vessels totalling 16,245 tons, with a further 600 boats from other areas. Unfortunately the situation did not last; in the 1790s catches were down, and the fickle herring deserted the coast altogether by the end of the century. The Rutland complex is a remarkable eighteenth-century survival, owing no doubt to the encroaching sands, the lack of attempts to revive the fishing industry (although this was much discussed) and its remote location. Indeed, more remains of the eighteenth-century fishing station than of the Congested District Board fishery works on Edernish 100 years later.

Burton Conyngham's ambitious improvement scheme also had a social impact on the Rosses. He needed a range of ability from outside the district and duly appealed to American loyalists for their fishing skills, English farmers for converting bog to agricultural land, and a range of craftsmen for building work. He is generally believed to have been relatively unsuccessful; only one of the three planned residential streets for this skilled workforce was built. Some families from outside the district did, however, arrive and stay after the enterprise failed, taking positions at the post office or customs. Burton Conyngham had a poor view of the native inhabitants of the area, calling them his 'ignorant and indolent tenantry'. Most of their dwellings were swept away to make room for the new station, but a few did survive and their inhabitants are mentioned in the estate papers of the early nineteenth century as continuing to be resident on the island. Local people did have skills to offer: they knew their local fishing grounds, acted as pilots and knew how to make hemp nets and a little salt. It seems that some of them found a place within the new scheme. Nevertheless, Burton Conyngham's new tenants were intended to set an example to the locals. Not only would the process of fishing be large-scale, modern and efficient, but the houses constructed for new workers stood in direct contrast to the one-room cabins of the islanders. Built of dressed granite and red brick with slate roofs, the houses of the street presented a typically Georgian, symmetrical façade. The interior of each house was subdivided into rooms, reflecting new ideas on space, order and standards of privacy. The houses were two-storey, an uncommon sight in rural Ireland until the mid-nineteenth century (Pl. 81). The little colony also introduced new items further reflecting 'polite' society. Surface collection of artefacts eroding from Conyngham Quay and the gardens behind the street yielded not only functional blackware (probably used as herring jars) but also a fragment of a salt-glazed stoneware plate. This was part of a set of matching tableware. Dining with individual crockery and cutlery was also a part of modern 'civilised' society, and these items would not become available to islanders until cheap imitations were produced in the nineteenth century.

While some inhabitants of the Rosses found a place within the Rutland fishery, the majority were excluded, and at least some regarded the scheme as a threat to their livelihood. Accustomed to moving cattle from the mountains to the islands in winter, they supplemented their diet by fishing local waters. The massive building work and its intention to harvest local stocks efficiently must have seemed like one more way for a reforming landlord to harness a resource hitherto regarded as commonage. Their response is recorded in the *Belfast Newsletter* of May 1786, which noted an incident of the mountain tenants attacking the Rutland settlement and driving out the inhabitants. Although ultimately unsuccessful in disrupting the progress of the works, the action does show the degree of alienation felt towards the scheme. There is no record of Burton Conyngham taking any steps to alleviate such hostility; like most improvers, his actions were primarily intended to secure greater profits for his estate without necessarily involving or improving the lives of his tenants.

As an antiquarian, no doubt William Burton Conyngham would have been surprised and bemused to learn that future archaeologists would take an interest in the monuments he created. Antiquarians of the eighteenth century generally disregarded the monuments of recent centuries in favour of cromlechs and Dane's raths of the distant past. Nevertheless, archaeological techniques can sharpen our view of the 'familiar' past, and test accepted historical interpretation. By examining Burton Conyngham's endeavour we can learn not only about the organisation of the fishing station, its facilities and fate, but also about the attitudes of both the landowning class and the impoverished. To modern eyes, the degree of social exclusion evident in the scheme is questionable, but to Burton Conyngham and his contemporaries many facets of the changes being wrought on Donegal society and landscape were considered normal and desirable. All archaeologists work within the values and attitudes of their own period, and this is as true today as it was in Burton Conyngham's time. Inevitably, the archaeological work we carry out and the interpretations we make in our time will also become subject to shifting social attitudes and archaeological analyses.

Acknowledgements

I wish to thank the Heritage Council, who sponsored a further phase of the survey work on Rutland Island under the 2003 Archaeology Grant Scheme.

Select bibliography

Forsythe, W. 2006 Improving insularity: an archaeology of the islands off the north coast of Ireland in the later historic period, 1700–1847. Unpublished Ph.D thesis, University of Ulster, Coleraine.

Kelly, J. 1985 William Burton Conyngham and the north-west fishery of the eighteenth century. *Journal of the Royal Society of Antiquaries of Ireland* **115**, 64–85.

Trench, C.E.F. 1985 William Burton Conyngham (1733–1796). *Journal of the Royal Society of Antiquaries of Ireland* **115**, 40–63.

Trench, C.E.F. 1987 William Burton Conyngham, 'profound scholar and antiquary', 1733–1796. *Ríocht na Midhe* **8** (1), 113–28.

Waddell, J. 2005 *Foundation myths: the beginnings of Irish archaeology.* Bray.

23

A stitch in time: fastening the 'Tara' brooch

Niamh Whitfield

One effective way of studying ancient technologies and processes is through experiment. Such experiments have taken many forms. In England, for example, there is Butser Farm in Hampshire, which aims to create a working version of an Iron Age farmstead so that results can be compared with evidence excavated from archaeological sites. In Denmark the Lejre Experimental Centre carries out projects on such diverse topics as Bronze Age and Iron Age burials, prehistoric science and stone tool manufacture in the absence of flint. A well-known Irish example of experimental archaeology is the late Professor M. J. ('Brian') O'Kelly's cooking experiments with *fulachta fiadh*, pits in which water was brought to the boil by heated stones.

In contrast, my own endeavours in this field have been modest and low-tech in the extreme. In the tests I am about to describe the only 'tools' I needed were a darning needle, a ball of wool, a pair of scissors and a length of tweed. How did I come to present myself at the Victoria and Albert Museum in London and the Ulster Museum in Belfast bearing such items, together with a camera to record what I did?

The problem I was hoping to solve concerned the 'Tara' brooch (Pls 84 and 85), an object made in the seventh or eighth century AD, probably in the early medieval kingdom of Brega between the Boyne and the Liffey. In the stratified society of early medieval Ireland such a splendid object was worn as an insignia of rank. But it probably also served the practical purpose of fastening the woollen cloth worn over a tunic by its aristocratic owner. The question I wanted to answer— 'How did it work?'—could not be resolved by looking at the object in its glass case in the Treasury of the National Museum of Ireland. Something else was needed.

I was prompted to think about this by the following events. As everyone

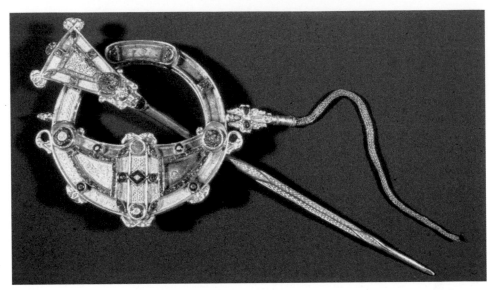

Pl. 84—The front of the 'Tara' brooch, showing (i) the loops at the junctions of the hoop and terminals probably for stitching; (ii) the silver chain; (iii) the projecting beast head on the perimeter opposite the attachment for the chain, which acts as a stop when the brooch is worn. The pin cannot lie at the angle shown here when the brooch is fastened. (Photo: National Museum of Ireland.)

Pl. 85—The back of the 'Tara' brooch, showing, in addition, (i) the C-shaped loop on the back of the pin head through which the hoop slots; (ii) the lug on the back of the H-shaped link for the chain to which a cord may have been attached (photo: National Museum of Ireland).

knows, one sure way to learn is to teach. The first thing that had spurred me into action occurred five years ago, when I led a group of my adult students from Morley College, London, around the Treasury in the National Museum. We were accompanied by, among others, Marian Campbell of the Metalwork Department of the Victoria and Albert Museum, an expert in the metalwork of the Middle Ages. As we stood looking at the 'Tara' brooch, many people's eyes were particularly caught by the matching small holes on the left and right at the halfway point at the junction of the hoop and the terminals. What were they for? I had not given this serious consideration before and was not able to come up with a very satisfactory answer. But afterwards Marian discreetly took me aside and told me that in the later Middle Ages it was common for heavy brooches to be sewn in place through similar little holes on the perimeter. Perhaps, she suggested, the 'Tara' brooch was also stitched in place.

This made me think again about the accuracy of a drawing that I had earlier asked the archaeological illustrator Nick Griffiths to do on my behalf, showing the 'Tara' brooch as it might have been worn. This was based on guesswork, and I wondered if it was right.

It seemed to me that a new drawing was needed, and I asked Nick if he would do one. He looks at things with an independent eye and a big advantage of working with him is that it is always a collaborative venture. But how exactly would the 'Tara' brooch look if it was stitched in place? Nick and I just could not agree, and I was left wondering how to resolve the issue. I could hardly ask the curators in the National Museum to take the 'Tara' brooch, one of their greatest treasures, out of its case just so that I could play with it to see how it worked. The answer would have been a very firm 'No', and such reputation as I may have had for common sense would have been shredded. I was stuck.

Then I remembered that the Victoria and Albert Museum's fine collection of nineteenth-century replicas of Irish brooches includes a very accurate one of the 'Tara' brooch by the nineteenth-century jeweller Joseph Johnson, which is to scale and about the right weight. Would Marian allow me to try out various fastening methods on this? She was as interested as I was in resolving the dilemma and agreed. The Ulster Museum has a slightly different replica of the 'Tara' brooch by Edmond (not Joseph) Johnson and Co., and the then Keeper of Antiquities there, Richard Warner, also kindly said that I could do some tests. So I was in business.

Why was the question of how the 'Tara' brooch fastened so hard to answer? The reason is that it followed a new design that made attaching it to the cloak especially difficult.

Previously, in the sixth to seventh centuries, the fashionable type of cloak-fastener in Ireland was the penannular brooch. As its current name (derived from

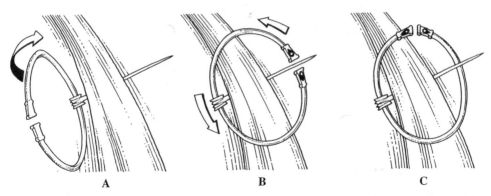

Fig. 31—Three steps in the fastening of a penannular brooch (drawing: Nick Griffiths).

the Latin *paene*, 'almost', and *annulus*, 'a circle') suggests, this was almost completely circular, but had a break through which a moveable pin attached to the hoop could slot. Brooches of this type are extremely easy to fix in place. As Fig. 31 shows, all one has to do is to stick the pin though two overlapping bits of the cloth. The pin itself must be pinned at exactly the desired angle, because it stays put. But the brooch head can be picked up and swivelled round. The aim is to get the pin to lie *over* the hoop. To achieve this the brooch head is rotated until the pin lies in the gap between the two decorative expanded 'terminals' flanking it. One terminal is then passed *under* the pin and the brooch head is rotated some more. Once this is done, the brooch becomes firmly locked in place and cannot be dislodged without rotating the brooch head backwards. Indeed, it anchors the brooch so firmly that in Morocco and Tunisia, where penannular brooches are still worn, heavy components such as medallions or chains are often suspended from very small penannular brooches. All this may sound complicated, but it isn't. Try testing a simple penannular brooch made out of bits of wire cut from a coat-hanger, and you will see for yourself.

Irish penannular brooches of the sixth to seventh centuries were made of copper alloy and decorated chiefly, if not always exclusively, on the terminals with either dainty spiral patterns set against an enamel background or with minuscule multicoloured patterned glass pieces ('millefiori') set in enamel. Though by some standards such brooches were very ornate, they must have seemed very dowdy and old-fashioned to their owners when in the sixth and seventh centuries the Irish, through their missionary activities, came into contact with the glittering gold and garnet jewellery worn by the aristocracy of Germanic Europe, particularly by the Anglo-Saxons, Franks and Lombards.

The Irish were clearly impressed, because they completely redesigned their traditional penannular brooch to produce a new compass-drawn type, of which the 'Tara' brooch (Pls 84 and 85) and the larger Hunterston brooch (discovered on the coast of Ayreshire in south-west Scotland) are the two finest surviving examples.

Like Germanic disc-brooches, the new Irish type was decorated on the front with gold filigree, colourful inlays and ornate studs, but it also retains many of the features of the earlier penannular brooch. In each case the brooch is attached to the garment by a pin that swivels around the hoop. There is a buffer at each end of the hoop to stop it slipping off, and beyond these buffers there are decorated terminals. But from a practical point of view there is one very important difference in design between the old and the new: on the new style of brooch, the gap through which the pin of the penannular brooch slotted has been closed. The type is labelled 'pseudo-penannular' because, although the presence of a gap between the terminals is acknowledged in the design, the brooch is fully circular. Simpler terms used to describe each type are 'open-ring' and 'closed-ring' brooch.

Closing the gap meant abandoning the very effective fastening method of the penannular or 'open-ring' brooch, and a new method of attaching the brooch to the cloak had to be devised. What could this have been?

Before trying to answer that question, it is important to explain that the pin on the 'Tara' brooch is attached to the brooch head by means of a large, reversed C-shaped loop on the back of the pin head, which cannot be removed (Pl. 85). The relatively large size of this loop makes it possible to rotate the pin head in two planes. First, it can be moved back and forth around the circumference of the hoop from approximately 9 o'clock to 3 o'clock. This is why the pin head appears in different positions in different photographs. Second, the pin as a whole can be picked up and rotated on its own axis from front to back to describe almost a full circle of 360°. Therefore the pin, as Pls 84 and 85 show, can lie not only *under* the brooch head but also *over* it. It will be remembered that the latter is what occurs when the penannular brooch is fastened.

I should also explain what type of textile I used in my experiments. I was not able to obtain a precise replica of any known weaves, which in any event represent a very small sample of what originally existed. Instead I used the fairly lightweight piece of tweed illustrated in Pls 86–89 (Harris, I fear, rather than Donegal, since this is what was most readily available in London, where I now live). It was not very thick but was strong enough to support the weight of even the heaviest brooch. Moreover, although it was not especially loosely woven, it was easy to stick the thickest brooch pin through the fabric without damaging it. When the pin was withdrawn a small hole was left, but it was easy to return the cloth to its original appearance by running one's finger over the hole. Purple was the colour of the cloaks worn by the most powerful members of society in early

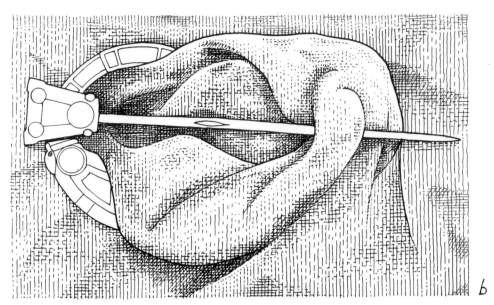

Fig. 32—A possible way of fastening the Hunterston brooch by pulling the fabric through the hole in the brooch head and sticking the tip of the pin through the fabric before pulling it back through the brooch head (drawing: Nick Griffiths).

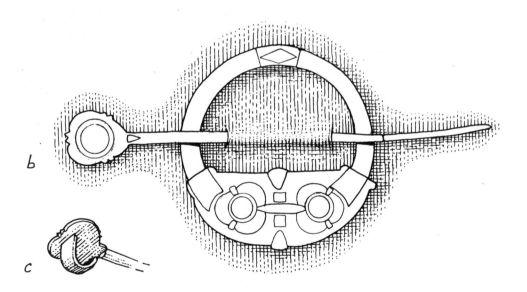

Fig. 33—Fastening the County Cavan brooch by detaching the pin, including back view of pin head showing the gap at the base of the loop and the pin head (drawing: Nick Griffiths).

medieval Ireland, surely the class to which the owner of the 'Tara' brooch belonged. But I confess that I again broke with authenticity by using a piece of brown tweed: that was what was available in the shop.

So what did my tests reveal about the way the 'Tara' brooch could be fastened? The first thing I found was that some methods, feasible in other cases, could be ruled out.

One was to mimic the fastening method of the penannular brooch and make the pin lie *over* the hoop by the rather drastic means of pulling enough cloth through the hole in the centre of the brooch head to make it possible to skewer the cloth with the tip of the pin before pulling it back through the hole. The Victoria and Albert Museum's collection includes a replica of the Hunterston brooch from Ayrshire, similar in many respects to the 'Tara' as well as many other early Irish brooches, and I found that in the case of the former it was possible to attach the brooch in this way (Fig. 32), though I had to be very careful not to damage the replica.

The critical factors are the size of the hole in the centre of the brooch head and the length of the pin. The pin of the Hunterston brooch is broken and now at least fairly short, but I could have pulled more cloth through if necessary. The Hunterston brooch is large (external diameter 12cm; maximum width of the central hole *c.* 8.5cm), and, as just explained, the broken pin now, at least, is short (length *c.* 13.1cm). The 'Tara' brooch, on the other hand, is relatively small (external diameter 8.6cm; maximum width of the central hole *c.* 6.4cm), but the pin is long (*c.* 22.1cm).

Handling the Johnson replicas of the 'Tara' brooch in both the Victoria and Albert Museum and the Ulster Museum made it clear, even without taking the risky step of trying, that it would have been impossible to pull the tweed through the hole in the centre of the brooch head. Before finally abandoning the idea I asked the Ulster Museum's specialist on early medieval metalwork, Cormac Bourke, to have a look, and he agreed. The hole is just too small. The replicas may not be as precious as the original 'Tara' brooch, but they are still valuable and need to be treated with respect. Even though my piece of tweed was lightweight, trying to pull it through the hole in the head of the 'Tara' brooch replica was just not on.

A solution to this difficulty adopted in the case of some Irish pseudo-penannular brooches was to make the pin detachable by not closing the loop attached to the back of the pin head. This was pointed out to me at a seminar at TCD in February 2003 by Nirvana Flanagan, then a student of the History of Art there, which again shows how much one learns through teaching. The loops of some elaborate pseudo-penannular brooches, such as the County Cavan brooch (Fig. 33) and the Lagore brooch, are not fully closed. In such cases, as

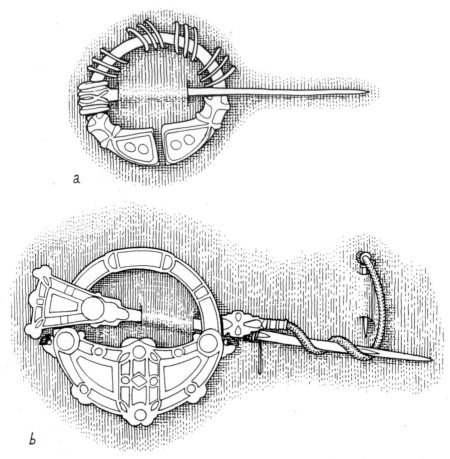

*Fig. 34—The fastening of a penannular brooch and the 'Tara' brooch compared.
(a) Fastening of a zoomorphic penannular brooch from Castledermot, Co. Kildare,
with the pin lying over the brooch head, held, in addition, by four wire coils that are
not strictly needed to hold the brooch in place.
(b) Fastening the 'Tara' brooch with the pin lying under the brooch head, with
additional support from (i) stitching through the perforations at the junctions of the
hoop and terminals; (ii) a cord attached to the back of the H-shaped link that is
wound around the pin shank; (iii) the silver chain that also wound around the pin
shank (drawings: Nick Griffiths).*

Nirvana noted, the brooch can be attached to a garment with minimal strain as
follows. First, the pin is removed from the hoop. Second, the brooch head is
placed on the cloth. Third, a small amount of cloth is pulled through the hole in
the brooch head. Fourth, the pin is threaded through the cloth and slotted back
into place onto the hoop. Fifth, the cloth is smoothed.

But this second method does not work in the case of the 'Tara' brooch,

Pl. 86—Replica of the 'Tara' brooch worn by Richard Warner of the Ulster Museum in the manner proposed in Fig. 34b (photo: N. Whitfield).

because the loop on the back of its pin head is closed and the pin is not detachable (Pl. 85). Yet another system must have been used to fasten it, but what could this have been?

It was clear that the only option was to pin the brooch in place with the brooch head dangled in front of it. So in this case the pin must lie *under* the brooch head, not over it, as in the case of a truly penannular brooch. But pinning alone won't suffice, because movement has the effect of dislodging the pin gradually and also causes the brooch head to flap about. A *de luxe* item such as the 'Tara' brooch was probably worn only on ceremonial occasions. More needed to be done to make the wearer confident that it would not fall off at the wrong moment.

Four features on the brooch (Pls 84, 85 and 86; Fig. 34) provide clues to what the additional fastening devices may have been.

First, there is the chain. This could be wound around the shank of the pin to anchor it in place. This fastening technique had a very long life in Ireland, and perhaps elsewhere too. It may have originated as long ago as the Bronze Age, when it appears to have been used to affix bone pins with perforated heads through which a cord was threaded. Perforated pins made of bird bone have been discovered in late Bronze Age contexts at Dún Aonghusa in the Aran Islands, and similar pins made of other types of bone occur in early medieval contexts in Ireland (Fig. 35c). Moreover, as the late Tom Fanning of UCG (now NUI, Galway) pointed out, a cord wound around the pin shank was also used to secure

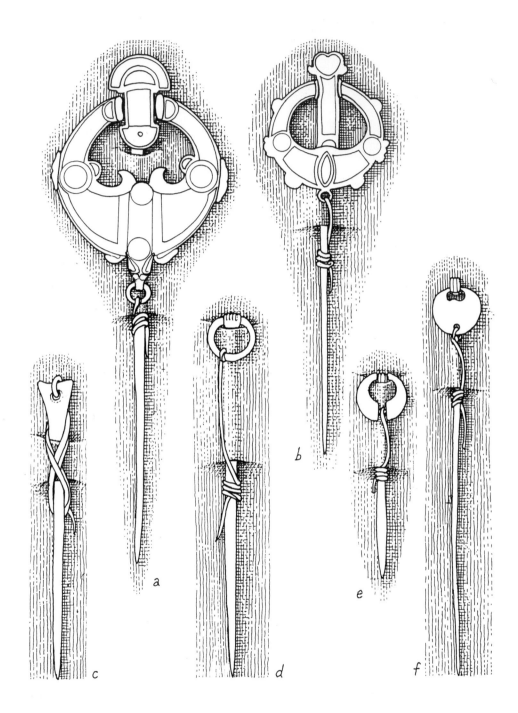

Fig. 35—Various types of early medieval Irish dress-fastener worn with vertical pin held in place by a cord wound around the shank (drawing: Nick Griffiths).

simple metal pins with a small ring at their head, so-called 'ringed pins' (Fig. 35d). Indeed, actual cords, happily not removed by tidy-minded curators, have survived attached to the ring in two cases, one interestingly made of purple silk. This method was also used in Ireland to secure other types of early medieval dress-fasteners, e.g. brooch-pins (miniature brooches) (Figs 35b, 35e and 35f) and later kite-brooches, which continued to be worn into the twelfth century. So by using the chain to anchor the pin the designer of the 'Tara' brooch was using a familiar method of securing a dress-fastener.

It is sometimes stated that the chain on the 'Tara' brooch has been cut, but examination under the microscope shows that this is not the case. Something that has now been lost probably *was* attached to the tip, however, if only to give the chain a neat ending. In Nick's drawing we showed a pin (Fig. 34b). This is guesswork, but there is some basis for the guess, because a similar pin is attached to an early medieval Irish ring and chain from Lagore, now in the Walters Art Gallery in Baltimore in the USA. Moreover, some seventh-century Anglo-Saxon jewellery also has pins at the end of chains, e.g. the shoulder-clasps from the great burial in Mound 1 at Sutton Hoo, and also a rather Irish-looking blue glass stud attached to a chain from Roundway Down, Wiltshire.

Second, there is a small pierced lug on the back of the H-shaped link between the brooch and the chain. I suspect that a cord was attached here, perhaps to a missing small ring, which was wound around the shank of the pin for extra security. Unfortunately, I was not able to try this out, because on neither replica was the lug pierced as it is on the original brooch. But this pierced lug must have had some function, and acting as an anchor for a cord is the most likely.

Third, there is a relatively inconspicuous element, a small projection from the edge of the hoop opposite the chain. I had always assumed that this was a decorative feature put there to match the H-shaped link for the chain opposite it. It was only when I experimented with replicas of the 'Tara' brooch that I realised that this has an important practical use, because it acts as a stop for the pin head. Its role was to ensure that if the brooch is worn with the terminals downwards the pin lies more or less horizontally across the brooch, so that the chain, and presumably also the cord, can be wound around the shank without putting too much strain on the link.

I was quite excited to discover this, but realised later that the original owners of the 'Tara' brooch, Waterhouse and Co., jewellers, of Dame Street, Dublin, understood this long ago. They had acquired the brooch soon after it was discovered in 1850 by a child playing near the strand at Bettystown, Co. Meath. Unlike every photograph published since, Waterhouse's fine wood-engravings of the front and back of the 'Tara' brooch published in 1851 correctly show the pin in the position in which it would have been worn if the terminals are downwards

Fig. 36—Wood-engraving of the front of the 'Tara' brooch published by Waterhouse in 1852 soon after the discovery of the brooch, showing the pin lying at the correct angle when worn.

(Fig. 36). The company's chief interest in the brooch was, of course, commercial, because they manufactured replicas of it under the grandiose (and saleable) title of 'The Royal Tara Brooch'. Working out how it would have looked when fastened would have been a priority for Waterhouse, though it must be added that in their replicas they cheated by adding a pin to the back, which was invisible from the front. (Sadly, when the brooch was in their care a number of panels were lost from the front, but that is another story.)

Last but not least, of course, there are the holes in the margin at each junction of the hoop and the terminals that my students and Marian Campbell had noted. There is plenty of evidence for sewing needles in early medieval Ireland, and I found that putting a few loose stitches through each hole with my darning needle could not have been easier. Nor was unpicking a problem. This could be done with the fingers or, if one was very careful, with a pair of scissors (or more authentically with a blade). What is more, when the 'Tara' brooch was stitched in place with the terminals downwards it hung beautifully, because a cross in a circle underpins the design and the holes were located at the tip of each of the horizontal arms of the hypothetical cross. So the balance was perfect. My tests convinced me that Marian was right. Even though the chain (and presumably also a cord) anchored the pin, it is very awkward to have the pin lie horizontally when the brooch head lies *over* the pin. Acting alone, the chain and cord could not have been guaranteed to hold the brooch. It would all have been just too

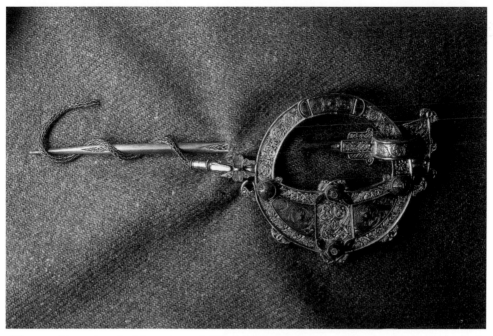

Pl. 87—Fastening the Victoria and Albert Museum replica of the 'Tara' brooch with the back showing (photo: N. Whitfield).

precarious. As Marian suggested, like many other pieces of jewellery throughout history, the 'Tara' brooch must have been sewn in place.

This fastening method, illustrated in Fig. 34b, not unworthy of Heath Robinson himself, really does work, as demonstrated by the photograph (Pl. 86), which shows how the replica looks when worn in the way described. My good-natured model is Richard Warner, then Keeper of Antiquities in the Ulster Museum, whom I commandeered in his office in the middle of the working day. He was busy and I was in Belfast for one day only, so we did not have the opportunity to dress him in an authentic cloak (*brat*) and tunic (*léine*), or to find a better background. But the photograph does show how inconspicuous the stitching is. It also demonstrates how the 'Tara' brooch looks when worn by a man on the shoulder in the manner prescribed by the Old Irish laws. A woman was to wear hers on the breast. The Old Irish laws also stipulated that compensation was due to anyone hurt by a projecting brooch pin. I did not notice until I saw the photograph of Richard that I had allowed the pin to project a bit too far, which shows how easily accidents could happen. On the high crosses, men are shown with their brooches tucked in from the shoulder: this is probably why.

I also found that it was not feasible to fix the brooch in place when worn, so

Pl. 88—Fastening a replica of one of the pseudo-penannular brooches from the Ardagh hoard, housed in the Victoria and Albert Museum, by tying white wool to the outer bar in the false gap between the terminals and winding it around the pin shank (photo: N. Whitfield).

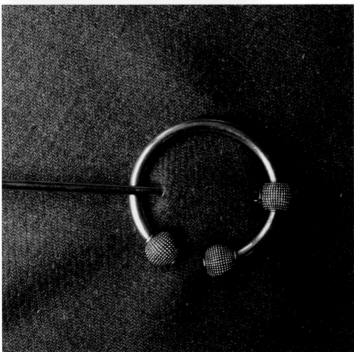

Pl. 89—Fastening a replica of the penannular brooch from the Ardagh hoard in the Victoria and Albert Museum (photo: N. Whitfield).

the 'Tara' brooch was probably stitched onto the cloak before it was slipped over the head of its owner, whether this was an aristocratic man or woman.

The 'Tara' brooch is beautifully decorated on the back, as well as on the front. A question that is often asked is 'Could it have been worn with the back on display?' I tried this out too (Pl. 87). The answer is that it could, but if it was worn in this way the back of the pin head would also be visible. I cannot categorically say that this never happened, but it seems unlikely to me. Hitherto I have assumed that the 'Tara' brooch was worn with the terminals downwards and the pin in a horizontal position. But, of course, once it is stitched in place it can be worn at any angle. Again, it is impossible to know what happened when it was in use, but when brooches are depicted on high crosses their terminals tend to be downwards, which I think makes this the most likely option.

Having the pin in a horizontal position on the 'Tara' brooch was decidedly awkward. So it is interesting to find that no other extant pseudo-penannular brooch with evidence for cleating follows this system. The cleating method survived, but with the pin worn upright with a lug for a cord or chain at the outer edge of the panel in the false 'gap' between the two terminals, rather than on the side of the brooch (Fig. 35). This worked with, rather than against, gravity, so the need for small holes for stitching became a thing of the past and fell out of fashion.

But when the Vikings made vast amounts of silver available to the Irish in the ninth century, pseudo-penannular brooches became more and more ostentatiously large and heavy. I tried cleating a replica of such a brooch, one of those from the Ardagh hoard, in the Victoria and Albert Museum (Pl. 88). I managed it, but it was so heavy that without supplementary stitching (for which there are no loops) it was not very satisfactory. This is probably why from the mid-ninth to the mid-tenth century the penannular form came back into favour in yet another make-over of the traditional brooch, the new Hiberno-Viking type being made entirely of silver, following Viking fashions (Pl. 89).

Testing the replicas of both penannular and pseudo-penannular brooches turned out to be very worthwhile. Of course, just because something works does not prove that it was done this way in antiquity. The Hunterston brooch, for instance, has perforations on the perimeter like those on the 'Tara' brooch, and was not necessarily fastened in the awkward way illustrated in Fig. 32. In the case of the 'Tara' brooch, however, after handling the Johnson replicas in London and Belfast, I would be prepared to bet a small sum that its designers adopted a 'belt and braces' approach, and secured it not only by its pin and chain but also by discreet stitches through the loops on its edge.

Bibliography

Fanning, T. 1994 *Viking Age ringed pins from Dublin*. Medieval Dublin Excavations 1962–81, Ser. B, Vol. 4. Dublin.

Whitfield, N. 2001 The 'Tara' brooch: an Irish emblem of status in its European context. In C. Hourihane (ed.), *From Ireland coming*, 211–47. Princeton.

Whitfield, N. 2004 More thoughts on the wearing of brooches in early medieval Ireland. In C. Hourihane (ed.), *Irish art historical studies in honour of Peter Harbison*, 70–108. Princeton and Dublin.

24

Discovering a sense of place: mental maps of Cork City

Colin Breen

This short piece is not about a discovery made during the course of excavation or extensive field survey. Such findings, while of intrinsic interest, are essentially a product of professional undertaking. They are somehow removed from one's social persona and are part of an artificially created exploration of the past as part of commercial archaeological practice or guided research questioning. Instead, this essay is about discovering an appreciation of the place we are from, about a constantly developing source of interest and, increasingly, a fascination with our own local landscape. It is about discovering a personal sense of place and feeling the need to return continually to that place (or places) to re-identify, re-associate and reignite not only one's interest in one's personal history but also those personal landscapes of memory. In a sense, then, it is a journey that investigates the distant past in the present through a mixture of knowledge, imagination and deep personal interest.

This journey begins physically and metaphorically in the locality where I grew up, in the southern suburbs of Cork City. It is a physical journey that I make often, but it is also a mental journey that continually evolves as the physical landscape is subject to change and remembrances take on new meanings. The journey is recounted here as a physical walk, and this walk has become a metaphor for a mental walk or journey that is continuing. The start of the walk is in Turners Cross adjacent to Christ the King Church, with its imposing Gotham-like figure of Christ towering over a sprawl of later eighteenth- and nineteenth-century artisan housing projects. These small, cottage-like houses line the roadway as far as Evergreen Road. They are of intrinsic social and architectural interest, remaining as a testament to the hundreds, or indeed thousands, of workers responsible for the physical development of the city. They do not possess the monumentality and impressive architecture of the larger

Pl. 90—Early twentieth-century photograph of Keyser's Lane below Elizabeth Fort (Cork City Council).

aristocratic mansions of the city's fathers and merchant princes, but maintain a sense of normality and presence, and in some ways a dignity, that has remained throughout their life-spans. Nestled within this complex are Quaker Road and the associated Quaker burial-ground. This quiet place, with its unassuming headstones and lack of pretension, remains symbolic of the idealistic contribution that many early Quakers made to city development. It is also reflective of the futility of overt materialism in this life and the attractions of peaceful resistance to the militaristic aggressions of contemporary governments, so explicit in the actions and teachings of the 'Friends'. Moving from Quaker Road to Barrack Street, the earlier aggressive government policies—for centuries dominated by conflict—are exemplified by the Elizabethan fort, a large artillery fortification built in the early part of the seventeenth century, dominating the old town's southern approaches. The fort has undergone many changes over the

Fig. 37—Detail of John Fitzgerald's early nineteenth-century watercolour of Elizabeth Fort and St Fin Barre's Cathedral (Crawford Municipal Art Gallery).

past 400 years and has recently undergone a programme of restoration that will hopefully, after years of neglect, place it as a historical attraction within this important quarter of the city.

Directly below the walls of the fort is a narrow lane that runs down to the river. Keyser's Lane bears testimony to the presence of the Vikings in the town (Pl. 90). The buildings on either side of the lane and in the immediate vicinity are of intrinsic historical interest: they are potentially late seventeenth-century and early eighteenth-century architectural survivals, and thus constitute some of the earliest buildings in the city. The many layers and fabrics that make up these types of buildings across the city represent continual redevelopment, repair and renewal, and so remain a major mine of information for further research. Standing at the riverside below the lane you are surrounded by some of the most important and imposing buildings in the city. Directly in front of you on the central island of Cork is the Beamish and Crawford Brewery, where porter was first brewed in 1792. To the immediate right is the limestone-arched South Gate Bridge, built in the eighteenth century and still facilitating one of the main arteries out of the town centre. On the far bank is the Sir Henry's site, now producing some of the earliest settlement levels in the town and the former home of a music venue, so formative in the lives of many of my generation. Did any of the excavations in the uppermost levels produce artefactual evidence of bygone gigs and hidden trysts? Immediately to your left, below the fort on the southern bank of the river, the opening to one of the original culvert schemes can be seen arching into darkness towards a Cathedral underworld (Fig. 37). I have often wondered what it would be like to follow that tunnel underground, possibly by canoe—a journey reminiscent, though not entirely comparable, to the more recent explorations of the classical period sewage and drainage system of Rome. Rather than entering the old town across the bridge, one can instead follow the river through Crosses Green, the site of former marshes and that of St Mary's of the Isle, a recently excavated Dominican priory. For many years this was a lost quarter of the town, dominated by warehouses of indeterminate function, but it has now been reclaimed by apartments and art-related retail units conveniently located close to the Art College.

At Wandesford Quay you cross over Clarke's Bridge and turn immediately left down Hanover Street. A stone carving of a beehive can be seen above one of the entrances into the elaborate storehouse on your right, marking the site of the former Hive Ironworks, operating since the opening of the nineteenth century. We can now cut across the marshes and head northwards through Nile Street and Henry Street towards the North Gate Bridge. Although rebuilt in modern times, foundations of the original crossing-place can be seen abutting the northern bank to the left of the bridge at extreme low tide. The rather dubious nature of the water quality and passing public attention has always prevented me from diving on this feature and assessing its historic character. Walking down Pope's Quay, you can take any left turn up one of the narrow, stepped lanes and you immediately enter a myriad of passageways and maze-like laneways. Innumerable tenements formerly lined these lanes, sections of which survive architecturally. A large number of smaller cottages and houses also remain, again bearing witness to the multifaceted social fabric that is woven together to make up the urban tapestry of this town. The walker will invariably end up at Shandon steeple, or St Anne's, the well-known landmark on Cork's northern skyline. Of especial interest adjacent to the church grounds is Skiddy's Almshouse, originally built in 1718 and admirably refurbished to again serve a social housing need.

Moving again, we turn southwards and wander in the general direction of Patrick Street, passing the rear of the Lady's Well Brewery in Blackpool before crossing the river again over Patrick's Bridge and the mercantile centre of the city. A final destination is South Terrace with its synagogue (Pl. 91). For me this has always represented an imposing presence in an otherwise bland, secularised political landscape. I have always wanted to see the inside of this building, but its imposing doorway and wrought-iron gates have always remained firmly shut. The same sense of mystery and intrigue also strikes me when I pass the Masonic

Pl. 91—The synagogue on South Terrace.

lodge on Tuckey Street, or the churches of many different faiths briefly glimpsed down side lanes throughout the city. Intrinsically associated with the synagogue is the area traditionally known as 'Jewtown' or the Hibernian buildings, settled by significant numbers of Jewish families in the later part of the nineteenth century. The census of 1901 records 55 Jewish families living in this complex off the Albert Road. There is a prevailing sense of a different place here, one with different meanings and values. The buildings are reflective of past diversity that was not always accepted. The architecture of the place is identical to many other housing projects around the city, but it is the intangible heritage or sense of 'heritage memory' that is especially important to this place. The initial difficulties this community endured both in Cork and elsewhere around the country has immediate associations with the present day as new immigrant communities make parts of the city their own, a process that is to be both welcomed and celebrated. For a town or city to develop a truly cosmopolitan and urban character it requires continual updating through new arrivals, new ways of thinking and new negotiations of social and economic space. The surrounding landscape is dominated by remnants of Cork's industrial past, including port complexes, gasworks and train facilities, the storage tunnels of which served a generation of youth admirably.

Endings

Invariably, something new is noticed or discovered each time you travel through 'town'. You are constantly finding out new things that you had not previously seen or known about, and you can learn to appreciate things that you had formerly ignored or casually overlooked. Without necessarily trying, you are continually absorbing more about your place, simply by being part of it. There is, however, a certain difficulty or worry that by learning too much about a place you may eventually devalue the experience, as the mystery disappears to be replaced by a form of academic complacency or removed understanding. Do you also reach a stage where you become afraid to discover more? Will too much knowledge serve to negate your interest? Perhaps travel and the discovery of other places can compensate somewhat. To travel to wonderful cities like Edinburgh, London or Mombasa can certainly renew one's interests and prompt new explorations and investigations. Travel of any sort challenges this sense of complacency and comfort and serves to reignite our energy and interests, not only in exotic foreign places but also in our own more familiar world. Ultimately, though, you will probably find yourself drawn time and again to look anew at your home town in an attempt to rediscover something of yourself, your 'people' and your background.

Bibliography

Crowley, J.S., Devoy, R.J.N., Linehan, D. and O'Flanagan, P. (eds) 2005 *Atlas of Cork City*. Cork.
O'Flanagan, P. and Buttimer, C.G. (eds) 1993 *Cork history and society*. Dublin.
Rynne, C. 1999 *The industrial archaeology of Cork City and its environs*. Bray.

25

On pilgrimage to Glendalough

Aidan O'Sullivan

In the Middle Ages, people went on pilgrimage to the shrines of saints or the distant sites of miracles for different reasons. They walked long roads to their pilgrimage destinations to see and touch the relics of a saint and to seek his or her blessing. They travelled along long-established pilgrimage routes as penance for their sins; in the hope of finding a cure for an illness or injury; to fulfil a sacred vow; or to give thanks for good fortune. It is even known that some medieval criminals—particularly from the thirteenth century onwards—were expelled from their communities and sent on pilgrimage for their crimes, and their experience would have been less pleasant. Sometimes, too, people travelled the pilgrims' path—and we know this because bad-tempered medieval clerics condemned them for their frivolity—merely out of curiosity. For a time, they could escape from their ordinary lives in close-knit villages, become strangers (the literal meaning of the word 'pilgrim'), and seek out new places and experience new things beyond the horizon.

Since the early medieval period—and undoubtedly before—people in western Europe equipped themselves with a staff, scrip (a leather pouch) and hat and set out on long journeys to a range of different pilgrimage centres. The most famous destinations were probably Jerusalem in the Holy Land, Rome (the city of Peter and Paul, with its graves of the martyrs) and Santiago de Compostela in north-west Spain, which was probably the most popular destination in medieval Europe, while Canterbury, Cologne, Aachen and Trondheim in Norway were also significant. Along the way, they would stay in some of the countless hostels and lodgings devoted to them, and stop at churches and convents.

In the Middle Ages, pilgrims were entitled to expect lodgings for the night and food while on their journey. This hospitality was provided by the Church and, in particular, the various significant monastic establishments associated

Pl. 92—*Images from Glendalough and Templeteenaun, Co. Wicklow.*

with the pilgrimage. On the pilgrim roads to places like Santiago de Compostela, there would have been up to half a million pilgrims a year; this must have placed a huge burden on the monastic economy, so they began to establish smaller hospices managed by clerics close to the routeways. During the peak of the pilgrimage phenomenon in the twelfth and thirteenth centuries, these hostels were situated at such regular intervals along the route that a person could travel for a day and still expect to find a roof over their head by nightfall—although their lodgings would probably only include a bed of straw and a meagre meal.

People who made such momentously long journeys to places like these were transformed forever; they were pilgrims when they came home, and their lives would always be associated with their prestigious journey. Indeed, archaeological excavations in British and Irish churches and graveyards have occasionally found individuals who were buried with pilgrims' badges such as scallop shells from Santiago de Compostela, probably signifying that they were ever afterwards known as pilgrims in their community.

When, however, these international pilgrimage foci became difficult of access for reasons of war with the Arab world, plague, disease or other obstacles, people also travelled to places closer within their own countries, or to regional or local pilgrimage centres. Indeed, these short pilgrim journeys to minor centres at local churches and monasteries must have been a normal religious practice for most people. In medieval Ireland there were quite a few of these pilgrim centres, famously including Clonmacnoise, Kildare, Armagh and Glendalough.

The pilgrimage to Glendalough was probably all the more significant because of the difficulties involved in getting there, located as it was in a remote, inaccessible valley in the heart of the Wicklow Mountains. In medieval pilgrimage the journey was often perceived as being every bit as important as the destination itself; its dangers, difficulties and uncomfortable experiences were seen as metaphors for the transformation of the self, the spiritual redemption that the pilgrim ultimately sought. For most pilgrims travelling there, it was a journey that required days of walking across the Wicklow Mountains. This was a remote and dangerous home of wolves and outlaws, while also being a landscape subject to unexpected changes in weather that can suddenly close in and make it a place of cold comfort. On a summer's day, though, there could have been no finer place to be, as the mountains, woods and bogs faded into a heat haze and the larks sang above the pilgrim's head as he or she walked along the trail.

The west Wicklow Mountains have a range of archaeological sites that testify to that medieval pilgrimage journey. There are medieval churches, crosses, cross-inscribed boulders, bullaun stones and other features situated along the most obvious route—the Kings River valley that runs down from the Wicklow Gap and provides access to Glendalough from the well-populated plains of Kildare and south Dublin. An ancient road known as St Kevin's Road provided pilgrims with a route to travel on, and there are various archaeological sites along it that signify its importance as a pilgrims' route. Most notably, the Hollywood Stone once lay in a field (it is now in the Glendalough Heritage Centre) near a fording-point of the Kings River. This is a massive block of granite on which is carved an intricate labyrinth—which was, of course, also a metaphor for the pilgrim's journey right across medieval Europe. The original location of the Hollywood Stone (today a meeting-place of two roads from Valleymount and Hollywood on the way to Glendalough) was probably a station or place of pause along this pilgrims' road. St Kevin's Road is traceable as an archaeological feature in several locations along the valley floor and is today most visible as an ancient stone-laid pathway at the very top of the Wicklow Gap. From there, the pilgrim could have seen the Glendasan Valley to the south descending towards Glendalough, its holy churches, shrines and monastery.

What a wonderful place it must have been to arrive at as a pilgrim—and there are historical records of important royal and ecclesiastical pilgrims arriving there in the tenth, eleventh and twelfth centuries. In the twelfth and thirteenth centuries, when pilgrimage was at its most popular in medieval Europe, Glendalough already had ancient churches and ruins that were centuries old. Founded by St Kevin in the fifth or sixth century AD, it had developed into a major monastic centre by the tenth century. The early medieval church of Reefert is located at the edge of the upper lake; its cemetery was a burial-ground for local kings anxious to lie with the saints, and the church also saw building in the later periods. Templenaskellig—a remote church and settlement at the southern edge of the upper lake—was undoubtedly a hermits' settlement far from the busy monastic enclosure. Close to Reefert is a stone enclosure, some pilgrim *leachta* and early medieval crosses that mark the route of the pilgrim *turas* or route up the valley. The main Glendalough monastic enclosure is situated lower down the valley, where most of the archaeological sites that we can see today are located. Most of these churches probably originated in the late eleventh and twelfth centuries, when a period of royal patronage and monastic wealth led to the construction and ongoing use of the medieval cathedral, the priest's house, St Kevin's house, the gatehouse marking the entrance into the monastic enclosure and, of course, the round tower that was already there and stood as a beacon for medieval pilgrims. In our imagination we must add to this what we cannot see: the medieval monastic clerics, students, craftsmen, tenants and labourers, and their dwellings, fields and animals, that made Glendalough one of the wonders of Ireland.

* * * * *

I was born and raised in Valleymount in the west Wicklow Mountains. I was taught by my parents, who were both teachers in the village's National School. My childhood memories are of the mountains and the lake, and of many car trips to play hurling and football matches on the other side of the county. We often drove up through the Kings River valley and across the Wicklow Gap—today still the only routeway across the mountains—to the towns (and GAA pitches) of Arklow, Avoca or Aughrim. Often, when we reached the top of the Wicklow Gap, the oppressively heavy clouds that had hung over west Wicklow suddenly disappeared to reveal a sunny day on the 'other side of the gap', providing splendid views down towards east Wicklow and beyond to the distant Irish Sea. Our return home was always heralded by the sight of the monastic round tower at Glendalough, telling us that we were nearly home in Valleymount again (with or without the Championship Cup).

But we did more than drive through these mountains, we walked most of them: Tonelagee, Moanbane, Silsean, Fair Mountain, Church Mountain, Slievecorragh, as well as the lanes and pathways of Granabeg, Granamore, Togher, Ballyknockan and Oakwood. My mother and father were great walkers and they had plenty of time after school, and two young sons and a dog to entertain and exercise. So, most evenings and during many weekends in summer and winter, we could be found somewhere in the Wicklow Mountains or seen walking along the banks of the brown-watered Kings River as it surged over the rocks on its way down the valley. I remember one St Stephen's Day, in particular, when my Dad and I walked through the snow from Valleymount, climbed the mountain above Carrigacurra and descended down the far side into the remote valley of Glenbride. I remember we dropped in to one of the families there and were given (very) big glasses of whiskey to warm us up. We had to phone my mother to bring us tipsily home in the darkening evening.

My father, John O'Sullivan, was born in Kilkee in 1938. He grew up on a small farm in east Clare and he knew the names of trees, flowers and birds. He had obviously had an idyllic life in Creeveroe, outside Killaloe, where there was always time after work on the farm for swimming in the River Shannon, for hurling in the local fields and for walking the Slieve Bearnagh hills with his beloved Uncle Jack, in search of rabbits or brown trout. He played senior hurling for Clare in the late 1950s and never lost his love for that sport—or, indeed, his native Clare accent. But he left Clare as a young man to train as a teacher, and on his first appointment in north Wexford he met my mother, Kathleen. They married there and came to teach in west Wicklow in the early 1960s, first in Lacken and then in Valleymount. Dad and Mam settled into their life there as the village teachers for 40 years. My Dad was the schoolmaster, played football for Valleymount, established hurling in the unpromising soil of west Wicklow, and taught generations of mountain children in Valleymount School. He was interested in most things, and was fascinated by history, folklore and archaeology—and the stories that local people told him of past times and historical events. Many of our walks in the mountains were to archaeological sites: to the Neolithic cairns and tombs on the hilltops, to Bronze Age standing stones, stone circles and barrows, and to medieval churches, crosses and enclosures.

Above all, my Dad loved Glendalough. Through the years, John and Kathleen would travel over to Glendalough in the evenings to walk amongst the ancient ruins and to stroll along the lakeshore. Over the decades he was continually to return there on a pilgrimage to the cathedrals, churches and crosses of that extraordinary monastery. Its founding saint, St Kevin, was always there in the background of our lives in the west Wicklows, and even the juvenile hurling and football teams that we played for were named after him. Any relation or friend from far away who visited us in Valleymount would inevitably be brought by my Dad to Glendalough to explore the monastic ruins, to walk in the oak woods or to stand by the upper lake. At the very end of the National School year, Dad used to bring his sixth-class students to Glendalough on a summer day-trip. He was bringing them to a place he loved, before he sent them off to secondary school and into the rest of their lives.

People often ask me how I became an archaeologist—and I always say that my Dad decided that this would be one of my subjects in university! I should explain that our house was always full of his archaeology and history books— some that we bought him as Christmas presents, some that he had bought himself (such as Françoise Henry's *Early Christian art*), and a suspicious number of others that he had simply 'forgotten' to return to Kildare County Library sometime in the late 1960s (when he was studying archaeology in UCD as a BA evening student). These books and others were to be liberated further. My own copy of Máire and Liam De Paor's classic *Early Christian Ireland* was 'borrowed' from his library and never returned.

In the mid-1980s, when I was contemplating going to UCD to study Arts, Dad wrote to Professor Michael Herity as one of his former students and enquired of him where I should study archaeology. While other universities were praised in the reply, inevitably UCD was proposed as the best! Unfortunately, when the time came in September 1985 to enrol for first-year courses in UCD, I was lying in a bed in Naas Hospital after a hard tackle in a GAA football match. Dad went happily along to the university on my behalf and joined the queues of young students for brief introductions to the various subjects (English, history, geography and so on). He obviously had a good time, and was delighted by the way he was treated by the lecturers at the information tables, who didn't bat an eyelid when he sat down for the interview (I never got around to telling him that these academics were well used to mature students and hardly saw him as odd). By the time he arrived back at my hospital bed after his enjoyable day in UCD, he was all chat about the various academic options and careers open to us—or me, I should say. Unfortunately, he said, archaeology couldn't be combined with English (our favourite subjects), so he had signed me up for archaeology, history and philosophy instead. Although sleepy from painkillers and dazed from my recent surgical operation, I could see that all this was as much to do with Dad's fascination with learning as with my own scholastic future. I could have changed subjects, of course. But when I emerged from Seamus Caulfield's enthralling first-year introductory lecture on archaeology, I knew that this was what I wanted to do with my life.

Throughout my time studying in university, Dad and I kept up our interest in the archaeology of the Wicklow Mountains. We explored much of the archaeology and history of the pilgrimage route to Glendalough—not really in a serious or academic way, but merely because they were nice places to walk and explore. Our trips to Glendalough grew more frequent too, but with an added interest in the archaeological remains.

One sunny day, probably in 1986, we found ourselves thrashing through the forestry plantation on the hillside at Templeteenaun, in the mountain townland of Ballinagee. Dad had been there before and wanted to show it to me, but it was a difficult place to find in the closely spaced coniferous trees. But then we suddenly broke into a grassy, open area of oak trees. We moved through these and found ourselves standing inside a large enclosure defined by a low stone bank. This was Templeteenaun church and graveyard, reputed to be an ancient site. Dad had been told about it by local families who lived up here. We explored it for a while, examining the walls of the enclosure, the entrance gap into it and the various stones seemingly haphazardly scattered around the interior. At the north-west corner we could see the ruins of an ancient rectangular stone building, now only visible as moss- and grass-covered foundations, but this was obviously a medieval church with its nave and chancel structure and east–west alignment. The forest was silent—apart from the Kings River babbling in the valley below us—and we stood in quiet contemplation there for a while, gazing at the ancient, mossy stones, before we walked back down the hill to the car and moved on to search for some booley huts that we had heard about from our neighbours.

* * * * *

Almost twenty years later, I stood again on the Templeteenaun enclosure wall and watched Dad climb the hill up to the site. It was again a sunny day and the sounds around us were still of larks singing and the babbling river, but also of the clink of trowels on stone and the chatter of UCD undergraduate students. Dad was coming up to visit our archaeological excavations at Templeteenaun church. It was August 2004, and the UCD School of Archaeology's students were working on their summer field school in the Wicklow Mountains. My colleague Graeme Warren and I—lecturers in archaeology at UCD—were leading the excavations that were one element in our landscape archaeological research project on the Kings River valley.

Templeteenaun church and graveyard are located almost at the top of the Kings River valley, only a few miles short of the Wicklow Gap itself. Even today it is a remote location, situated well above the last houses in the valley. In the past, it must have been a similarly isolated place, but it is situated on a hillock overlooking the route of St Kevin's pilgrim's road. The site itself as Dad and I had seen it years before was intriguing rather than impressive, but our archaeological excavations had now revealed a few interesting things about the history of this quiet, remote spot. The church is a large enough building, is aligned east–west and was simply constructed of unmortared granite stones, with a doorway located near its south-west corner. In its present form it probably dates from the eleventh to twelfth century, though it may have earlier origins. It stands at the north-east corner of a stone-walled enclosure, beside the main entrance. Our excavations suggest that this enclosure was built in the medieval period and that it served to define a sacred space around the church itself.

We also know now that people approaching the church and enclosure in the medieval period would have climbed a steep slope and found themselves walking up a narrow laneway, defined on either side by a stone and earthen bank. This lane obviously saw a lot of human or animal traffic in the past as its surface has been eroded down into the subsoil. As you walk that laneway today and approach the site entrance, you can see to your left a small stone structure—seemingly a house—built of rounded stones gathered from the land around. This may have been a pilgrim hostel, a place for people to sleep overnight outside the church bounds, or it may have some other function. Scattered between this small house and the outer edge of the enclosure we have recovered hundreds of pieces of pottery from a medieval midden deposit. Claire McCutcheon, one of Ireland's best-known pottery specialists, has told us that this collection includes types of medieval pots known as Leinster Cooking Ware (a crude native pottery probably made locally) and green-, red- and brown-glazed Dublin-Type Wares (imported from medieval Dublin) that can be dated to about the twelfth to thirteenth century. There were also a few iron objects, including a medieval horseman's rowel spur, with its distinctive spiked wheel that could be used to goad the horse forward. This midden of broken pottery, charcoal, burnt bone and rusted iron objects was obviously where the rubbish of the dwelling-place was thrown, just outside the entrance into the enclosure.

Our medieval traveller walking past this and moving through the narrow enclosure entrance would then have found himself or herself looking at the church to the left, the settlement and cemetery space in front, as well as some other interesting features. To their right, down the slope, this observer may also have seen (if it existed then) a strange rectangular platform defined by a kerb of granite stones and surmounted by other stones. Our excavation of this rectangular platform has also revealed that sometime in the past people came to Templeteenaun and to this structure and placed water-rolled granite and quartz stones on top of it. These stones could not have been found around the site and had to be brought from a riverbed, perhaps the Kings River itself. On many early medieval ecclesiastical sites (e.g. Inishmurray, Co. Sligo; Glendalough, Co. Wicklow; Illaunlough, Co. Kerry), people deposited such quartz stones on rectangular, outdoor altars (often known as stations or *leachta*) as a mark of piety, as a prayer or as a plea for spiritual succour. This 'station' at Templeteenaun may well have been a medieval pilgrims' station, but of course it could be later in date too.

Overall, our archaeological excavations at Templeteenaun indicate a settlement presence there in the Middle Ages (i.e. the house, medieval pottery and other finds indicate that people were living there), particularly in the twelfth to thirteenth century, precisely when the pilgrimage to Glendalough was at its peak. Templeteenaun was also usefully located along St Kevin's Road, the main pilgrims' way to Glendalough across the mountains. Although Templeteenaun may have been an isolated church serving the spiritual needs of a remote mountain community, it may also have been a church-supported hostel on the pilgrims' road, a place to pause, rest, pray and take shelter overnight before the final leg of the journey down to the monastery of Glendalough.

* * * * *

With his interest in all things and our shared discovery of it, my Dad loved visiting Templeteenaun while we were working there, and I loved to see him come; he came regularly while we first surveyed the site in 2003, and then during the digging seasons in 2004 and 2005. He was well known to my colleagues Graeme Warren, Robert Sands and Conor McDermott, and he often visited while I was away too. When he arrived at Templeteenaun, he and I would walk around the site together looking at all the archaeological features, and we would open up the cardboard finds boxes and pore over the ancient sherds of medieval glazed and turned pottery and discuss their origins, uses and abandonment. Dad would tell us about the families who lived on the mountains and the stories about Oakwood, a settlement we could see across the Kings River, and its role in the 1798 rebellion. Dad often visited when other people were there too— interested walkers, people from Hollywood and Valleymount, and once Con Costelloe, the well-known local historian and editor of the *Kildare Historical and Archaeological Journal*. My mother told me later that they often used to sit in O'Connor's pub in Valleymount, discussing history and politics over a pint of stout. Even the Coillte officer who supported our excavations was well known to Dad; Frank Reid was a local man who had played with him on the 1964 Junior Football team that brought a rare County Championship to Valleymount.

Not long after his retirement from Valleymount National School, Dad discovered he was suffering from a rare lung disease that deprived him of oxygen, left him breathless and hindered his ability to walk. From then on he found it increasingly difficult to deal with the steep slopes of Templeteenaun, and would drive along the Coillte access road to us instead, until finally he was unable to visit us at all (and so I would bring home the site plans and finds in the evenings to show him over the kitchen table). In the spring of 2006 he visited us on Conor McDermott's archaeological excavation on St Kevin's Road itself, but he was now unable to leave the car and could only look at the site through binoculars while I explained to him what had been found. My father, John O'Sullivan, died peacefully in Peamount Hospital, Co. Dublin, on 14 October 2006. His passing was much like his life—gentle, kind and good—and we were all there with him. But when I stood up from his bedside that morning, I turned and looked out the hospital window towards the distant Wicklow Mountains, their slopes illuminated by bright autumn sunlight, and I knew, however much I might long for it, that I would never walk in the mountains with my Dad again.

We travelled to Glendalough again a few weeks later, though, my mother and I. It was a dark winter's day and we were dazed by the days and weeks behind us. My little nephew and young niece walked with us around the monastery, under the churches and round tower, under the wooded mountains that rise above that place. I explained to Aideen what the medieval cathedral of SS Peter and Paul would have been like, trying to give her a sense of what a prodigious and wonderful sight it must have been for all the weary pilgrims who arrived in hope at Glendalough, and what they must have felt on reaching the end of their long journey. In that small moment, I realised yet again that I was travelling—as a university teacher and archaeologist—along a well-loved road that my father had set me upon.

26

Coloured rags and discarded food: archaeology and memory

Nick Maxwell

The difference between false memories and true ones is the same as for jewels: it is always the false ones that look the most real, the most brilliant. ~ Salvador Dali

The past is never dead, it is not even past. ~ William Faulkner

My one and only experiment with a hallucinogenic substance had me lying on my back watching a mentally generated movie on the ceiling of the damp bedsit I lived in during 1969. It was a complicated plot involving cowboys and much guitar music. And so I am afraid the spoiled preacher in me itches to draw the trite analogy that memory is like an old movie played on the ceiling of one's decaying mind to the soundtrack of life. But cheesy sermons apart, writing about events gone by is necessarily a memory construct, a screenplay, a fiction. And writing about one's involvement with archaeology involves a double dose of construction, because archaeology itself is like memory. It's a slice, a CAT-scan if you will, of a version of reality. So trying to revisit what moved you emotionally from your involvement in archaeology can find you steering into a twilight zone of created facts. They may or may not have happened as you tell them, or the archaeology involved may or may not have happened, but perhaps the tale told is better for that. Perhaps archaeology does not accurately fix the past but says much about our present needs (prejudices!) from the way we interpret the material cultural remains. Thus, in the grim first three-quarters or so of the last century, Ireland was interpreted through its archaeology as the home of a great artistic and linguistic movement, part of a greater European cultural cutting edge, which we were definitely not in those bleak times. It is interesting to note that while archaeologists are coming to grips with that 'appalling vista', an Iron Age without the Celts (Ó Donnabháin 2000), others with a hunger for spiritual direction see an equally spurious Celtic spiritual inheritance as part of our heritage (MacConville 2006). The movie of our past is once again to be accompanied by the echoing, haunting strains of the harp, the lonely laments of the pipes, but now set amid the 'spiritual' landscapes of Cork, Kerry, Offaly or Meath.

But what of my personal memory-movie—what is lost and found in my memory? Or, to echo Austin O'Malley's madwoman, what coloured rags have I kept, what food have I thrown away?

The screenplay of my memory takes me to County Tyrone and the excavation by Claire Foley of the lovely court tomb at Creggandevesky, near Carrickmore (Pl. 93), bypassed by the plantations but not by the troubles. A young man who looks a lot like me, and who, incidentally, is almost completely ignorant of the Neolithic, has the extraordinary privilege of slowly uncovering, beneath the cairn of covering stones, the elegantly curved court area of the monument for the first time in maybe 5,000 years. To memory it seems a moment of religious intensity, of awe and deep emotion at what is being revealed after having been hidden for thousands of years, and perhaps it is best to leave it at that reality.

But the joy of archaeology is really only infrequently connected to the magical moments of major finds. That movie is frequently more *Carry On* than Kieslowski, even though we would like it to be the latter. But the incidental plot lines complement, improve and reinforce the archaeological experience. While digging at Creggandevesky we stayed in the Sunnyside Guest House (the name more a reflection of the personality of the owner, Mrs Toal, than the weather to be experienced in May in County Tyrone—it snowed, or am I thinking of a Cary Grant movie?). Here was ancient Ireland played out before our eyes, from the quality of the plumbing to the huge dinners laid out in every room on the ground floor on the morning of a funeral. Mrs Toal's establishment was the nearest thing to a hotel in Carrickmore, and she would roast great joints of beef and provide industrial quantities of whiskey (always a southern brand) for mourners.

For us permanent guests the beef provided a welcome change from the ubiquitous chicken, not to mention the packed lunch of banana sandwiches that was provided for us on every single day of our stay there. I like to think that this was a genuine misunderstanding built into the plot. Mrs Toal's daughter remarked to me on my last day on the site: 'You like bananas, don't you, Nick?'—I can hear the canned laughter even now. A more pretentious writer than me might point out that it seemed that ritual was as important in the Sunnyside Guest House as it had been in the court of the tomb on McCartan's land at Creggandevesky.

Mrs Toal's attitude to life also said more about Ireland, old and new, than

Pl. 93—The court tomb at Creggandevesky, near Carrickmore, Co. Tyrone (with thanks to the Environment and Heritage Service, Department of the Environment, Northern Ireland).

perhaps any monument or historical treatise could tell. She was hospitable in the way that people are who are steeped in its obligations. When we called in to see her with our small baby a year after we had left the site, she immediately produced steak and Guinness, which you refused at your peril. She viewed the *punt* and the pound sterling as equal currencies (which they certainly were not at that time), and she was, I guess, republican but passed no judgements on any person because of their background, particularly when you were under the protection of her roof.

The McCartan boys, whose family had for generations owned and farmed the land where the site was located, provided us with another link to the past: handsome, charming, with a casual love for their inherited landscape and an unspoken pride in the monument that we were digging. Memory has them appearing hollow-eyed after yet another night of being rousted from their beds by the British Army. They were courteous but cautious with us, and I can see them standing watchful and silent during the time we were paid a visit by the British Army. The soldiers crawled up the hill to the site on their bellies after landing from a helicopter in an adjoining field. That unnecessary bit of military posturing was followed by a very polite but well-informed interrogation about my expertise in the Neolithic by the officer in charge. This piece of intimidation by the forces of law and order was not lost on these young men; they knew who it was really aimed at. The reality and meaning of Irish history came close to us on that day and was perhaps more instructive than any reality provided by the monument.

Later that night (or again it might have been another night) we ended up in Fox's pub. Inexplicably (because it was usually quiet) it filled with youngish men and a singsong developed. All good Irish fun, you would think; the songs were the traditional songs of Irish freedom-fighting, but mixed with the Kevin Barrys and Croppy Boys were, more chillingly, songs written about the local heroes of the Provisional IRA killed or wounded quite recently. Strangely, a living tradition was being casually displayed, born out of real horror and death. The songs of Irish freedom didn't sound so good after that.

Now these snapshots, and more I haven't disclosed from County Tyrone, in retrospect assume a significance that they may or may not have had at the time. Memory is like a poetry of the mind: its recollections, gathered after the event and collated, assume a coherence, a rhythm and a design that alter the reality. Archaeological interpretation likewise performs a similar operation. It puts together snapshots to form a view that is only one possibility, a view that can and sometimes does make much too much of partial evidence. Is the broken pot in the court tomb just that or does it have more meaning? Does it have meaning because we want it to, because our current prejudice demands it? Very few sane people would classify any archaeological writing as poetry, yet it could be seen as explaining the unexplainable in a way that conveys its meaning largely by how ideas are presented.

But this contribution should be about the emotion engendered by specific discoveries and monuments, and so we move to another scene in the memory-movie. Did this happen? Two young men stand nervously outside the hoardings surrounding the Fishamble Street side of the Wood Quay site, determined to stop bulldozers destroying medieval parts of the site (Pl. 94). Did I really say, like John Wayne in *Flying Leathernecks*, to the tyro archaeologist (now Professor) Gabriel Cooney, 'We're going in'? I rather like to think I did. Particularly as the attempt quickly descended back into *Carry On* territory, as the agile Cooney sprang lightly over the fence and I was left scrabbling for a foothold until he came to my rescue by throwing a ladder back over. Thus we both managed to halt, at least for a few hours, an attempt to destroy quite early material behind the city walls. Yet when I think back to those days of working on the Wood Quay site there are better memories, and I can conjure up clips from the picture-show that was the excavation.

The men recruited from the dole queues to work the site were extraordinary

Pl. 94—An earthmover overcoming the best efforts of Cooney and Maxwell.

characters (Pl. 95). One grew tomatoes and potatoes on the spoil-heap, a few waited only to get paid so they could drink themselves insensible, while others gambled away every penny of their wages. One man sacked by the site director (now Museum director Dr Pat Wallace) blithely came back to work the next day because, he said, his sister told him to! Another got taken on for his ability to name the famous Waterford hurling team of the '50s (in my book, as reliable as any fancy recruitment method). Another called us 'penny c**ts' after being sent home for boozing too much at lunchtime. Pat, when taking him back on the next day, took the view that he was referring to recent site discoveries of eleventh-century silver pennies of King Cnut. The measure of Dr Wallace is that to this day he recalls this incident with great humour and enjoyment. Another workman came to work on his first day and just started digging a huge hole when he wasn't immediately given something to do.

Those were dark days for such men in Ireland. Many were rejects from the building trade or too old for it, but the majority had an innate sympathy for what we were doing, and some developed great skill as diggers; many knew more about the artefacts than the collection of university graduates employed to supervise them. Theirs is a story replicated on many an archaeological site from the 1930s to the 1990s. And the story of such men is as much a story of Ireland as that of the earliest settlers or of the Vikings. Archaeology's greatest weakness is that it rarely reveals people as individuals, often seeing them as merely the sum

Pl. 95—Some of the excavation team at Wood Quay, forever fixed in time if not in memory. Many of the work force were refugees from the building trade or considered too old for it, but the majority had an innate sympathy for what we were doing, and some developed great skill as diggers; many knew more about the artefacts than the collection of university graduates employed to supervise them. (Photo: Hugh MacConville)

of their body parts. It is interesting and instructive, therefore, that it is always the people who are involved in and around excavations who provide the fun, the insight and the drama. Con Manning's affectionate memoir of the Kells, Co. Kilkenny, excavations is testament to that.

I will end this movie with one final scene. It's a cold winter's morning at the height of the Wood Quay controversy; the Museum and Dublin Corporation have decreed that no one is to be allowed to view the work on the site, and all visitors are banned. I pass the gate just as somebody knocks on it; I open the gate and recognise Mike Murphy, at that time a very well-known TV presenter with an interest in the arts, a great supporter of the fight to save the site. I was determined to show him the site despite the ban on visitors, and took him on a tour. About halfway through the tour I was summoned to the presence of the then Museum director, Dr Raftery, an archaeologist and civil servant of the old school, who demanded to know who I was showing round the site. 'It's Mike

Murphy, Director', I said. 'Who is Mike Murphy?' he replied (though I suspect he knew well enough). Could I really have replied, as if addressing an aged High Court judge, 'I believe he's a popular entertainer, Doctor'? Anyway, Mike Murphy was ejected and I narrowly escaped the sack. God knows what would have happened had Dr Raftery appeared when we were showing Spike Milligan the site. I rather think it would have been a worse crime to show the site to an anarchic comedian than to a 'popular entertainer'.

So, as the sun sinks over the horizon, we say farewell to my memories of working in archaeology in the 1970s. The callow youth with a sketchy knowledge of the Neolithic (and, if the truth be told, most other periods) has ended up as an archaeological publisher (and now, by definition, with a sketchy knowledge of most things) pushing what he sees as unreliable memories and theories on an unsuspecting public and trying to convince himself that it is poetry.

References

MacConville, U. 2006 Mapping religion and spirituality in an Irish palliative care setting. *Omega* **53** (1–2), 137–52.

Manning, C. 2006 The Kells Priory excavations—personal memories of working on the site. *Archaeology Ireland* **20** (4), 13–15.

Ó Donnabháin, B. 2000 An appalling vista? The Celts and the archaeology of later prehistoric Ireland. In A. Desmond *et al.* (eds), *New agendas in Irish prehistory*, 189–96. Bray.

27

Admiral Nelson: my part in his downfall

Franc Myles

The actual events surrounding the physical creation of an archaeological site are central to the formation of the archive from which our argument expands and from which our discoveries are contextualised and fed to the theory mill. It is rare indeed when those events can be linked directly to the personalities responsible for their creation. Such, however, are the joys of engaging with our contemporary past, although this is not to suggest that things are as cut and dried as they might initially appear. The *dramatis personae* of this particular narrative rounds up a cast of Dubliners, headed by what today would be referred to as 'dissident republicans', namely Liam Sutcliffe and Joe Christle. Depending on whom one believes, either or both were responsible, at exactly 1.32am on the morning of Easter Monday, 8 March 1966, for depriving Dubliners of the landmark that had provided a convenient reference point for the centre of their city since 1808: Francis Johnston's 134ft (40.8m) Doric monument to Horatio Nelson.

Of course, those responsible for the erection of what was inaccurately known as Nelson's Pillar should not be forgotten. This was a cross-confessional committee made up of elements of the aristocracy along with prominent members of the Catholic merchant class, all of whom, as Maurice Craig has pointed out, were doubtless grateful to Nelson for reopening the shipping lanes. Arthur Guinness was among their number. If one person is responsible for having the site of the pillar excavated, however, the plaudits must go to another quintessential Dubliner (who was in fact a Tyrone man), the very personification of Flann O'Brien's 'the brother', Michael Ó Nualláin. Plans to replace the pillar with Ian Richie's 120m 'Monument of Light' were stymied by Ó Nualláin, who pursued every opportunity available to scupper the proposal, eventually forcing Dublin City Council to commission an Environmental Impact Assessment of

303

the proposed scheme.

The EIA, undertaken by Annaba Kilfeather, established the likelihood of the foundations of the pillar surviving under the central median of O'Connell Street. As these would have to be removed to facilitate the erection of the pillar's replacement, an archaeological solution was required, and this writer got the job. Such were the circumstances surrounding the excavation of a 6.6m-square foundation of indeterminate depth, a structure which was neither protected as a fragment of the city's architectural heritage nor recognised as an archaeological monument in its own right.

Prior to the excavation proper, it was decided to assess the site by mechanically opening a series of trenches across where we thought we would locate the foundation. The site had yet to be hoarded off, and our activities interfered with the thousands of pedestrians trying to make their way to work. Few respected the notional area of operations demarcated by the crowd control barriers, and many people stopped to chat. The first paving slab had just been lifted when a member of the public beckoned me over and in a conspiratorial hush, barely audible over the early morning traffic, enquired if I was 'after the coins'. A Dub of the old school, he was somewhat overdressed for the bright September morning; I could just about see a shirt and tie beneath a woollen scarf tucked into the upturned collar of his Crombie. He was to return on a daily basis to offer titbits of information and occasional words of advice.

Indeed, he was the first of many. By the second day we had become an attraction in our own right, with what appeared to be most of the population of Dublin demonstrating an alarming awareness of archaeological theory and practice. Several suggested the unlikelihood of encountering anything of significance and suggested we dig across the river in Temple Bar. Most appeared pleased that the remains of the pillar were about to be exposed, and several of these saw it as an opportunity to ditch Richie's proposal and rebuild the original structure. One lady thought that such a course of action might persuade Northern Unionists to 'rejoin the Republic'. When it was suggested that Nelson could be replaced with a more contemporary figure, she agreed wholeheartedly and nominated Garret FitzGerald. Some broad-minded and forward-looking folk were delighted that the foundations of Nelson's Pillar should be the subject of an archaeological investigation and were to return on a regular basis for updates on our progress.

Day one was almost an unqualified success. Not alone had we established the exact location of the pillar, we also succeeded in finding George P. Beater's 1894 entrance on the southern side of the monument. Unfortunately, we had also managed to whack the steel housing for the city's largest Christmas tree, which was placed right in the centre of the column in a circular space backfilled with

Pl. 96—The ground-level masonry courses of Nelson's Pillar, with G. P. Beater's entrance to the south (background). Note the centrally placed Christmas tree housing.

demolition rubble. This accident was reported to the project manager, who didn't seem too disappointed: there would soon be something else more permanent put up, and the tree would have to find another seasonal home.

Still under the gaze of the general public, over the next few days the upper courses of the foundation were exposed and cleaned up, an added bonus being the survival in plan form of Beater's porch, replete with white ceramic bricks and electrical fittings that sparked every so often (Pl. 96). The iron base of the entrance turnstile survived, twisted out of shape and presenting a health and safety risk to those members of the public who hazarded a closer look. At 400mm below the pavement, the shape of the column in the centre of the square plinth was evident to all, although the steps rising up through the central circular cavity had been replaced by the aforementioned Christmas tree housing. The reverential poses adopted by the archaeological crew as the area was being brushed up for a photograph left none of the bystanders in any doubt as to the importance of the task being undertaken. A polite round of applause followed a final adjustment of the ranging rods and the taking of the first photograph.

Many people shared their memories of the pillar with me. I met one couple who had become engaged at the entrance when waiting for a tram there in 1954.

They'd had their photograph taken against the pillar by a street photographer and almost 60 years later we replicated the shot, the half-erected timber hoarding a poor substitute for the original background. My new friend in the Crombie looked on, occasionally calling me over and informing me how many steps had led to the top (166), or what the entrance fee had been (a constant 6d over the years). He appeared, however, to have something more pressing on his mind and declined all requests for an elaboration of his interest in the matter. One gentleman, affording me a deference I was entirely unworthy of, asked me to settle an old dispute he had with a friend: he wanted to know which of Nelson's many victories were carved into the four sides of the plinth and which one of them faced the river. I protested my lack of knowledge, my competence in this instance relating only to matters below ground. He returned the following day with his friend, who, if disappointed at not remembering Trafalgar, at least had the satisfaction that evening of telling his grandson that he'd walked again through the entrance of Nelson's Pillar.

At this point it was decided to excavate mechanically along the eastern side of the foundation to ascertain its depth, which was found to be a manageable 3.45m below the level of the paving. Before one of the crew had multiplied 3.45 by 6.6 by 6.6 (not the present writer), someone else had calculated how much stone there was to be removed. I was then asked by the project manager, who had been developing an unhealthy interest in the size of my trowel, what exactly my approach would be. We withdrew to the barrier and contemplated the mass of limestone below us.

'He'll dig it backwards.'

We looked around. My friend in the Crombie had been listening in to our conversation and wasn't in the least shy with his opinion.

'You mean arseways?' I rejoined.

'No, backwards,' he replied. 'First in, last out.'

That seemed fair enough, and we treated our friend with a new regard from then on.

The excavation of what was left of the pillar was not exactly fraught with difficulties. The possibility of finding a hoard of coins somewhere in the masonry, as signalled by our friend in the Crombie, had been explored in the method statement submitted with the application to excavate the site. Only one (near-) contemporary account of the events of 1808 mentions the existence of coins within the foundations. Warburton, Whitelaw and Walsh recorded the deposition of 'various coins' in a recess covered by a brass plate. They had also credited William Wilkins with the design of the monument, a claim that was discredited by Patrick Henchy in his article on the pillar in the *Dublin Historical Record* in 1948.

There appeared to be a greater likelihood of recovering the foundation stone, which had been placed in position by Charles Lennox, duke of Richmond, the lord lieutenant of the day, on 15 February 1808. The best account of the ceremony was given in the *Freeman's Journal*, a publication not noted for its advocacy of king and empire. Although at times a certain bemused tone is evident in the report, the newspaper acknowledged that publishing the names of the previously anonymous committee would 'contribute to silence the strictures that our Correspondents are in the habit of making upon their [the committee members'] taste, designs and motives'.

The *Freeman's Journal* report is worth quoting in full, if only as a mirror image of the archaeological procedure followed 194 years later, as hinted at by our friend in the Crombie.

'When his Grace entered the pailing, the company within immediately took off their hats; he then descended the board placed there for the occasion. A Freemason's apron was then put around his wastc [*sic*] by Mr Johnston, the Architect.

The stone was suspended from a triangle, with the place ready prepared to receive it, when his Grace ordered it to be lowered, and taking the Trowel in his hand, placed some mortar upon it . . .

Her Grace the Duchess of Richmond came within the pailing and descended a few steps. She was attended by Sir Charles Vernon, and seemed to participate in the sentiments which actuated everyone around. She wore a deep and becoming mourning, but appeared to enjoy uncommon health and spirits. She nodded at many gentlemen who attended the ceremony particularly the Provost. His Grace was dressed in Regimentals and wore a black scarf upon his left arm. His Aide de Camp and Pages accompanied him to lay down the foundation stone. When the stone was placed, a Brass Plate was handed to his Grace by the Architect, Mr Johnson [*sic*]. After perusing the inscription on it for a few minutes, his Grace placed it on a bed made in the foundation stone. Some melted rosin was powered around it, and another stone placed over it. Thus concluded the ceremony.'

The report concluded that, 'notwithstanding the concourse of people assembled [which] exceeded we believe, that on any former occasion, not the slightest accident occurred'. This was all the more surprising when one considers that, after the stone had been positioned, the yeomanry had discharged three volleys, followed immediately by the artillery. This was followed by three cheers from the spectators, which may possibly have silenced the cries of the wounded.

Just prior to the bulk removal of the masonry, the site was finally hoarded in and several holes were cut at eye level to facilitate those wishing to observe the proceedings. Our friend continued to peer balefully through one of these holes and would often appear at the gate as we emerged for lunch, obviously upset at his relegation to observer status. On one of these occasions, after we'd removed Beater's porch and the upper courses of masonry from the foundation plinth, he decided to up the ante and inquired after the time capsule.

'The time capsule?' I'd heard it all now.

'The time capsule,' he confirmed. 'The coins are in the time capsule.'

This exchange took place on the morning of 12 September 2001, when most peoples' minds were concentrated on the events of the previous day, events which, beyond the obvious human and political reverberations, had archaeological implications of their own. We nonetheless reread the report in the *Freeman's Journal* and noted the inscribed brass plaque on the foundation stone, so carefully placed in position by Lennox. There were other archaeological considerations at play, however, and more opportunities to pursue. The insertion of steel shuttering along three sides of the foundation had left an access ramp to the south, where it quickly became apparent that earlier buildings were present under the central median of the capital's main street.

Relatively little is known about this early development on the lands formerly belonging to the abbey of St Mary, which were granted to the Moore family, later the earls of Drogheda, in 1619. The area was set out in lots in 1682, and Marlborough Street, where construction began between 1700 and 1710, formed the eastern extent of the built estate. Charles Brooking's map of 1728 depicts the grid pattern of the old Drogheda estate (since 1714 under the ownership of Luke Gardiner), and shows the enclosed slob lands east of the North Strand Road as being still liable to flooding.

The three cellars recorded to the south of the pillar's foundation certainly relate to the period of the first buildings on the site and belonged to narrow, three-bay Dutch Billies, which probably date from the last decade of the seventeenth century. The buildings as depicted on Rocque's *Exact survey of the city and suburbs of Dublin* reflect the disjointed approach taken throughout this early period of the city's modern development, with unequal plot widths, differing plan types and serrated street frontages. Their long plots extended to stabling that fronted onto Prince's Street, their widths corresponding to those depicted by Rocque in 1756. The buildings above were presumably cleared by the Wide Streets Commissioners' widening of Drogheda Street, what was now Sackville Mall in the 1790s.

The excavation of the cellars provided a brief diversion from the job in hand,

and if my friend appeared impatient at the amount of time we were spending on the earlier structures, he would rarely mention it. At this stage he was permitted to enter the hoarding to view the excavation in greater detail, an honour he accepted as his rightful due. He appeared satisfied with our *modus operandi*: each course of masonry was graded off by machine, the dressed stone around the edges being carefully examined for masons' marks or other graffiti, the discovery of which would help justify our presence and relieve somewhat the tedium often experienced in mid-excavation. As each day progressed, less and less of the GPO was visible above us, until finally we were left with the apex of the pediment and the 1993 replica of John Smyth's *Hibernia* above.

The lower course of masonry was exposed by one o'clock on 2 October. Our work nearly finished, we crossed the river and sat at the bar in the Palace, where we prepared to wash the ancient dust from our throats while fielding the usual questions from the bar staff and lunchtime drinkers. Just as the glass was raised to my lips, my mobile rang and I recognised the number of Gerry, one of the contractor's men seconded to the archaeological crew for the duration of the excavation. The conversation was brief.

'They've found the time capsule', I told Simon, sitting beside me.

His response was lost in the rush to get back across the river and back to 1808.

And there, at the very centre of the column, was our friend, still in the Crombie, at the end of a shovel, attempting to prise off what appeared to be a Portland stone plate centrally placed on the surface of a huge granite block. This was held in the very core of the column and had been obscured earlier by the loose rubble that had been placed into the central cavity after the stone had been positioned. He was unapologetic, and possibly expected our thanks for assisting in the discovery of the time capsule, which was doubtless filled with coins of the realm and various important documents. The bashful avoidance of eye contact on the part of the contractor's men indicated that he had not acted alone. Indeed, quite a large area had been shovel-scraped to a satisfactory degree, and we were not unhappy that this onerous task had already been undertaken. Our friend was nonetheless escorted up the ladder and encouraged to continue his observations from one of the viewing holes, which by now were completely useless, all the action taking place several metres below the pavement.

The foundation stone consisted of a cut granite block with a rectangular cavity in its upper surface (Pls 97 and 98). The block measured 660mm by 550mm and was 300mm deep, although its depth was not immediately obvious, being buried in the ground. The cavity measured 410mm by 250mm and was 80mm in depth. In its centre was a second, much smaller, roughly cut cavity. This was dovetailed, being longer at its base than at the surface, and had been

Pl. 97—The foundation stone in situ in the lowest foundation courses.

Pl. 98—Detail of the foundation stone.

used for lowering the stone into position with a mason's device known as a Lewis.

The main cavity was cut to accommodate a brass plaque that was placed into it and then sealed with resin. The now-solidified resin filled the Lewis recess and created a thick sealant layer under, around and over the top of the plaque. The thickness of the material on the surface of the plaque varied from 1mm to 5mm, suggesting that it was poured in as a liquid and not applied with a brush. The upper surface was polished and engraved with an inscription eulogising Nelson and a list of the members of the pillar committee, although admittedly this was not immediately evident. There were six holes in the plaque, suggesting that it had initially been intended to screw it into position. The contents of the block were finally protected with a lid of Portland limestone placed inside the granite cavity.

The loose material around the foundation stone was cleared away prior to its removal. This was undertaken by carefully removing the mortar crust adhering to the base of the stone to a sufficient extent to allow straps to be placed underneath. The stone was parcelled in bubble-wrap before the straps were inserted and it was carefully lifted out of the trench by the excavator bucket. It was immediately brought to the conservation laboratory at Collins Barracks with the assistance of Eoin Sullivan and his trailer.

The recovery of the foundation stone generated considerable public and media interest. Even as the stone was being prepared for its journey to the conservation lab, the press was pushing the time capsule story despite all initial evidence to the contrary. Exiting the hoarding that evening, we pushed through crowds of bystanders who appeared to be there by word of mouth alone. Our friend in the Crombie was outside, modestly recounting his own part in the day's events. Our previous unpleasantness forgotten, we shook hands and went our separate ways.

The question of the missing coins was broached again after the foundation stone was opened under laboratory conditions in Collins Barracks. The absence of a cavity within the stone containing artefacts of the day was noted and much commented upon. Rumours had swept the city in 1966 of the existence of a hoard of coins in the foundations that was not recovered in the rubble. The ruined pillar had been subjected to some pilfering before the site was cleared, and although the admiral's head was recovered from a London auctioneer, his sword is still missing. The writer's attention was subsequently drawn to a sale at a Dublin auctioneer's, which had taken place in September 2000, where a lot comprised of three low-denomination coins of George III was offered for sale. The lot consisted of an 1805 George III halfpenny and penny along with a farthing of 1806 and included the lead sheets they were stored in. The coins, according to the catalogue, were 'apparently [from] under the foundation stone of Nelson's Pillar', and a provenance was given to Buckley's Auction Rooms, Sandycove, Co. Dublin, *c.* 1985. The catalogue referred to the fact that 'the high points of the coins were slightly flattened by the pressure of the masonry on top of the lead protector', but otherwise the coins were 'extremely fine' and 'unevenly toned'. The estimated price was given as IR£400/IR£500.

On the basis of the effort required to reach the lower courses of the foundation plinth, the provenance of the coins was obviously unsatisfactory. It did not appear likely that coins of such a low denomination would be deposited within such an important civic monument. On the other hand, the fact that there was no reference to such a deposition in any of the contemporary newspaper accounts could not be taken at face value. So where were the coins from?

There are several buildings in the city dating from the first few years of the nineteenth century which have not survived into the new millennium. Much of Gardiner Street was under construction during this period, as was the area around Hardwicke Place. The former was disassembled throughout the 1970s and 1980s, whereas much of the latter had been removed by Dublin Corporation in the 1950s. On the other side of the city, Richmond Barracks, which was built in 1807, was named after Charles Lennox, the last person to have handled the foundation stone before our nameless friend took it upon himself to expedite the final moments of the excavation. Most of the complex was demolished in the late 1960s, with further demolition taking place in the 1980s. Perhaps the coins were recovered from the demolition works here and given a more interesting provenance to achieve a higher price?

The explosion that demolished most of the pillar was for several years afterwards rumoured to be the work of Basque nationalists engaged in a hands-on training exercise with some local republicans of a socialist bent. It is recognised now, however, that by the mid-'60s the Basques were probably more *au fait* with the use of explosives than their Irish counterparts. The accepted story outside of republican circles credits Joe Christle with both the idea and the execution. Christle, a well-known cyclist, boxer and Dublin character, had long ago left the mainstream republican movement and was now lecturing in law at the College of Commerce in Rathmines. Liam Sutcliffe's alleged involvement with what was apparently called 'Operation Humpty Dumpty' emerged in April 2000, when he described in some detail how the gelignite and ammonal were placed in the pillar just before the gates closed for the evening. The media interest in Sutcliffe's admission possibly encouraged the creation of an alternative provenance for the coins to be sold the following September. Two days before the auction, however, he was arrested under Section 30 of the Offences Against the State Act and invited to repeat his story to an audience of Special Branch detectives in Store Street. He declined and the matter was dropped.

Perhaps the most pertinent report on the time capsule that never was appeared on a satirical website, the *Evil Gerald*, the headline of 15 October of which proclaimed 'Time capsule reveals "same old shit"'. From another angle, the 'morning prayer' spot on the radio appropriated the story to illustrate the theme of disappointment, presumably our own disappointment at not finding the time capsule we were looking for.

The excavation of the pillar foundation brought home to me the extent to which archaeology can be made relevant to what was, literally in this case, the man in the street. Our friend in the Crombie had surely as much right as we had to participate in the rediscovery of Nelson's Pillar, and who knows, perhaps his was a more fundamental engagement, invisible to our eyes, blinkered by our preoccupation with creating the archaeological archive. Most people we encountered at the hoarding had their own memories of the pillar to excavate, and among those I include the several republicans who regretted their initial enthusiasm for its destruction. I sometimes wonder, though: if Liam Sutcliffe had actually been charged with his part in the explosion, would this have been the first time the state has prosecuted an individual for *creating* an archaeological site?

Select bibliography

Bolger, W. and Share, B. 1976 *And Nelson on his pillar: 1808/1966. A retrospective record*. Dublin.

Craig, M. 1952 *Dublin 1660–1860: a social and architectural history*. London.

Henchy, P. 1948 Nelson's Pillar. *Dublin Historical Record* **10**, 53–63.

O'Regan, J. (ed.) 1998 *A monument in the city: Nelson's pillar and its aftermath*. Kinsale.

Walsh, P. 1998 Dutch Billys in the Liberties. In E. Gillespie (ed.), *The Liberties of Dublin*, 58–74. Dublin.

Warburton, J., Whitelaw, J. and Walsh, R. 1818 *History of the City of Dublin*. Dublin.

Whelan, Y. 2003 *Reinventing modern Dublin: streetscape, iconography and the politics of identity*. Dublin.

Whyte's Auction Catalogue, 23 September 2000. Dublin.

28

The excitement of archaeology

Ian Blake

S ummer 2006, I have e-mail: 'The M3 will bring unspeakable destruction to Ireland's heritage particularly at the massive floodlit interchange planned for Blundelstown at the foot of the Hill of Tara . . . A motorway attracts development and the planning permissions are already being lodged for property at the foot of the hill in the Tara/Skryne Valley'. It is to go ahead despite TD Ciarán Cuffe's warning that 'Carving a motorway through the Tara landscape would be an act of sacrilege', and Deputy Michael D. Higgins's condemnation: 'this is an appalling decision which will affect not only this generation, but generations to come . . . This has important implications not only for the people of Meath, but for people throughout Ireland.'

How can this happen in Ireland in 2006? And, irony of ironies, in County Meath of all places, the setting of perhaps some of the most thorough and comprehensive archaeological campaigns ever seen in the British islands, namely the Discovery Programme's research of Tara and Professor George Eogan's four decades of exemplary fieldwork and continuing publication at Knowth. Back in the seventies, public opinion forced authority to exercise control over development that was threatening the proper recovery of the evidence of Viking Dublin. There are now a higher percentage of graduates than ever before and the public today is quite capable of appreciating the subtleties, nuances, refinements and techniques of modern archaeological research, yet we seem to have regressed. Why?

I suggest that it is because television, particularly the example set by the BBC, has done more to damage the public concept of archaeology as a proper academic study of mankind which necessitates rigorous clear thinking than any barbaric medieval book-burning. The average viewer, asked 'What is the real purpose of archaeology?', will almost certainly suggest that it is glorified treasure-hunting.

While it is certainly true that Howard Carter, looking through the hole into Tutenkhamun's tomb, replied 'Marvellous things!' in response to the question 'What can you see?', rarely mentioned are his decades of hot, dusty, hard work which preceded eventual discovery in that final season, the last that Lord Carnarvon was prepared to finance. The legitimate excitement of archaeology lies in that special moment of realisation that results from patiently putting together largely undramatic fragments of evidence which emerged slowly, bit by bit.

Television presents a quite different and utterly erroneous picture. Week after week, woolly-hatted wallies of *The Time Team* swoop down on an archaeological site. In a matter of days, or even hours, they 'discover' some epoch-changing evidence and seduce a credulous audience into believing that it solves, at a stroke, some problem that has baffled stuffy old academic archaeologists for decades, if not centuries, before vanishing back into the clouds like mythical gods. Neither the weeks of tedious preliminary labour nor the subsequent hours of careful research required for publication ever feature. Such persistent travesty has insidiously mis-educated the archaeologically naïve into categorising archaeology as a trivial pursuit indulged in by amiably dotty eccentrics from a comic-cuts academic world. Unhappily, it has evidently corrupted the understanding and integrity of those very ministers and senior civil servants specifically charged with guarding our heritage and preserving from the JCB the historic surroundings of sites like Tara.

During the more than 40 years that Professor Eogan has been researching Knowth, television has persisted in treating archaeology as 'hot' news (encouraging viewers to expect the melodrama of murder, robbery, political scandal or an incident in a war zone) instead of as a documentary and building, season by season, a picture of the progress of careful scientific work, conveying the *gradualness* of the revelations that provide the intellectual excitement for the genuine archaeologist. Oh for an archaeological David Attenborough, whose patient documentary programmes have educated millions into a proper understanding of, and respect for, the wonders of the natural world.

In 1968 I was castigated in *Antiquity* for an article in the *Irish Times* in which I deplored the astonishing 'attack'—the only word for it—on Silbury Hill in Wiltshire. With the tacit approval of virtually every other eminent archaeologist, all of whom should have known better, and against every principle of archaeological stratification, Professor Richard Atkinson was allowed to drive a horizontal tunnel into the base of this mysterious monument. His 'poetic', not to say highly imaginative, speculation—'I believe, therefore, that Stonehenge itself is evidence for the concentration of political power, for a time at least, in the hands of a single man . . . Who he was, whether native-born or foreign, we shall never know . . . Yet who but he should sleep, like Arthur or Barbarossa . . . beneath the mountainous pile of Silbury Hill?' (Atkinson 1956, 165)—undoubtedly seduced the BBC into anticipating the discovery of some gold-decked Neolithic king 'in the quiet darkness of a sarsen vault'. They funded the work, quite clearly expecting a news 'scoop'—'STONE AGE TUT FOUND IN WILTSHIRE?'

The tiny village of Mir Zakah lies on the ancient trail from Afghanistan to Pakistan and, in the third century, there was dumped into a roadside watering hole 'the most amazing hoard in history'. In 1947 a villager discovered a gold coin, and it led to the recovery of 13,000 more, all of which were illegally dispersed. When, in 1992, heavy rain turned up another coin, 'A rough alliance of warlords, gangsters, antiquities dealers and greedy collectors converged . . . One coin became . . . finally more than half a million . . . the well yielded more than four tons of coins and 770 pounds of other gold and silver artworks . . . It was as if somebody found a world-class museum at the bottom of a well—only to sell off the contents without a moment's regard for its value to the common heritages of history and humanity' (Holt 2006, 7).

Fortunately Silbury produced virtually nothing significant in the way of archaeological, let alone reliable, evidence, and proved an expensive, humiliating, news disaster. Otherwise no doubt 'antiquities dealers, greedy collectors' and misguided archaeologists would have persuaded television into vandalising other ancient sites as crassly as Canon Greenwell's barrow-burrowing in the nineteenth century. As it is, Silbury remains a shameful reminder of an academic disgrace. (How ironic that, in 2008, almost exactly 40 years after I was castigated in *Antiquity* for daring to question the methodology employed at Silbury, it has been necessary to conduct an emergency 'rescue' operation to shore up the collapsing Atkinson/BBC tunnel, which is destabilising a unique English prehistoric monument, and to hear on the radio a young archaeologist patronisingly observe that 'they knew no better at the time'.) While we should not perhaps condemn the uneducated impoverished inhabitants of Mir Zakah, we should at the very least be able to pride ourselves on having 'in authority' those who can be trusted to cherish the complex of historic and prehistoric evidence, all that remains to us of 'the common heritages of history and humanity', that evolved over millennia to ring through Tara's halls.

Television has never learned the lesson. It signally fails to show how the legitimate, intellectual, excitement of archaeology lies not at all in sudden discoveries of some spectacular single treasure or 'find' but in how, after many seasons of slogging work, the disparate pieces at last begin to fit together and a new, often unsuspected, picture emerges.

There is nothing quite as thrilling as when, cutting the first turf on a new site, a tell-tale sherd confirms that you are on the trail—not of the great and the rich, with their palaces, but of men and women who, without your efforts, would, in the words of Ecclesiasticus (XLIV, 9), 'have no memorial, who had perished' so long ago that they 'are become as if they had never been'. To piece together and interpret what little they left behind into a reliable picture of their lives is hard, delicate, often frustrating but nonetheless exciting work. Yet this fascinating process is rarely, if ever, the stuff of television archaeology.

There can also be the very different, but very satisfying, excitement of proving 'accepted' theory wrong. As undergraduates, two of us were rather patronisingly allowed to investigate an allegedly Romano-British enclosure and 'Roman barrow' in Dorset. Excavation revealed that the 'barrow' was in fact a dump of WWII army junk, petrol cans etc., and that the mysterious depression nearby was the relic of a searchlight battery temporarily sited there. It could be precisely dated: at the bottom of the pit, beneath an army gas-cape, lay a perfectly preserved 1941 Woodbines cigarette packet, although in the course of our work it had become clear that we were indeed excavating within the one remaining unploughed segment of a vast ditched enclosure—but very early Iron Age, not Romano-British.

Gradually our volunteer team uncovered an impressive entrance—and a mystery. The ditch end to one side of the gateway had been refilled for some twenty feet, the rubble, including 'unweathered' tabular flint, still sharp-edged, freshly broken. In other words, it had been refilled immediately after it had been dug in antiquity. Why? On top of this, at one end was laid a human longbone and at the other end half of a human skull. Finally, all twenty feet had been capped by tight-packed flint nodules so firmly 'cemented' in puddled chalk that it was difficult to shift them even with a pickaxe. If this was a defensive ditch, why refill it at this point so vulnerably close to the gate? Superstition? Sacrifice? Commemoration? We still do not know. But one day, somebody at another site may uncover evidence that will resolve this intriguing mystery.

In our second season, the discovery of post-holes cut into the rock-chalk that underlay the shallow turf led our self-appointed adviser to assure us that it would be a 'typical Iron Age roundhouse, sixteen feet (4.8m) diameter, with a roof-supporting central pole'. Three weeks' work revealed that it was indeed an Iron Age roundhouse—but nearer 60ft (18m) in diameter and with no trace of a central pole.

I remember the excitement (and trepidation) as I looked down on indisputable evidence of a huge wooden building carved into the chalk over two millennia before the manufacture of the precarious 60ft hydraulic tower, which the German army had once used for artillery spotting, from which I was photographing the site. There was further excitement months later: putting the depth of each post-hole onto the master-plan. It became evident not only that all the posts were of the same diameter but also that they had not all been sunk to the same depth; the deeper holes were on the higher part of the slight slope, obviously to ensure that the tops of the posts were all level. Thus not only were the posts of the same diameter but they had been pre-cut to the same length. All this implied highly organised prehistoric forestry and coppicing, to say nothing of quantity surveying and advanced building techniques—a far more sophisticated early Iron Age society *c.* 500 BC than the woolly-knickers-and-woad savages some of our Romanists would have had us believe.

Twelve years later I was filming, week by week, the revelatory reconstruction of our Pimperne roundhouse by the late Peter Reynolds, himself a TCD graduate. As he went along he worked out techniques used by the Iron Age builders, who had used no nails, and demonstrated why they needed no central pole to support a massive conical thatched roof.

In between had come the very different excitement of exploring the Wilderness of Judea, then in Jordan, which would never have come about had I not gone to TCD as an undergraduate in 1960 and attended lectures by the late Dr Frank Mitchell, SFTCD. His exposition of the archaeology of Ireland was a revelation. My primary interest was in the prehistory, but he opened my eyes to an aspect of which I had been woefully ignorant—Early Christian Ireland. Although fascinated by the exquisite workmanship of the Ardagh Chalice and the Book of Kells, the tingle in my spine came when, on field-trips, we found a carved cross in a remote field, stood awed by the great High Cross at Kells, or wandered among the towers and moss-covered graves of anonymous monks at Glendalough.

Professor Mitchell was supervising the doctoral thesis of George Eogan, then compiling his invaluable work on Irish bronze swords and about to begin work at Townley Hall and Knowth, who told me that he had held the Excavation Studentship at the British School of Archaeology in Jerusalem and encouraged me to apply for it in 1962.

So it was that I found myself a site supervisor on the hill of Ophel under the iron heel of Dame Kathleen Kenyon, excavating sad ruined terraces of the city sacked by Nebuchadnezzar. One rest-day we made an excursion led by the great Biblical scholar Roland de Vaux of the École Biblique to Qumran, which he had excavated. He also showed us the caves in the soft marl cliffs from which he had recovered Dead Sea Scrolls. I remember gazing south through the heat haze and asking what sites lay along there. 'None. Too arid,' I was assured by everyone I questioned. Subsequently, looking at maps and talking to a hydrologist, I learned that along the shore of the Dead Sea, 390m below Mediterranean Sea level, there were almost certainly occasional freshwater springs. Surely there *must* have been settlement?

After graduating from TCD in 1964, I returned as Senior Research Scholar to make a lone survey in the Wilderness of Judea. The only previous explorer had been the naturalist Tristram *c.* 1860. I set up camp close to the Wadi Darajah, on top of precipitous cliffs that drop almost vertically 1,300ft to the shore. It is very, very hot. I tramped cane-brake by the edge of the Dead Sea, tasting various springs. Many were bitter, but two or three were sweet and cool. There was no sign of ancient habitation. *They* were obviously right, there was nothing there.

Deflated and disappointed, I returned, this time trudging along the foot of the great tumble of scree some 40m or 50m back from the edge of the Dead Sea. After a bit I registered that I had been walking very easily, and realised that beneath my feet was a great block almost 2m long and 0.5m wide and thick. There was another ahead of me. I glanced back and could scarcely believe my eyes. I had been stepping from one great block to another—a great curve of huge blocks—for well over half a mile.

I had been walking along the remains of a massive terrace wall, built to retain scree from the near-vertical cliffs above. Then came realisation: it was to preserve what were in fact tiny 'gardens' of fertile soil from being 'drowned' by scree. As I followed this astonishing wall, there, tight against it, I eventually came across the stone foundations of a house with a small courtyard and a scatter of pottery. I took photographs and returned to the School in Jerusalem, where I persuaded the then director, Crystal Bennett, to come back with me and verify that I was not imagining it all.

It was a marvellous, unforgettable moment; we stood there, the evidence before our eyes. Received opinion was wrong: there *had* been ancient settlement in this arid place after all. The pottery dated it to about 700 BC, almost certainly one of the half-dozen lost so-called 'Cities of the Wilderness' listed in the Book of Kings.

Has all this anything to do with Ireland?

High on the cliffs above Ain Turabi is a shallow cave in which I had found some sherds dating from *c.* AD 500. Washing them, the hair stood up on my neck: two of them had very faint writing on both sides. Ostraka. The Greek is too faded to make coherent sense, but they began with what was definitely a cross: letters between a Byzantine Christian hermit and his 'lavra' at the Wadi Kharitoun.

In 1966, a postgraduate at Balliol, Oxford, I returned in December to make exploratory excavations of some of the sites I had found. I persuaded George Eogan to join me, and asked him to supervise excavation of that cave. One morning he sent one of his small 'gang' with a cryptic note, suggesting that I should come up. I realised that he had found something but did not want to

Pl. 99—Excavation in the 'utter wilderness': Ain Turabi, Dead Sea shore, January 1966. George Eogan, with white shirt and mattock, stands next to the author; also pictured are (Dr) K. Prag, Rosemary Hunt, Hamid (cook), Yusef Labardi (Department of Antiquities) and Ay'id (interpreter).

attract undue attention from the Ta'amri workmen who were excavating the site at Tarabi that I was planning, as they might suspect 'treasure' or scrolls. I scrambled up the steep scree. It was already well over 100 degrees, though only nine o'clock.

He had most carefully excavated, in section, two large Byzantine water-jars which had been buried up to their necks in the floor of the cave. Although now cracked and fissured (the area is subject to earth tremors), these humble everyday vessels, though empty, were still complete (an enormous tribute to meticulous excavation) and *in situ* as they had been left 1,500 years earlier. Made of porous clay, they enabled the water to seep out very slowly and, by evaporating, keep the remainder cool. They were the anonymous hermit's 'reservoir' and would have been regularly replenished from goatskins filled, no doubt, from the fresh spring at Ain Tarabi below. Most touching of all, still in place over the mouth of each jar was a flat stone which had been carefully put there to prevent dust contaminating the water. Had he ever, or never, returned?

The photograph in front of me (Pl. 99), taken on the Dead Sea shore, shows us with what today must look like a contingent of El Qaeda insurgents but were in fact our workmen. George, in his white shirt, holds a small mattock. How appropriate that it should be an Irish archaeologist who recovered, from that remote cave in the cliffs above, evidence of a hermit seeking seclusion to contemplate his faith, just like those early Christians inhabiting similarly remote cells and hermitages on islands and in caves about whom I had first heard in Frank Mitchell's lectures five years before.

A year later came another 'coded' message.

I had, at the time, a vacation job as sub-editor on the *Irish Times*. A telephone call was passed to me. 'George here.' Pause. Then, very deliberately, 'So glad you're coming out to see us *tomorrow*'. Although I had regularly visited his excavations in the previous seasons, I was aware of no plans for me to do so in the immediate future. Then I remembered his summons to the cave. 'Of course,' I said, asking no questions, and made immediate arrangements to borrow a car. Early next morning I set out for Knowth.

'I wanted you to be the first journalist to see what we've found.'

Unlike Newgrange, Knowth had conventionally been classified as a 'blind' mound. Now, after several seasons spent patiently investigating small, undramatic supernumerary features, what they had discovered was the passage and chamber which received opinion agreed did not exist.

Foot by foot, I was led along a passage of great stones and into a chamber. His team were the first for some 4,000 years to stand there, perhaps the first ever to see it in such detail by virtue of the modern lighting at their disposal. It was a marvellous moment, the culmination of half a dozen seasons of careful preliminary (but in television-speak insignificantly unrewarding) work. *Time Team* archaeologists would have given up on it long before.

I knew exactly how he felt. His belief that *they* were wrong and that there *must* be a passage was triumphantly justified. I had felt the same in that moment when I knew *they* had been wrong and there *had* been settlement along the Dead Sea shore. In the subsequent season, George and his team discovered a second passage and chamber in the once 'blind' mound of Knowth, and have followed it up with decades of research and publication.

No gold, no jewels. No 'treasure', but a treasury of decorated stones that continue to defy conclusive interpretation and will excite archaeologists and invite theories for years to come. The Rosetta Stone was only 'decoded' after decades of speculation; maybe some future archaeologist will uncover, somewhere, evidence that will clarify beyond doubt the message and purpose of these tantalising decorated stones. Perhaps it will be somebody reading these words even now?

Archaeology is an exciting detective story but, as in real detection, enlightenment comes only gradually after methodical research over a long time. Television deludes itself that it is Sherlock Holmes; if only it had had the humility to admit that it had more in common with plodding Dr Watson, it might have had the vision to look in at Knowth quietly, once or twice a season, from the time excavation began in the early 'sixties. This would have given viewers the opportunity to appreciate that gradual unfolding of an enthralling exploration of the past wherein lies the legitimate excitement of archaeology. And what a priceless archive would be available to us now.

Although 'the pride of former days' has indeed 'become mute', perhaps television can still be persuaded to cover the day-by-day destruction of a historic landscape, as the M3 and ensuing commercial development is bulldozed through the prehistoric complex surrounding Tara. This would at least provide an archive every bit as embarrassing and shaming as that BBC footage of Silbury Hill 40 years ago—an invaluable lesson in what *not* to do for future archaeologists.

Bibliography

Atkinson, R.J.C. 1956 *Stonehenge*. London.

Atkinson, R.J.C. 1960 *Stonehenge*. London.

Blake, I.M. 1967 Dead Sea sites of the 'utter wilderness'. *Illustrated London News*, Arch. Section 2263, 4 March 1967, 27–9.

Eogan, G. 1965 *Catalogue of Irish bronze swords*. Dublin.

Harding, D.W., Blake, I.M. and Reynolds, P.J. 1988 *An Iron Age settlement in Dorset: excavation and reconstruction*. University of Edinburgh Department of Archaeology Monograph Series No 1.

Holt, F.L. 2006 Ptolemy's Alexandrian postscript. *Saudi Aramco World* **57** (6) (November/December), 6–9.

Moore, T. 1808–34 The harp that once through Tara's halls. In T. Moore, *Irish melodies*, Vol. 1.

Author biographies

Dr Mike Baillie is Emeritus Professor of Palaeoecology at Queen's University, Belfast. His original degree was in Physics before moving to Palaeoecology, where he was one of the team responsible for the construction of Ireland's long oak dendrochronology and the calibration of the radiocarbon timescale. His interest in high-resolution chronology prompted an interest in catastrophic environmental events, and he has spent many years attempting to reconstruct the effects of volcanic eruptions and extraterrestrial impacts. He is recognised internationally as an expert in tree-ring studies and chronology and was elected to the Royal Irish Academy in 1990.

Dr Ian Blake was the archaeological correspondent of *The Irish Times* from 1967 until 1974. A graduate of Trinity College, Dublin, he edited both *TCD* and *Icarus* and won the Vice-Chancellor's Prize for English Verse. He was a research scholar at the British School for Archaeology in Jerusalem until the sites were overtaken by the Six-Day War. He obtained his D.Phil. at Balliol, Oxford, supervised by Dame Kathleen Kenyon, Assessor for Wainwright Near Eastern Archaeological Essay Prizes. A winner of the Petra Kenney and Neill Gunn poetry competitions, he lives in Wester Ross, looking over the sea to Skye. His poems appear regularly in *Poetry Scotland*, and his novel *School Story* (written as 'Iain Mackenzie Blair') was published in 2005.

Cormac Bourke is from Dublin and has been Curator of Medieval Antiquities at the Ulster Museum, Belfast, since 1983. He is the author of several papers on the archaeology and history of the early Insular Church, and his catalogue of hand-bells in Ireland, Britain and Brittany is in preparation. He is the Honorary Editor of the *Ulster Journal of Archaeology*, an Associate Editor of *Medieval Archaeology* and a Fellow of the Society of Antiquaries.

Dr Niall Brady's research interests and experience lie in the study of agrarian technology and in underwater archaeology. His particular focus is on the medieval period in its broadest sense. As Project Director of the Discovery Programme's Medieval Rural Settlement Project (2002–8), he and his team are producing a series of four monographs that examine different aspects of settlement and land use across Ireland during the later medieval period.

Dr Colin Breen studied archaeology at University College Cork, the University of St Andrews, Scotland, and the National University of Ireland, Galway. He worked for a number of years at Queen's University, Belfast, before moving to Dúchas, then the state body with responsibility for archaeological survey and protection in Ireland. He is currently a lecturer in historical and maritime archaeology at the University of Ulster. He has published a number of books and articles on varying aspects of archaeology in Britain, Ireland and sub-Saharan Africa.

Anthony Corns is currently employed as the IT manager at the Discovery Programme. He received a Master's degree in Geographical Information Science (GIS) from the University of Edinburgh in 2000. He specialises in the research and application of technology to the field of archaeology, covering aspects of GIS and three-dimensional survey and modelling.

Ian W. Doyle was appointed Archaeology Officer with the Heritage Council of Ireland in 2003. He is a graduate of Trinity College Dublin and University College Cork and completed his Master's thesis in 1996 on the subject of imported pottery in early medieval Ireland. Since his graduation he has worked on a wide variety of fieldwork projects, in addition to a survey of unpublished excavations on behalf of the Heritage Council. He directed excavations on the River Nore (Kilkenny City) Drainage Scheme at John's Bridge and at No. 1 Irishtown (2001–3), and on a ring-barrow at Kilmahuddrick, Dublin (2000). He is currently managing the archaeological conservation of the former Bishop's Palace in Kilkenny City.

Joe Fenwick is Field Officer in the Department of Archaeology, NUI Galway, specialising in field research and scientific survey techniques. Among other major research projects, he has contributed to the investigation of the royal landscapes of Tara, Co. Meath (the Discovery Programme, Dublin), and Rathcroghan, Co. Roscommon (the ArchaeoGeophysical Imaging Project, NUI Galway). He is co-director of the Brugh na Bóinne Research Project, which is conducting a programme of archaeological and geophysical survey at Newgrange, Co. Meath, as part of a wider landscape study.

Wes Forsythe is a researcher at the Centre for Maritime Archaeology, University of Ulster. He previously worked for the government's Maritime Archaeology Unit (then part of Dúchas) and as a freelance archaeologist. He has worked on a range of coastal and underwater archaeological projects both in Ireland and abroad.

Dr Pauline Garvey is a lecturer in the Anthropology Department, the National University of Ireland, Maynooth. She conducted doctoral research in Norway, and was awarded a Ph.D from University College London in 2002. Her areas of specialisation include the anthropology of Scandinavia, material culture and domesticity, and she has published several articles on consumption and the home in Norway. Current research into the socio-politics of design and IKEA consumption is funded by the Irish Research Council for the Humanities and Social Sciences.

Michael Gibbons is an independent archaeologist with over 25 years' experience in the profession. He is a former member of the Archaeology Committee of the Irish Heritage Council and former co-director of the National Sites and Monuments Record Office. He has worked with the Department of Antiquities in Jerusalem and the Museum of London City Excavation Programme. His special interests include maritime and mountain pilgrimage landscapes and the intertidal zone archaeology of County Galway. A member of the Croagh Patrick Archaeology Committee, Michael has contributed to their recently published book, *Croagh Patrick: Ireland's Holy Mountain* (2005). His recent work includes a book on Connemara (2004) and articles on the Mesolithic, *Purpura* dye and Viking Age archaeology.

Myles Gibbons graduated in 2003 from NUI Galway, where he studied History and English as part of his BA degree. He has co-authored articles on subjects such as Mesolithic settlement in Ireland, Viking Age fortifications and Lord Charlemont's travels in the Mediterranean. At present he lives in Clifden, Co. Galway.

Professor Dennis Harding was Abercromby Professor of Prehistoric Archaeology in the University of Edinburgh from 1977 to 2007. He gained his doctorate at the Oxford Institute of Archaeology under the supervision of Professor Christopher Hawkes, and in 1966 took up a Lectureship in Celtic Archaeology in the University of Durham. In Edinburgh he spent ten years in academic administration, including terms as Dean of Arts and Vice-Principal of the University. For 25 years he held a private pilot's licence for air-photographic survey in northern Britain. His field research has focused on the Iron Age of Atlantic Scotland, and in 2004 he published a survey of *The Iron Age in northern Britain*. His new book, *The archaeology of Celtic art*, was published in 2007.

Noel Healy is a Ph.D Candidate at the Department of Geography, NUI Galway. His research interests include nature-based tourism, tourism impacts, the transformation of tourist destinations, globalisation and tourism, landscape policy and planning. Having spent a very successful research period at the University of California, Berkeley, in 2005 investigating planning and management in US National Parks, Noel's current research, funded by the EPA/ERTDI, focuses on visitor management strategies and sustainable tourism practices in National Parks and protected areas in Ireland.

Dr Kieran Hickey is a lecturer in the Department of Geography at NUI Galway. His main interests are in environmental change and human impact on the natural environment, particularly over the last 500 years. To this end Kieran is undertaking a number of research projects on the climate and natural history of Ireland, along with more specialised research on changing patterns of Atlantic storminess and their trigger factors and the climate/coastal interface. He has published extensively in national and international journals and has contributed chapters to a number of books and atlases. He is currently completing a book on the natural and cultural history of wolves in Ireland.

Heather A. King is an archaeologist with the National Monuments Service, Department of the Environment, Heritage and Local Government. She received a Master's degree from the National University of Ireland on the subject of late medieval crosses in Meath, and was subsequently awarded a scholarship to undertake a Ph.D (unfinished) on the late medieval crosses of Ireland in Trinity College, Dublin. She was employed as assistant director on the Urban Archaeology Survey of Ireland and has worked as site assistant at Knowth, Wood Quay, Moynagh Lough crannog and elsewhere, before directing excavations at Fourknocks, Church Island and principally at Clonmacnoise since 1990. Her publications include two volumes of Clonmacnoise Studies, along with a range of papers on excavations and on early, late and post-medieval sculpture and funerary monuments.

Dr Małgorzata Krasnodębska-D'Aughton, formerly of the UCD Mícheál Ó Cléirigh Institute, lectures in Medieval History at University College Cork. She has published on Irish illuminated manuscripts, manuscripts in Polish libraries and, most recently, on ecclesiastical art in the collections of the mendicant houses in Ireland. Her professional experience includes work on the current *Franciscan Faith: Sacred Art in Ireland 1600–1750* exhibition at the National Museum of Ireland.

Dr Brian Lacey studied Archaeology and Early Irish History at UCD, obtaining his D.Phil. from the University of Ulster. He lectured at Magee College, Derry (1974–86), and later set up Derry's Heritage and Museum Service. In the mid-1970s he directed a series of salvage excavations in the centre of Derry and, in 1980–3, the archaeological survey of Donegal. Since May 1998 he has been Chief Executive at the Discovery Programme and editor of the *Journal of the Royal Society of Antiquaries of Ireland*. He is author of *Cenél Conaill and the Donegal kingdoms, AD 500–800* (2006). His most recent book is '*Terrible Queer Creatures': A history of homosexuality in Ireland.*

Nick Maxwell runs the publishing company Wordwell Ltd. He also manages and publishes *Archaeology Ireland* and *History Ireland*. He doesn't live in Surrey with a labrador.

Dr John McDonagh is a Lecturer in the Department of Geography at NUI Galway. His main research interests focus on rural geographies, sustainable environments and landscape evolution, conservation and management. He is currently completing a book (with Tony Varley (NUI Galway) and Sally Shortall (QUB)) entitled *A living countryside—the politics of sustainable development in rural Ireland* (to be published by Ashgate) and has published two previous books, *Renegotiating rural development in Ireland* (Ashgate, 2001) and *Economy, society and peripherality* (ed.) (Arlen House, 2002).

Franc Myles is married to Maria and they share a house with Tommy and Meabh in Inchicore. He has excavated swathes of the inner suburbs of Dublin and is presently involved in a community archaeology project in County Clare, excavating an early eighteenth-century church in Tulla prior to its conservation as a ruin. He is employed as an archaeologist with Margaret Gowen and Co. Ltd and is based in Dublin.

Dr Muireann Ní Bhrolcháin is a senior lecturer in the Department of Medieval Irish and Celtic Studies, National University of Ireland, Maynooth. She completed her BA and MA degrees at the National University of Ireland, Galway. She received her Ph.D for an edition of the prose *Banshenchas* (The Lore of Women) in 1981 and published *Maol Íosa Ó Brolcháin* in 1986. She has written articles on women in early Irish literature, Maol Íosa, the *Banshenchas*, and most recently on the Gabhra Valley. She has received prizes for and published a number of books in Irish for younger children and teenagers.

Dr Jenifer Ní Ghrádaigh is a medieval art historian whose particular research interests are Romanesque art and architecture in its political and social context and the study of pre-Norman material culture from early Irish sources. She received her doctorate from the Courtauld Institute of Art, University of London, in 2004 for her thesis on 'The Romanesque architectural sculpture of the medieval kingdoms of Meath, Bréifne and Airgialla', following which she joined the School of Celtic Studies, Dublin Institute for Advanced Studies, as a research scholar. She is currently the CACSSS Fellow at the Department of History of Art, UCC, and joint Honorary General Secretary of the Royal Society of Antiquaries of Ireland.

Dr Elizabeth O'Brien is a graduate of UCD, where she obtained an MA and an M.Phil. in Irish Studies, and of the University of Oxford, where she obtained her D.Phil. She has excavated on many different types of sites in Ireland. Her specialist subject, on which she has published articles in Ireland and Britain, is the study of Irish early medieval burial practices. She is the author of *Post-Roman Britain to Anglo-Saxon England: burial practices reviewed* (Oxford, 1999). She is a Fellow of the Society of Antiquaries of London.

Dr Aidan O'Sullivan was born and raised in Valleymount in the west Wicklow mountains and is a Senior Lecturer in UCD School of Archaeology. His main research interests are early medieval Ireland, landscape, maritime and wetland archaeology. He is the author of *The archaeology of lake settlement in Ireland* (Discovery Programme/Royal Irish Academy, 1998) and *Foragers, farmers and fishers in a coastal landscape: an intertidal archaeological survey of the Shannon estuary* (Discovery Programme/Royal Irish Academy, 2001), and is a co-author of *Rethinking wetland archaeology* (Duckworth, 2006) and *Maritime Ireland: an archaeology of coastal communities* (Tempus, 2007).

Matthew Seaver graduated from Bradford University in 1995 with a BSc. in Archaeology. This entailed a one-year work placement including education experience in archaeology for York Archaeological Trust at the Archaeological Resource Centre, York. He subsequently completed an MA in Archaeology at University College Dublin in 1997 with a thesis on medieval boroughs in County Meath. He has worked on a wide variety of archaeological sites and gained a licence to direct excavations in 1999. His excavation work has focused on a multi-period landscape at Laughanstown, Co. Dublin, and at the early medieval complex at Raystown, Co. Meath. He is a native of Kilkenny and now lives in Lusk, Co. Dublin. He currently works for CRDS Ltd.

Robert Shaw has been employed as a geo-surveyor at the Discovery Programme since 2002. He studied Topographic Science (Geomatics) at the University of Glasgow, graduating in 1988. Following a number of jobs in commercial land surveying and cartography, he discovered the world of archaeology in 1992 when he began work as a surveyor with the Royal Commission on the Ancient and Historical Monuments of Scotland in Edinburgh. His current role allows him to further his interest in the application of new technology to the specific challenges of archaeological survey. In 2003 he became a full member of the Institute of Irish Surveyors.

Dr Rory Sherlock graduated from UCC with an MA in archaeology in 1997 and began working in contract archaeology. Having spent a year directing an archaeological survey of north-west Cavan in 1998–9, he returned to the world of excavations and worked in Kerry and Limerick before returning to Cork in 2001. He worked as a site director with Sheila Lane and Associates in Cork for a number of years before completing a Ph.D in NUI Galway on the social environment of the Irish tower-house.

Professor Roger Stalley is Professor of the History of Art at Trinity College, Dublin. His research has focused on medieval architecture and sculpture in both Britain and Ireland. He has written over a hundred articles in periodicals and journals and is the author of seven books, including *Architecture and sculpture in Ireland* (Dublin, 1971), *The Cistercian monasteries of Ireland* (London and New Haven, 1987) and *Early medieval architecture* (Oxford, 1999). He was recently elected a member of Academia Europaea.

Professor John Waddell is Professor of Archaeology in NUI Galway. His research interests lie mainly in the archaeology of prehistoric Ireland and in the prehistoric relationships between the island of Britain and continental Europe. His publications include *The prehistoric archaeology of Ireland* and *Foundation myths: the beginnings of Irish archaeology*. Fieldwork has included work on the Aran Islands and at the royal site of Rathcroghan, Co. Roscommon.

Dr Niamh Whitfield received her initial training at University College Dublin, where she obtained a BA and MA in Archaeology. She went on to complete an MA in the History of Art at the Courtauld Institute of Art, London, and a Ph.D in Medieval Archaeology at University College London. Having married an Englishman, she now lives in London. She divides her time between research, some part-time teaching and organising and leading archaeological study-tours to various parts of Ireland. She is a regular lecturer at conferences in Ireland and abroad, and has published extensively on early medieval Irish metalwork, paying particular attention to the 'Tara' brooch.